Latina Evangélicas

Latina Evangélicas

A THEOLOGICAL SURVEY
FROM THE MARGINS

Loida I. Martell-Otero,
Zaida Maldonado Pérez, and
Elizabeth Conde-Frazier

CASCADE *Books* · Eugene, Oregon

LATINA EVANGÉLICAS
A Theological Survey from the Margins

Cascade Books
An Imprint of Wipf and Stock Publishers
199 W. 8th Ave., Suite 3
Eugene, OR 97401

www.wipfandstock.com

ISBN 13: 9781498212366

Cataloging-in-Publication data:

Martell-Otero, Loida I., 1953–

Latina evangélicas : A theological survey from the margins / Loida Martell-Otero, Zaida Maldanado Pérez, Elizabeth Conde-Frazier ; Foreword by Serene Jones.

xiv + 164 p. + 23 cm.—Includes bibliography and indexes.

ISBN 13: 9781498212366

1. Hispanic American Theology. 2. Protestant churches—Doctrine. I. Maldonado Pérez, Zaida. II. Conde-Frazier, Elizabeth. III. Jones, Serene (1959–). IV. Title.

BT83575 L100 2013

Manufactured in the USA

Chapter 5, "Evangélicas Reading Scriptures: Readings from Within and Beyond the Tradition," includes work from "Seeking Guidance from the Word: U.S. Latino/a Religious Communities and Their Scriptures" by Efrain Agosto, Brian Clark, Elizabeth Conde-Frazier and Jacqueline Hidalgo, Presented to Reading Scriptures, Reading America Conference at the Institute for Signifying Scriptures of Claremont Graduate University, October 16, 2009. Research for this report was done under the auspices of the Institute for Signifying the Scriptures and its Scriptural Ethnologies Project.

Loida: To Vitelva Ortíz and Francisca (Paquita) Flores for
teaching me about the Bible and the love of Jesus.

Elizabeth: To all the women who taught us theology
through their *vivencia*.

Zaida: A las mujeres valientes y luchadoras en mi vida: mi madre,
Ruth, mi hija, Jazzlin Ruth, mi abuelita, Perfecta, mi maestra de escuela
dominical, Mery, y las muchas más que Dios conoce.

Este mañana es tuyo, nena

(This "tomorrow" is yours, girl)

By Zaida Maldonado Pérez

September 7, 2012

Mañana, mañana, mañana
Bursts from yesterday's grip
Biding, compelling, inciting
¡Get up, *mi Reina! Pa'lante, ¡Sí, se puede, nena!*
Life is yours, mine, ours
What are you waiting for?!
Strut that beautiful body toward the prize
Walk it, jump it, crawl to it, run it
However and whatever it takes, *mami*
You got it 'cause God gave it to you
You got *el Padre*, you got *el Hijo* and you got *Espíritu Santo*
You got *coraje!*
It runs through your veins as Taíno, African, Mayan and Spanish blood
It's warrior blood
The kind that doesn't give up or fret *cuando la cosa se pone dura**
This is your hour upon the stage
Show us what you got, *chula*
Bless us with the light that you see
The *candela* that drives you
The truth that carries you to the many
Mañana, mañana, mañanas
Oh, and while you are at it,
Look back! . . . look back
To the trail of women that follow you
The cola of *mujeres* that you have inspired
And, be blessed, *mamita,* be blessed

*when things get difficult

Contents

List of Contributors | *ix*
Foreword by Serene Jones | *xi*
Acknowledgments | *xiii*

one
Introduction: *Abuelita* Theologies | 1
Loida I. Martell-Otero

two
Dancing with the Wild Child:
Evangélicas and the Holy Spirit | 14
Zaida Maldonado Pérez, Loida I. Martell-Otero,
and Elizabeth Conde-Frazier

three
From *Satas* to *Santas*: *Sobrajas* No More:
Salvation in the Spaces of the Everyday | 33
Loida I. Martell-Otero

four
The Trinity *es y son familia* | 52
Zaida Maldonado Pérez

five

Evangélicas Reading Scriptures: Readings from
Within and Beyond the Tradition | 73

Elizabeth Conde-Frazier

six

Ecclesiology: A *Dabar* Church;
Pentecostal and Communal | 90

Elizabeth Conde-Frazier

seven

Neither 'Left Behind' Nor Deciphering Secret Codes:
An *Evangélica* Understanding of Eschatology | 108

Loida I. Martell-Otero

eight

Epilogue—*Hablando Se Entiende la Gente* | 127

Loida I. Martell-Otero

Glossary | 139
Bibliography | 145
Subject and Name Index | 155

Contributors

Elizabeth Conde-Frazier is Academic Dean of Esperanza College of Eastern University in Philadelphia. Among her contributions, she has published *A Many Colored Kingdom: Multicultural Dynamics for Spiritual Formation* and *Listening to the Children: Conversations with Immigrant Families*.

Serene Jones is President of Union Theological Seminary in the City of New York and Roosevelt Professor of Systematic Theology. Her publications include *Trauma and Grace: Theology in a Ruptured World*, *Feminist Theory and Christian Theology* and *Calvin and the Rhetoric of Piety*.

Zaida Maldonado Pérez, Dean of the School of Urban Ministries at Asbury Theological Seminary, Florida-Dunnam Campus and Professor of Church History and Theology. Her publications include *The Subversive Role of Vision in Early Christian Martyrs*, and *An Introduction to Christian Theology*, coauthored with Justo L. González.

Loida I. Martell-Otero is Professor of Constructive Theology at Palmer Theological Seminary of Eastern University, King of Prussia, Pennsylvania. She coedited *Teología en Conjunto: A Collaborative Hispanic Protestant Theology* with José D. Rodríguez and has published on topics related to Christology, soteriology, vocation, and spirituality.

Foreword

RARELY DO I COME across a book in the field of systematic theology that by the end of the first page has stirred in me three very different reactions. It made me think very, very hard. It surprised me with the newness of its idea. And best of all, it caused me to smile. How is it that one book can provoke all three?

The thinking hard part was elicited by the seriousness these scholars bring to the old-fashion work of systematic theological reflection. It's an example of classical doctrinal refashioning at its best. The surprise part was stirred by the freshness of their approach, in both content and style. I promise you the ideas and narratives written on these pages are unlike any you have encountered in previous texts. The smile part—well, it has numerous roots. I smile with admiration for a project whose time has come. I smile with appreciation for hard work poured into the book: its scope is broad, its waters deep, and hence its labors most certainly were long. I smile at the vivid images that came dancing across the page towards me as I read. The thoughts, ideas, theology, and stories that compose *evangélica* theology are alive, playful, one might even say pregnant with theological meaning.

In this book, three leading North American Christian theologians take up the ancient theological task of helping "faith seek understanding" for the sake of the present day church and its witness in the world. For Loida Martell-Otero, Elizabeth Conde-Fraizer, and Zaida Maldonado Pérez, this seeking is not general or abstract, however. They undertake the task of theological reflection with their feet firmly planted in the church community that formed them—the rich world of Protestant Latina women's lived experience. They seek, on behalf of that community, to name themselves as *evangélica* rather than be named by others. That their feet are planted in the soil of a community that, according to recent demographic studies, is the largest group of Protestant women in the world today makes the work even more prodigious and important. That they are speaking out and writing about a religious reality that has been silenced for too long makes the work truly historic.

The existential reality of *evangélica* women, as described in this book, is distinctive. It is pluriform, mestizo/sata; it is especially grounded in the everyday and in popular religion; and it is inherently ecumenical and collaborative. So too the book's aims are postcolonial and feminist, appreciative of Catholic theologies while not subsumed beneath them. Building on both the Catholic and Protestant heritage, they embrace Scripture study and tongues in the midst of a sacramental worldview that takes God's presence in the everyday as axiomatic. An emphasis on the Incarnation leads to the language of *evangelic@*, gospel-bearing, people.

At the heart of the project is a powerful image: the Holy Spirit as the wild child of the Trinity. As Martell-Otero describes her, she is creative, uncontrolled, and musical. She moves between people, making connections, bringing life to the party, inspiring fresh vision and grand stories. She also brings her wild comfort to places of pain and despair, and she is honest. Sometimes she dances in line with others, finding good partners in her Trinitarian trot. More often than not, though, she breaks with tradition and improvises, impishly, wisely, delightedly. When she breaks into such an improvisational dance, the world around her is suddenly made light with creative, unmanaged possibility.

Read the book carefully but with a light and open heart. The goodhearted intentions that flow through these pages are testimony to the hospitable nature of the *evangélica* reality they narrate. Watch for the importance of salvation, both christological and social, as found in practices of song and testimony; the practicality of *evangélica* reading and reception of Scripture; and the holistic character of *evangélica* eschatologies. There is much to be learned here, especially, about the Holy Spirit. There is much to be pursued here, academically, in the years ahead. There is much to be garnered here, in terms of deepened insight into Latina women's faith experiences. Most importantly of all, there is abiding wisdom here that, offered for all, cannot help but enrich the faith of those who engage it.

Blessings to the authors for their courage and creativity. I eagerly await your next installment in what I hope is an emerging, comprehensive theological vision. We need it!

Serene Jones
President, Union Theological Seminary
New York, 2011

Acknowledgments

THE AUTHORS HAVE MUCH to be grateful for and realize that a project such as this would never have seen the light of the day had it not been for the support of so many people. We want to thank Cascade Books, and especially K. C. Hanson and Christian Admondson for their support, patience, and help throughout the past two years as we brought this book from idea to concrete fruition. Their wisdom and expertise were of great help to us. Thanks as well to Ulrike Guthrie who believed in us from the start and for making better writers of us all. A special word of thanks to Dr. Serene Jones, President of Union Theological Seminary of New York City, who believed in this project and took time from an overworked schedule to contribute a foreword to the book. We want to thank José Rodríguez, Heather Biscoe, and Jesse Nietzer, our student assistants, for their help in editing the bibliographic data. We are mindful of the support provided to us by our respective schools and library staff, and by colleagues who gave us feedback. We want to thank the Hispanic Theological Initiative and the Wabash Center for their ongoing support and partnership. Our thanks to Frank Colón for sharing his gifts of music and his invaluable information about *coritos*. We are especially grateful to our spouses, families, and friends who patiently understood when we sacrificed weekends, vacation days, and trips to the movies, who listened to us as we talked out our passions and our ideas, and read our manuscripts for what seemed liked a hundred times. Thanks to be to the God of our faith who gave us a vision, to the women of faith who taught us to believe, and the communities of faith who continue to pray for us. *A todas y todos, gracias.*

one

Introduction

Abuelita Theologies

LOIDA I. MARTELL-OTERO

IN 1994 WHEN I wrote "Women Doing Theology: Una Perspectiva Evangélica," there was a dearth of Latina Protestant (*evangélica*) women with PhD degrees in the theological disciplines.[1] Daisy L. Machado was the first when she completed her degree in church history. Others, including Elizabeth Conde-Frazier and Zaida Maldonado Pérez, soon followed her. Seventeen years later the number of *evangélicas* has increased, thanks in great part to the efforts of some churches, organizations such as the Fund for Theological Education and the Hispanic Theological Initiative, and to countless individuals—some of whom will be named throughout the chapters of this book. Together they fought for greater representation of Latin@s in all arenas of theological education. Consequently, the Hispanic Theological Initiative estimates that as we write in 2011 there are more than eighteen such scholars representing various fields of theology throughout the United States, Canada, and Puerto Rico.[2] Of them, Conde-Frazier, Machado, and Maldonado Pérez serve as deans in different academic institutions. While we have not yet reached a "critical mass" in academia, with

1. Martell-Otero, "Women Doing Theology," 67–85.

2. I am grateful for the information supplied by Joanne Rodríguez, director of the Hispanic Theological Initiative, Princeton Theological Seminary, March 2011.

new *evangélica* scholars beginning academic and seminary studies all the time, it is imperative that we begin to articulate what defines us.

What defines us are the theologies that we have inherited from our *abuelas, madres, comadres,* and *tías*—that is to say, the wise women of our faith communities who gave us a firm foundation of the gospel, and taught us to love the Lord and to demonstrate that love in the world.[3] Yet, our theology transcends the theologies we inherited. Those wise women taught us about the power of prophetic words and the responsibility we have to seek and hear them. They did not simply pass on *el evangelio* (the gospel) as a set of accepted dogmatic statements. They nurtured us with a keen sense of the Spirit's ability to create anew. While their teachings were our starting points, an ongoing communal collaborative effort to constructively expound upon various themes from the perspective of *evangélicas*—a *teología en conjunto*—leads us to critically discern aspects of our inherited traditions that have been colonized. Thus this book also represents a postcolonial reinterpretation of our theologies.

The increase in the quantity and quality of resources that address theological themes from the perspective of Latin@s in the past two decades has been gratifying to see.[4] However, many of the books and articles published, particularly those written by Latinas, represent Latin@ Catholic perspectives. The contributors to this book are grateful for the rich theological lode provided by such notable scholars as Ada María Isasi-Díaz, Jeannette Rodríguez, María Pilar Aquino, and a host of others with whom we have collaborated in the past; but we also recognize a need to provide a voice that is distinctively Protestant, or *evangélica*. A few other books have done this. Justo L. González's *Mañana: Christian Theology from a Hispanic Perspective* was an early salvo in 1990.[5] *Teología en Conjunto: A Collaborative Hispanic Protestant Theology* was published in 1997 as a means to articulate an *evangélic@* perspective, but it was not necessarily geared to specifically Latina voices.[6] Subsequent publications were meant to represent Protestant Latin@ viewpoints but again lack an articulation of a specifically *evangélica* perspective.[7] While articles dealing with various

3. Grandmothers, mothers, godmothers, and aunts.

4. Latin@s is a gender-inclusive term that will be used throughout this chapter, and represents the more cumbersome "Latinas and Latinos" expression.

5. It was published by Abingdon Press in 1990.

6. See Rodríguez and Martell-Otero, *Teología en Conjunto*.

7. For example, the intent of González and Maldonado Pérez's *Introduction to*

themes by *evangélica* theologians have been published, this is the first book-length project that responds to the need to create awareness about naming ourselves as Latina *evangélicas*.[8] Therefore it demonstrates how we are distinctive from Latin@ theologians and Euro-dominant theologians in general, and from other non-*evangélica* Latina voices in particular.

This is a book about Latina theology from an *evangélica* perspective, yet its audience is not so narrowly circumscribed. Theology is a discourse whose truths become only proximate even with an increase in the diverse communities that participate in the dialogue. Contextual theologies have made clear that *all* theologies are socially circumscribed, and consequently have both creative insights and painful blind spots. The various viewpoints allow for an enriching and often prophetic conversation. The absence of Latina *evangélica* voices has impoverished this overall discourse. Our absence is not due to the fact that we have nothing to contribute, but rather has occurred because our traditions have too easily been dismissed. Some consider our *abuelita* theologies *sobraja* (leftovers)—marginal or derivative. We insist that they and we contribute a needed and valuable voice to Christian theological discourse from a distinctive social location, for we have each experienced the impact that our theologies has made upon the lives of our students and colleagues, whether Latin@ or not, in the classroom as well as in academic, professional, and ecclesial circles.

The authors of this book have resisted the tendency of non-Latin@ and Latino scholars to name us. When someone else names you, they have the power to objectify you and create you in whatever image they desire. White feminist, womanist, Asian North American, and Latin@ scholars have insisted upon the right to name themselves.[9] Scriptural texts attest to the power of naming. I believe that it is not coincidental that so many oppressed women in the Bible are also nameless. Many of the *evangélicas* that taught us, guided us, and inspired us also remain nameless to the wider world. As Latinas they have been objectified or rendered invisible. This

---

Christian Theology was not necessarily to present *evangélic@* theologies although it was coauthored by two Latin@ scholars. Later Pedraja published *Teología* in 2003, but its purpose was not necessarily or primarily to present a Latina *evangélica* theology.

8. In addition to "Women Doing Theology," there have been a number of articles by such *evangélica* scholars as Elizabeth Conde-Frazier, Nora Lozano-Díaz, Daisy L. Machado, and Zaida Maldonado-Pérez, among others.

9. See for example Isasi-Díaz, "*Mujeristas*: A Name of Our Own," 560–62. Schüssler Fiorenza, *The Power of Naming*, particularly her introduction to the volume.

book seeks to name our *abuelas* and to honor them by naming ourselves, our theologies, and our contributions to the Church and to the world.

Thus we begin with a fundamental question: who are Latina *evangélicas*? Latinas are women from a Latin American or Latin Caribbean background who either reside, or were born, in the continental United States. The controversy of using such broad terms as *Hispanic* or *Latina* has been discussed sufficiently elsewhere and will not be repeated here.[10] Suffice it to say that, technically, there is no such thing as Latinas or Latinos. Sixto J. García and Orlando O. Espín use the term *Latin@* to underscore that there is a "community of communities" in the United States composed of such disparate groups as Mexicans and Mexican Americans, Puerto Ricans, Cubans, Dominicans and other Caribbean Latin groups. Also included are the various ethnic, cultural, or national enclaves that arise from Central and South America. This community is currently one of the fastest-growing and largest "minoritized" groups in this country.[11]

The 2010 census count has estimated that there are 50.5 million Latin@s, making up approximately 16.3 percent of the total population—a 43-percent increase in the past decade, making them one of the fastest growing groups in the country.[12] This is a significant undercount that does not take into consideration the almost twelve million undocumented migrant workers inhabiting its borders, or the three million inhabitants of the island of Puerto Rico. Latinas compose almost half (48.3 percent) of the total US Latin@ population,[13] and their voices must be heard and their experiences taken into account.

Latinas are part of a community that though disparate, nevertheless faces a number of issues and shares common experiences of bilingualism, multiculturalism, popular religious faith, marginality, poverty, colonization, migration, and cultural alienation. They are undereducated, and underemployed. The likelihood that they are poor is double that of white women.[14] They are exploited. They lack access to quality housing and proper health care. Justo L. González's 1996 observation that "every negative statistic for Hispanics—employment, underemployment, poverty rate,

10. For example Segovia, "Hispanic American Theology and the Bible," 26–27; also Maldonado Pérez, "US Hispanic/Latino Identity," 93–110.

11. García and Espín, "'Lilies of the Field': Providence," 70.

12. Passel et al., "Census 2010," 1.

13. Pew Hispanic Center, "Statistical Portrait of Hispanics 2009," Table 8.

14. See Gonzales, "Hispanic Women, 2007."

school dropouts—has remained at a steady 150% of what it has been for the rest of the population" still holds true fifteen years later.[15] In the words of David T. Abalos, Latin@s lack "access to vital connections."[16]

Latin@s are not newcomers to this country. They are an intrinsic part of the history of the Americas. They are also an important constituency of the Christian church, composing an estimated half of the Catholic Church. They also contribute significantly to the membership of the US Protestant church; an estimated 25 percent of the Latin@ population is affiliated with some Protestant, evangelical, Pentecostal, or charismatic denomination.[17] Therefore it is important to know and understand their beliefs, particularly since religious faith is intrinsic to their cultural mores.

Themes discussed in this book are the theological reflections of women who arise from this cultural matrix and reflect upon the realities of this diverse community. Ours is what María Pilar Aquino and Roberto Goizueta call a *praxis of accompaniment*—a theology that arises from our experiences being part of the life of our communities.[18] So Latina theology is a grassroots reflection. Consequently, we can state that, like other Christian Latin@ theologies, it is distinguished by two primary characteristics. First, it is the distinctive expression of a people who reside in North America and live a pluriform existence. This existential reality has been denoted in various ways, including *mestizaje, mulatez, mezcolanza* (mixture), *nepantla* ("land in the middle"), and *sata/o* ("mongrel" or "mutt").[19] Each of these terms underscores the biological, cultural, linguistic, and religious mix, an inherent part of the Latin@ identity. This existential reality leads to a pluriform theology that is distinctive, though not necessarily unique. *Unique* implies a singularity, something that is unlike any other. *Pluriformity* precludes any singular or univocal description by its very nature. It implies an inherent multiplicity. It is an encounter of multiple elements, which takes place without effacing any of its individual constituent parts.

15. González, *Santa Biblia*, 57.

16. Abalos, *Latinos in the United States*, 118.

17. Maduro, "Sociology of Latina/o Religious Empowerment," 151. For a sample of the varying reports see Morales, "Latino Religion, Ritual and Culture," 194 ; as well as Espinosa, "Changements démographiques et religieux," 303–20 ; and Suro, et al., "Changing Faiths," 5, 7.

18. Aquino, "Theological Method," 27. Goizueta, "Mestizaje and Theological Method," 22.

19. *Mestizaje* has no clear translation, although it has often been mistranslated as "miscegenation" or "hybridity." See Elizondo, *Galilean Journey*, 5.

The particular dynamic of this encounter is what makes our pluriformity distinctive. Uniqueness is precluded by the fact that one finds elements of Latin American (which encompasses African and Amerindian beliefs and culture) and European theology in any Latina theological formulation because of its common heritage with these parent groups. Additionally, this encounter produces a third reality: a new *mestizo* or *sata* expression that is distinctively Latin@.

The second characteristic of a Latina theology is that it is a critical reflection based on the day-to-day, or popular, religious belief of the Latin@ community, whose faith forms what Espín has called the "epistemological womb" of daily life.[20] It is an integral part of *la vida cotidiana. Lo cotidiano* is more than the simple translation of "daily" or "everyday." According to Isasi-Díaz, it is that which "constitutes the immediate spaces of our lives, the first horizon in which we have our experiences that in turn are constitutive elements of our reality."[21] As such, *lo cotidiano* is not an object to be studied, but the very matrix of life as it is lived by the marginalized and oppressed. For cultural and historical reasons, popular religious faith is integral to *la vida cotidiana* of the Latin@ community. Thus Latina theology is not simply about a list of specific practices upon which Latina scholars reflect. Rather it is the articulation of a given praxis, a reflection on *una manera de ser* ("a way of life") in a community that struggles daily with issues of survival within a context of economic injustice and multilayered discrimination. Latin@ popular religiosity is both an epistemological tool and a hermeneutical lens that gives expression to a distinctive way of doing theology. This foundation of popular religious faith aids Latina theologians in articulating how a colonized, marginalized, impoverished, and exploited people continues to have faith in the God of salvation, and how such a faith has endured throughout the five hundred years since it was first introduced into the Americas.

In light of Latin@s pluriform and religious existence, it is notable that their theology is a deeply ecumenical and collaborative endeavor. *Teología en conjunto* ("collaborative theology") is a dialogical process that reminds us that genuine theology can only be done as a communal endeavor. For Latin@ theologians, there are no insurmountable boundaries between academic scholars and grassroots communities of faith. Protestant and Catholic Latinas often collaborate on projects and have formed alliances

20. Espín, "An Exploration of the Theology of Grace and Sin," 127.

21. Isasi-Díaz, *La Lucha Continues*, 95.

and friendships that transcend traditional religious animosities. Beyond sharing a common religious foundation that arose from historical factors relating to the conquest of the Americas, we share a common cause as we struggle against the sin of injustice and for the survival of our communities.

Notwithstanding our common theological history, Protestant Latin@s also acknowledge a caesura within that history that took place with the introduction of Protestantism in Latin America and the Caribbean in the late nineteenth century. Perhaps it would be more accurate to claim that a variety of "Protestantisms" entered and influenced religious thought in *mestiza* Catholic Latin America, since the missionaries that came represented a variety of religious traditions, including mainline denominations, Holiness/Wesleyan groups, the Moravian community, and nondenominational churches.[22] Later, Pentecostalism also exerted a significant influence.[23] The blend of common history with caesura provides *evangélicas* with a particular hermeneutical lens and praxeological belief, which this book will endeavor to explain.

The early waves of Protestant missionaries mixed social action and evangelization with a process—whether intentional or unconscious—of Americanization in their approach to the residents of Catholic Latin America and the Caribbean. New converts, in turn, tended to fold Protestant principles into the fabric of their inherited popular Catholicism. These principles include such evangelical beliefs as the insistence on the authority of Scripture, the belief that salvation is obtained through faith in Jesus Christ and demonstrated by a distinct experience of conversion, and the conviction that this "new life" must be evidenced through a praxis of piety.[24] Missionaries were concerned about this "transmutation" of the beliefs they had imported, at times accusing the newly minted Latin American Protestants of syncretism.[25] I witnessed this transmutation when my grandmother, a staunch American Baptist Sunday school teacher, would exclaim, "¡Ave María Purísima!" ("Hail Mary most pure!")—a common saying in

22. Costas considers Latin@ Protestantism to be influenced by a wide range of groups, including Anabaptists, Puritans, Moravians, German Pietists, Wesleyans and Holiness adherents; but also sixteenth-century Spanish mysticism, Social Gospel influences and charismatic/Pentecostal movements along with grassroots social movements. See *Liberating News*, 10–11

23. See Martin, *Tongues of Fire.*

24. Moore offers a somewhat condescending historical narrative of this process in Puerto Rico in *Puerto Rico para Cristo.*

25. Ibid., 2/2.

Puerto Rico. Another example of this transmutation is the *evangélica* adoption and adaptation of the Free Church or Anabaptist belief in the unmediated presence of God accessible to each believer. *Evangélic@s* reinterpreted this belief through the lens of a sacramental worldview, which acknowledges God's mediation in the everyday, as well as through the lenses of their Amerindian and African roots, according to which music is a means for such mediation.[26] The issue of God's mediation, in turn, affects *evangélica* ecclesiology, worship, and belief. I believe that this understanding of divine mediation contributes to the strong belief in *presencia* (God's presence) and to the concomitant emphasis on the incarnational in our theologies.

The pluriform *manera de ser y de creer* (way of being and believing) that arises from the coexistence of a common history with a subsequent caesura has led us to denote ourselves as *evangélicas* rather than as evangelicals or Protestants. Unlike the English *evangelical*, *evangélic@* does not have any theological connotation per se. A straightforward translation of the term would imply that *evangélicas* identify with a distinctive group within US Protestantism, one that defines itself in a specific theological and political manner.[27] This is simply not the case. For Latin@s, *evangélic@* is the identifier of those who understand themselves, generally, to be a people who preach the gospel—*el evangelio*. While synonymous with *Protestant*, this latter term is not as commonly used in Spanish because it seems to imply that somehow *evangélicas* are protesting against something. Thus my coauthors and I, along with other Latina Protestant scholars, have chosen to name ourselves with the nontranslated *evangélica* to denote the distinctive nature of Latin@ Protestantism as a popular religious faith. *Evangélic@* underscores that it is a product of the encounter of the *mestizo*, *mezcolanza*, or *nepantla* popular Catholicism common to all Latin@s and Latin Americans with the various forms of spiritualities and religious practices that were introduced by the sundry Protestant missionaries who worked in Latin America, and further influenced by more contemporary charismatic movements. It denotes a pluriform or *sat@* popular Protestantism.

This book highlights the various *evangélica* theological themes that we believe are distinctive from those of our Latin@ Catholic brothers and

26. For more on Free Church ecclesiologies stemming from the Left-wing Reformation, see Kärkkäinen, *An Introduction to Ecclesiology*, chapter 5. Espín has coined the term "sacramental worldview" to describe the belief that there is an inherent relationality between God and the created world in "Pentecostalism and Popular Catholicism," 27n34.

27. For a discussion of the various meanings of *evangelicalism*, see Marsden, ed., *Evangelicalism and Modern America*.

sisters. However, its primary purpose is not to underscore how *evangelic@* are *distinct* from Latin@ Catholic theologies. As Conde-Frazier states so well, we honor their contributions, particularly those of Latina *feminista* and *mujerista* scholars. We seek not to debate but rather to engage in dialogue. Thus this project is above all the articulation of what it means to be *evangélica* in the United States, written from our particular experiences and perspectives, and through our particular epistemological lenses. While the faith and teachings of our *abuelitas* serve as a foundation for our theologies, we also honor the Protestant principle of *ecclesia reformata et semper reformanda*—the church reformed and always reforming—that allows us to grow, contextualize, question, and provide constructive suggestions to the traditions we have received. In particular, we seek to provide a postcolonial construction of our faith. While this volume is written from a Protestant perspective, the specifically *evangélica* outlook of the book transcends Euro-American, Latin@ Catholic, and male *evangélico* perspectives. We speak out of our experience as *evangélicas* seeking to understand our faith. Indeed, we believe that we have been called to such a task.

One element that distinguishes *evangélicas* is our traditional emphasis on the importance and presence of the Holy Spirit. We believe that the Spirit is the One who not only empowers women but also legitimizes their calling—an important role for those whose voices are often suppressed within patriarchal and racist social and ecclesial structures.[28] Given the pneumatological strand that runs throughout all our theological discussions, we authors believed that the book should begin with a discussion of an *evangélica* understanding of the Holy Spirit. Thus, in a true spirit of *teología en conjunto*, in chapter 2 all three of us engage in a collaborative discussion about the role of the Holy Spirit in the lives of *evangélicas*. Beginning with Maldonado Pérez's description of the Spirit as "wild child," the chapter focuses on *evangélicas'* affinity for the person and role of the Spirit as one who saves, heals, affirms, calls, empowers, and transforms persons and communities. The Spirit is the subversive One who pours out charisms and enables women as *personas llamadas* (called) to do *trabajo personal* (God's work) in peripheral places where others hesitate to go, because where the Spirit is, there is God. Spirit is evidence that God is *presente* (present). To be called is to be *sanctificada* (sanctified). This sense of being "set apart *for*" also means that *evangélicas* are "set apart *from*" certain

28. Martell-Otero, "Women Doing Theology," 77–78. See also Conde-Frazier, "Hispanic Protestant Spirituality," 141; as well as chapter 4 of this book.

roles patriarchal ecclesial structures have assigned to men. Throughout the chapter, the authors integrate pneumatology in Trinitarian, soteriological, and incarnational themes, particularly as it explores the role of the Spirit in worship and *lo cotidiano*. It is a highly personal chapter that closes with Maldonado Pérez's *testimonio* (witness) about her experience of the Spirit who "goes native."

The second most important distinction of *evangélica* theology is its soteriological emphasis. It is related to Christology—indeed, the doctrines of salvation and Jesus Christ are often treated as one unified subject. One could say that an *evangélica* Christology *is* a soteriology. After all, the term *evangélica* emphasizes that we consider ourselves a people who embody the hope of the "good news." Yet, soteriology is not necessarily christocentric. In chapter 3, Martell-Otero examines three important sources that give insight into an *evangélica* understanding of salvation: Scripture, *testimonios* (witnessing), and *coritos* (musical refrains). She argues that soteriology encompasses pneumatological elements, and therefore is undergirded by a functional Trinitarian foundation. She further asserts that salvation for *evangélicas* is an incarnational reality encountered within the context of *lo cotidiano*, rather than solely as a transcendent reality that helps one "go to heaven." Jesus is the divine *sato jíbaro* (mutt or country peasant) who lives to bring life to communities crushed by death-dealing powers. The Spirit is the One who heals personally and communally (*katartismos*) in light of institutional injustice. Martell-Otero argues that particularly for *evangélicas* salvation is experienced as the humanization of women who have been treated as *satas* and *sobraja*. In Christ and through the power of the Spirit, they discover themselves to be beloved daughters of the living God—*santas* who can witness to God's purpose for us all.

When one examines closely the above-mentioned pneumatological strands in *evangélica* theology, one perceives that the Spirit is not simply another God along with the Father and Jesus. The Holy Spirit is important for *evangélica* precisely because the Spirit is God—the Third Person of the Triune God affirmed by Nicene and subsequent ecumenical councils. However, in contradistinction to the Trinitarian tradition that focuses on abstract formulations and leads to cognitive dissonance for evangelicals today, *evangélica* faith is based on a functional Trinity. This praxeological approach to Trinity gives them the freedom to call on Jesus or *Papito* (God the Parent) or the Spirit, understanding that each Trinitarian Person is distinct while also knowing that each is God.[29] In chapter 4, Maldonado Pérez examines the particular ways in which *evangélicas* perceive the Trinity, and the role of Trinity in *la vida cotidiana*. The triune God is not simply an article of faith, one that is affirmed through the Apostles' Creed and other documents of the church. For *evangélicas*, the Trinity underscores three lived realities: *la familia* (family), *la comunidad* (community), and *la presencia* (the abiding presence of God in the spaces of the everyday). Maldonado Pérez especially views the Trinity from the experience of a reconstituted *familia*, positing a way to understand brokenness through the lens of God's promise to create (and thus have us behold) something new. She approaches her Trinitarian formulation through these foundational concepts.

In chapters 5 and 6, Conde-Frazier examines two important and intricately related topics: the roles of the church and of Scripture in *evangélica* theology. Both areas are vital because they contribute to the empowerment of *evangélicas'* voices. Church is often the place where *evangélicas* are trained and live out not just their faith but also their vocation. It is the place of community and *familia*, a place of cohesiveness and sanctuary for a people who experience loss and chaos in a racist and dehumanizing society. Specifically in chapter 5, Conde-Frazier discusses how *evangélicas* structure their ministries in the community as an integral part of their service to God, emerging from their "neighbor consciousness" in relation to their Spirit consciousness. She further examines how *evangélicas* negotiate ecclesial spaces, shaping their congregations, and thereby create new models of church through their daily practice of prayer and discernment, as well as through creative ministries. According to Conde-Frazier, a biblical foundation, a deep sense of vocation that is divinely inspired, and experience as Latinas serve to inform and shape an evangélica ecclesiology. Experience includes compassion for the suffering and oppressed, anger over injustice, and passion for God and for justice for the world—which Conde-Frazier considers part of the ministry of reconciliation. Conde-Frazier underscores the incarnational aspect of ecclesiology as she relates ministry to the concept of *dabar* (verb): that is to say, that a true church cannot just be satisfied with preaching or saying the right things. She reminds us all that the church is a Spirit-led community and the body of Christ, tasked to bring to life and enflesh the good news it preaches. It must be the very incarnation of light, love, and hope to all people, but especially "to the least of these," to the forgotten and the downtrodden of the world.

29. In some *evangélica* communities the appellation *Papá Dios* is used.

Ada María Isasi-Díaz has alleged that Scripture plays a minimal role among Catholic Latinas.[30] This is not the case for *evangélicas*, who consider Scripture foundational for practice and belief.[31] Nevertheless, Scripture exerts a praxeological authority for *evangélicas*; unlike some Protestants who hold a traditional understanding of Scripture's authority, *evangélicas* say that Scripture is important, not because of some a priori theoretical argument of infallibility or inerrancy, but rather because it speaks to actual life realities facing the Latina community in the spaces of the everyday. Scripture has authority because it witnesses to the presence of a saving tri-une God in the space of *lo cotidiano*. This reading of Scripture is reflected in the celebration of *testimonios* (witnessing). Conde-Frazier examines this distinctive practice of *evangélicas* in chapter 6. She explores the primary role of Scripture among *evangélicas*, and also discusses the hermeneutical tools of discernment important for them. In light of the important post-colonial work being carried out in biblical studies, Conde-Frazier reviews how colonizers used the Bible and how the colonized interpreted it. She then discusses how such practices impact current interpretive readings in *evangélica* churches, and how they have been surpassed in prophetic ways liberative for women. Part of Conde-Frazier's methodology is to feature the voices of *evangélica* pastors, laywomen, and scholars.

Emphasis on *lo cotidiano* has not robbed *evangélica* theology of the transcendent parameters it has inherited from its missionary forebears. Yet for *evangélicas*, transcendence does not necessarily imply pie-in-the-sky or escapist theologies. Martell-Otero argues in chapter 7 that the dimensions of spatiality in conjunction with temporality hold the key for an *evangélica* contribution to the discussions about eschatology. To speak about eschatology from an *evangélica* perspective is to go beyond the dichotomies of now and then. It is not an argument between dispensationalists, premillennialists, or other such eschatological camps—though such millennial beliefs abound in the *evangélica* churches. Martell-Otero revisits the Trinitarian language of *perichoresis* (understood within the framework of the biblical concept of the reign of God) as well as the meaning of *kairos* in its spatial rather than temporal sense. This permits her to define eschatology in terms of "place": the encounter of God's sacred space and time with creation space. Given the importance of place, Martell-Otero posits that *evangélicas* can understand eschatology as a vision of holistic community that entails

30. Isasi Díaz, *En La Lucha*, 46.
31. Martell-Otero, "Women Doing Theology," 76.

a healing of the historic rupture between God, humankind, and creation. This healing *takes place* by creating a living space for all, especially for those historically displaced. This vision, impelled by the power of the Spirit, is what moves *evangélicas* to work towards justice and the transformation of their communities.

Earlier in this introduction, we referred to *teología en conjunto* as one of the distinguishing characteristics of Latin@ theologies. Theology is never carried out in a vacuum, nor is it solely the expression of isolated cogitations. It is truly a discourse. This book is the product of such a communal discourse—among its authors, between the authors and their communities of faith, and between these communities and the Latin@ context in the United States. This aspect of our theologies is again reflected in the dialogical nature of chapter 8. We model that agreement does not necessarily mean uniformity, nor does diversity and divergence lead to division. Rather, such a praxis of *en conjunto* amid diversity leads to an enriched and enriching theological conversation that blesses each of us. We hope that our responses in this chapter will answer some questions and raise others by you, the reading audience, as you engage with each topic alongside us.

Theology does not arise just from specialists in the field. Indeed it is our claim that *evangélicas* are profoundly theological women who reflect on the presence of God and its implications in the spaces of the everyday. Nevertheless, theology can sometimes be daunting because of a tendency to use specialized jargon (e.g., words like *eschatology* and *perichoresis*). We want this book to be accessible not just to theologians in the academy but to our *abuelitas* and other *evangélicas* in the pew. For this reason, we have included a glossary of technical terms. While all Spanish terms are defined throughout the book, most are also included in the glossary. Each chapter also includes questions to stimulate further conversation among all of us. We hope that the contents of this book will be a gift to our communities, which have gifted us with their faith, their vision, and their theologies.

t w o

Dancing with the Wild Child

Evangélicas *and The Holy Spirit*

ZAIDA MALDONADO PÉREZ, LOIDA I. MARTELL-OTERO, AND ELIZABETH CONDE-FRAZIER

INTRODUCTION (MALDONADO PÉREZ)

I LOVE THE HOLY Spirit. She is like the wild child of the Trinity, anywhere and everywhere moving, calling forth, and stirring things up.[1] She is wonderfully illusive yet also fully present.[2] She is untamable, full of possibilities and creative potential. She is the *salsa* beat in our daily foxtrot and the *un-dos-tres-bachata* in our electric slide. She is and will be unconventional, even uncultured.[3] She is the miracle of the mélanges that terribly confound some but keep others praising the God who never ceases to surprise and amaze us. She is the wonder that moves our questions from, what does this all mean? to, what shall we do? She can forever alter our lives and change

---

1. Gen 1:2; Acts 2 et al.

2. Or, inscrutable. In another sense, Basil (fifth-century Cappadocian church father), refers to the Spirit not allowing us to "form the idea of a nature circumscribed." Basil the Great, *On the Holy Spirit* §22.

3. Mark 8:22–26; Acts 10; Rom 3:11b et al.

our world.[4] She is life-giving breath, wind, and fire. She is the *ruach elohim*, the flaming divine *pneuma* that is always "going native" because she wants to be encountered by all.[5] She is calming Spirit amid the storm. She is wisdom. Some in the early church didn't know what to make of her and tagged her on almost like an afterthought to the end of the first Nicene version of the creed that begins with "We believe" and ends with "And in the Holy Spirit." Much like a lingering question about which there was still much to ponder, the nature, person, and work of the Spirit eluded the early church's noetic grasp. Today she still eludes ours. But I love this about her! As part of the Godhead, she reminds us that she cannot be had or possessed as many claim when they say, *tengo el Espíritu Santo* ("I have, or I possess, the Holy Spirit" and therefore can order it about).[6] Rather, it is we who are the Holy Spirit's temple, God's vessel. Saint Basil the Great, a fourth-century theologian who wrote *On the Holy Spirit*, eloquently captures some of the "spirit" of this "unapproachable" yet "apprehendable" third Person of the Trinity. This poetic, almost panegyric tribute to the nature of the Person and work of the Holy Spirit is worth quoting here at some length.

> Intelligent essence, in power infinite, in magnitude unlimited, unmeasured by times or ages, generous of Its good gifts, to whom turn all things needing sanctification, after whom reach all things that live in virtue, as being watered by Its inspiration and helped on toward their natural and proper end; perfecting all other things, but Itself in nothing lacking; living not as needing restoration, but as Supplier of life; not growing by additions; but straightway full, self-established, omnipresent, origin of sanctification, light perceptible to the mind, supplying, as it were, through Itself, illumination to every faculty in the search for truth; by nature un-approachable, apprehended by reason of goodness, filling all things with Its power, but communicated only to the worthy; not shared in one measure, but distributing Its energy according to "the proportion of faith;" in essence simple, in powers various, wholly present in each and being wholly everywhere; impassively

---

4. Acts 1:12; 2:37, 38 et al.

5. Acts 2:3–4, 8 et al.

6. I am reminded of the many evangelists and some pastors who claim to be able to distribute the gifts of the Holy Spirit as if they controlled or "had an in" with the Holy Spirit. Acts 2:3 is an excellent example of the Holy Spirit being the one that distributes (the Greek says "distributing") as God wills. The Holy Spirit also reminds us that God cannot be "had" in the sense of being duped, deceived, or lied to (see Acts 5:1–11; Gal 6:7–8).

divided, shared without loss of ceasing to be entire, after the like-
ness of the sunbeam, whose kindly light falls on him who enjoys
it as though It shone for him alone, yet illumines land and sea and
mingles with the air. So, too, is the Spirit to every one who receives
It, as though given to him alone, and yet It sends forth grace sufficient and full for all mankind [*sic.*], and is enjoyed by all who share
It, according to the capacity, not of Its power, but of their nature.[7]

"Wholly present in each and being wholly everywhere," this "Sup-
plier of life" is God with us. She is the passion in the Word-become-Verbo
for us. She is God's animator, the "verb" in the Word, if you will.[8] As our
Advocate (Helper, Comforter, Counselor), the Holy Spirit is not only God
with us; She is God for us.[9] And, for *evangélicas*, the Holy Spirit especially
is God in us, the one in and through whom we commune with the divine.[10]
Filled, inspired, and moved by the Holy Spirit, *evangélicas* engage life from
the perspective of the One who is able to move over chaos, nothingness,
and death, speaking life into death-bearing situations and being midwives
to hope. The Holy Spirit emboldens us, even through the shadow of death,
to fight the good fight on behalf of those gripped by despair. And it reminds all, even those who would confuse patriarchy for orthodoxy, that
we do all of this as nothing other than *hijas de Dios*— women, mothers,
daughters, leaders, pastors, bishops, apostles, vessels and instruments of
God's will and glory.

---

7. Saint Basil the Great, *On the Holy Spirit*, §22.

8. Heb 4:12. Note: those of us who grew up with what was the most commonly used
translation of the Bible—the *Reina Valera* (1909), have been used to referring to Jesus
(and to the Greek *logos* in John 1:1) as the *Verbo* ("Verb"), not the "Word" (*Palabra*), as
do English translations. Although, grammatically speaking, the word *Verbo* as referring
to the person of Jesus would be a noun, the use of *Verbo* rather than *Palabra* makes a
substantial difference in the way Latinas/os understand and envision the Son. As the
Verbo, *Jesús* is an *active* agent (rather than passive) in the beginning, and throughout
history, with God (e.g. Gen 1:1 and John 1:1). The Holy Spirit, then, becomes a natural
procession from the Son, God's embodied activity of dynamic grace. The *Reina Valera
Gómez*, (2010) and other Spanish translations also have "Verbo" for the Greek *logos*. *La
Biblia de Estudio: Dios Habla Hoy* (1994) has "Palabra."

9. The *Theological Dictionary of the New Testament* has "advocate" as the "first clear
idea" corresponding to "Paraclete." Jesus is the one who intercedes at "God's bar in heav-
en" (Matt 10:32–33; Rom 8:34; Heb 7:25). Referring to its use in John, the contributor
claims no single equivalent for "Paraclete," deeming "advocate" the basic interpretation,
and "Supporter" or "Helper" as "perhaps the best rendering" (784).

10. Rom 8:26; 2 Cor 13:14, et al.

Beginning from the Scriptures and the Holy Spirit's own witness to us as one of the Persons of the Godhead, we explore in this chapter how the Spirit is God for us because She is God in us.[11] She is God's ¡presente! We argue that the Holy Spirit's act of dwelling with us and being in us (John 14:17) affirms our personhood not only as children of God (Rom 8:16) but as Latina women, instruments of God's reign in whatever way God deems. The Holy Spirit is divine *presencia*. Since She is Holy, we are made holy. We are sanctified, set apart for the work to which God calls us, and gifted accordingly. Hence we will also consider what these gifts or charisms are that *evangélicas* bring to ministry and how they witness to God's presence— God's *trabajo personal*—in and through us.

Although God sets us apart for service in the work of the church, we also encounter a movement that continually sets us apart from such ministries it sees as reserved for men only. This makes us especially sensitive to the importance of the Holy Spirit's call to "test the spirits" (1 John 4:1). Hence this chapter also considers the important role of discernment, its foundation, and the signs that help us distinguish between God's Spirit and our own. Finally, because the Holy Spirit is at every point of our experience deeply relational and so also deeply contextual, we end the chapter with a personal witness of a Holy Spirit gone native.

First, here is a note about our use of the feminine for the Holy Spirit. As *evangélicas* we believe that the Holy Spirit is one of the Persons of the Trinity, coequal, codivine, consubstantial with the Father and the Son.[12] Scripture says that God has no gender. God is not a man (Num 23:19); God

11. I like how Gregory of Nazianzus put it in his *Fifth Theological Oration, On the Holy Spirit*, ch. 7. "The Holy Ghost," he argues, "which proceedeth from the Father Who, inasmuch as He proceedeth from That Source, is no Creature; and inasmuch as He is not Begotten is no Son; and inasmuch as He is between the Unbegotten and the Begotten is God" (*The Nicene and Post-Nicene Fathers*, 2nd ser., 7:320). This is one of the five orations that Gregory, known also as, the Theologian, preached in Constantinople between 379 and 381 with the intention of refuting the claims, especially of the Arians and Eunomians, on the nature and interrelations of the Persons in the Godhead.

12. Gregory of Nazianzus underscores the Godhead of the Holy Spirit as follows: "But we have so much confidence in the Deity of the Spirit Whom we adore, that we will begin our teaching concerning His Godhead by fitting to Him the Names which belong to the Trinity, even though some persons may think us too bold. The Father was the True Light which lighteneth every man coming into the world. The Son was the True Light which lighteneth every man coming into the world. The Other Comforter was the True Light which lighteneth every man coming into the world. Was and Was and Was, but Was One Thing" (Gregory of Nazianzus, *The Fifth Theological Oration: On the Holy Spirit*, §3).

is Spirit (John 4:24; 2 Cor 3:17; Phil 3:3). This does not mean, however, that we are to refer to any of the Persons using the English neuter pronoun *it*, since this usage of the neuter obfuscates God's personal self-disclosure. Indeed, the Scriptures refer to each of the Persons using gendered pronouns, metaphors, and analogies (Isa 42:14; 46:3–4; 49:14–15; 66:12–13; Num 11:2; Luke 13:18–21; Matt 6:9; 23:37 et al.), reminding us that the Hebrew tradition, unlike the Christian tradition, is significantly more versatile and more at ease using both male and female language for God. Rather than a cumbersome use of both masculine and feminine pronouns for the Holy Spirit, and following the feminine form of the Hebrew term *ruach* ("breath," or "blowing," "air," "wind," or "soul"), we use the feminine pronoun when referring to the Holy Spirit.[13]

THE HOLY SPIRIT AS *PRESENCIA* (MARTELL-OTERO)

Evangélicas are very familiar with this Person, whom Gregory of Nazianzus once described as *theos agraptos* (the God about whom we tend to remain silent).[14] The Spirit indeed is the "no-body" that is often described as a "holy ghost," envisioned as an ephemeral misty nothingness. Too often the Spirit has been subsumed by christological and Trinitarian discussions, her role limited either to "pointing to Christ"—like a good hunting dog on a trail—or serving as a "bond of love" between the Father and Son. The Spirit is trapped either by ecclesial structures or within the interior cavities of pietism's safe spaces of privatistic enthusiasm. Such a Spirit can never be the wild child described at the beginning of this chapter, the dance partner who swirls us in a *bachata*, and who takes us to uncharted areas of faith and

13. *Pneuma*, is neuter in the Greek, *spiritus* in Latin is masculine. I am aware that the feminine form of the noun does not, therefore, imply gender. The intent of this work is not apologetical—I am not suggesting that we ought to refer to the Holy Spirit solely as She. It is simply my preference here, one based on biblical precedence. I am also not advocating for a Trinity that is one-third feminine and two-thirds masculine. It is clear that this does not solve the issue of patriarchy. However, it does alleviate, for me and countless others, the dissonance over an absolute and unbiblical insistence and, often, reification of the maleness of the Godhead (that becomes equated with God's roles as Father and Son. This borders on an idolatry of gender. We must remember that God is called Father because he is "begetter" of the Son and because he relates to the Son (and because of him, to us) as Father. God is, however, Spirit. For an extensive definition of *ruach*, see Congar, *I Believe in the Holy Spirit*, 3.

14. Or, literally, "the God about whom no one writes." Gregory of Nazianzus, "On the Holy Spirit," 194.

experience. Such a Spirit could never raise eyebrows. *He* would never raise the kind of controversial cries that followed the World Council of Churches gathering at Canberra after Chung Hyun Kyung's address brought such a wild child to the august meeting that dared to proclaim the theme "Come Holy Spirit," with the expectation that he would come dressed in a business suit or at the very least in clergy garb.[15]

Evangélicas know this wild child, who is often preferred as absence rather than *presencia* (presence) because we too have experienced being treated as no-bodies and invisible nothings. We recognize the social symptoms of being invited to places where we are not really wanted, and where we must dress in white in order to survive as a people of color who speak and dance in different rhythms and see life from different perspectives. We have learned to survive amid a dominant group who prefers to captivate and dominate, rather than partner and form communal relations in order to become *familia* to each other. It is not surprising that we resonate with such a Spirit who comes to us as this wild child, who opens up the arms of God's *ekstatic* love to us, and makes our hearts soar when we pray, "Come, Holy Spirit!" In response, we open our spirits and lives to the unexpected miracles that take place when we utter such a phrase.

For *evangélicas*, the Holy Spirit is first and foremost a Person. Writing from a Pentecostal context, Samuel Soliván notes that the "personalization of the Holy Spirit is important to Hispanic American pneumatology because the relationship of the Spirit to persons, in this case Latinas and Latinos who daily experience treatment as nonpersons, can provide a transformative model of personhood and self-esteem."[16] Dehumanized by the dominant society in myriad ways, by churches in overt and subtle ways, and by socioeconomic and political forces that shape our new globalized realities, we are suspicious of theologies that also seek to depersonalize the Spirit. To us the Spirit is never a force, a bond, or a disincarnate being with no fixed identity. The Spirit is unlike those who relate with Latinas from afar as feudal lords, impersonal government officials, or superior powers— persons accustomed to dictate where and how things can and should be done. Rather the Spirit is the One who draws near to speak, comfort, reveal,

---

15. See Chung, "Welcome the Spirit," 220–23. Subsequent responses are on 224–29. Also Balasuriya, "Liberation of the Holy Spirit," 200–205.

16. Soliván, "The Holy Spirit," 53.

touch, strengthen, anoint, encourage, heal, and bring to new life. The Spirit speaks *tú a tú* (face-to-face).[17]

Spirit is not just any Person, however. She is the Third Person of the Trinity. Spirit is God, and therefore is God active and present among us. *Evangélicas* are cognizant that as God, the Spirit is the One who comes to be in their midst but not as a secondhand messenger, for that would imply that *evangélicas* are an afterthought in God's eyes. *Evangélicas* are persons, daughters of the living God. The One who comes to them is One who together with the Parent and Son "is to be worshipped and glorified" and who is active not just in the church, but in the world.[18] As Third Person, Spirit is part of the story of salvation. Killian McDonnell identifies two "constitutive moments" in this soteriological dance: one christological and the other pneumatological.[19] The tradition, particularly as expressed by Athanasius and Gregory of Nazianzus, has often understood salvation through Jesus Christ as *theosis* or divinization. Yet, for *evangélicas* this *danza* also includes the redemptive power of Spirit to humanize. That is to say, the Spirit is the One who gives us a vision of what life is, and exposes the lies of the nonlife that have been constructed for us by oppressive social structures. Spirit is the One that leads us away from the *habitus* of death on a personal as well as an interpersonal level. She teaches us to be a holistic community, to be *familia sana*, and reminds us that the earth is the Lord's and not our plaything to destroy at whim. Spirit is God the Third Person, who treats the outcasts and nobodies like persons.

While Scripture does not have a doctrine, a pneumatology per se, its use of key words to describe the Holy Spirit clues us in to her identity. One such term is *ruach*. Because Spirit is breath of life, early church creedal statements often described her as life-giver and Creator, who breathes life into all of creation. Spirit is wind that blows. I have often heard preachers interpret John 3:8 to underscore the freedom of the Spirit to blow where it wills. However, a more accurate reading of the text indicates that it is we who are blown about by the power of *ruach*. Spirit is God's continual tie, or *vínculo*, to us: we live because God breathes (Psalm 104). Spirit is God's *dynamis*—God's power and active presence in the world. We cannot breathe

17. In Spanish, the formal you (*usted*) is used as a sign of respect but at times can also deliberately preserve or create emotional distance. *Tú* (singular "you,") is informal and often indicative of intimacy and trust. In Puerto Rican society, we treat as *tú* only those closest to us.

18. "Word and Spirit," 15.

19. McDonnell, "Determinative Doctrine of the Holy Spirit," 154.

without God! Spirit is the wild child that is God's gift to us, but whom we try again and again to possess as data rather than *donum*, as given rather than as *gratia*.

As God, Spirit is precisely *la presencia de Dios que se puede sentir* (the presence of God that can be felt). This sense of God's presence is wonderfully reflected in the *corito* (short refrain) called "Dios Está Aquí" ("God Is Here").

> Dios está aquí
> Tan cierto como el aire que respiro/
> Tan cierto como en la mañana se levanta el sol/
> Tan cierto que cuando le hablo Dios me puede oír/
> Lo puedo sentir cuando está a mi lado/
> Lo puedo sentir dentro de mi corazón.[20]

Sentir can mean "to feel" but also implies *sentido* (sense). God's presence makes eminent sense for *evangélicas* precisely because God is gracefull, Life-giving Spirit that permeates the world with breath and life. Where else could God be if not *here*? The *evangélica* notion of *presencia* is the affirmation that God the Spirit is present in the world bringing life, hope, and transformation to all its spaces, not solely to the spaces of "outer breath" or "inner love."[21] It is an acknowledgment that God's transcendence is manifested in God's immanent presence. Sin, evil, and death do not have the last word; God does.

As an immanent, personal *Presencia*, Spirit is never immaterial or disincarnate. An *evangélica* pneumatology is deeply incarnational, which also implies that it is always contextual. Spirit is *presente* and is especially present to the reality and lives of flesh-and-blood people. Spirit is not theory. She is not a thing to be bandied about, nor is she less than the other Trinitarian Persons. *Dios verdaderamente está aquí*, fully Person, fully present.

THE HOLY SPIRIT AND THE CHARISMS (CONDE-FRAZIER)

When we internalize the *presencia* of the Spirit, She does an internal work in our lives as women. Calling is a special way for the Sprit to usher in a keen awareness of the fullness of our energies created by God. The Spirit

20. God is here/ As truly as the air that I breathe/ As truly as the sun rises in the morning/ As truly as when I speak God hears me/ I can feel God when God is at my side/ I can feel God in my heart. (Loida Martell-Otero's translation.)

21. Heron, *The Holy Spirit*, 87.

works in us a oneness with God that awakens the fullness of who we are. This creates a space of freedom for us to be ourselves; it also gives us the strength to know, channel, maintain, and grow our life of freedom. Within this calling into fullness of freedom and life is an endowment, an infilling with the charisms of the Spirit. We become life giving and full of life. This may be called vocation.

The charisms or gifts of the Spirit are the expressions of God in us, a spiritual genetic inheritance that we receive as children of God. The Spirit makes no distinction between persons but pours herself out generously to all who ask (Luke 11:13)—regardless of age, ethnicity, gender, ableism, or sexual orientation—as a part of the Spirit's embrace and empowerment within a covenant of abiding. John Wesley's words express well this experience of God's Spirit: "God breathes unceasingly in the soul and the soul breathes unceasingly unto God."[22]

The charisms are not only those mentioned in the epistles and categorized in different ways (Rom 12:4–10; 1 Cor 12:8–11; Eph 4:11–13). They are the gifts or expressions of who we are. Our very being is a charism, as Jürgen Moltmann affirms: "Being a woman is a charism which must not be surrendered in favor of male ways of thinking and behaving."[23] These charisms are the unity between Jesus and the church. They find full expression in community, for they are meant for communal use (1 Cor 12:12–14). They are for the carrying out of the tasks of the church in the world: *diakonia, koinonia, leitourgia, kerygma, didache* and *propheteia*. They also become the ways in which the church contextualizes her ministry. The charisms become the fulfillment of Jesus' words to the disciples: "These things shall you do and even greater" (John 14:12, NRSV).

For *evangélicas* these charisms are for doing *trabajo personal* (personal work). This is the carrying out of one's ministry as a form of discipleship. *Trabajo personal* is one-on-one ministry. Such ministry takes many different forms in many different contexts. It may be visiting a neighbor to clean her apartment because she is ill, visiting those in prisons or hospitals, listening to and counseling someone, or discipling a new believer by engaging in Bible study. This is different work from that of a committee. It is a personal sense of calling to do a consistent work for the least of these. It may be done two by two or alone. It may be known to others or it may be done in secret. The reward for such work is not recognition but hearing

22. Wesley, *Sermons on Several Occasions*.
23. Moltmann, *The Source*, 57–58.

Jesus say to us, "Well done good and faithful servant" (Matt 25:21, NRSV). *Trabajo personal* is calling and charism in tandem, and it is the Holy Spirit who directs and empowers us in this work. This exercise of the charisms is for reasonable service in the everyday world.[24] Charisms are the evidence of the presence of the Holy Spirit. As Martell-Otero writes in chapter 7 on eschatology, "Spirit empowers as well as invites, grants charisms and provides the resources necessary to carry out the ministries needed to transform our suffering communities."[25]

Tongues

It is easy to see how the charisms of prophecy, wisdom, and healing help to transform our communities. The gift of tongues, however, is a bit more confusing and controversial for those Protestant communities who do not claim to be charismatic. For this reason I want to give a bit more attention to this gift. Tongues or an utterance of the Spirit is the Holy Spirit praying in us and through us. She prays "with sighs too deep for words . . . and intercedes for the saints according to the will of God" (Rom 8:26–27, NRSV). This is the language of the Spirit that taps into the rivers of the Spirit flowing within us even when these seem to go underground because we are depressed or oppressed. She brings us back our voice. She summons us to word and to creative work.

Tongues may also express joy, praise, and song. At a time of great crisis in my life when I could not pray, I opened my mouth in both desperation and faith that the Spirit would resurrect my strength. A song came forth, surprising me and stirring my feet to dance. After that moment, the joy from that deep well strengthened me, released me from stress, and broke the suffocating grip of depression in my soul and body.

When we are built up from the inside out, we are resurrected at every level of our personhood. We are empowered, and each time we give ourselves to the overflowing of the Spirit we are transformed. The transforming flow eventually brings us to an insight about ourselves, our circumstances, and God—an insight that is catalytic of new patterns of thinking and acting. This is not only a holy moment or religious phenomenon but a way to release life from within.

24. Moltmann, *The Source*, 58.
25. See p. 122 below.

Prophecy: A Word from God

Paul tells the Corinthians that the gift of tongues edifies the speaker (1 Cor 14:4). However, if accompanied by interpretation, it becomes prophecy and can edify others. A word from God comes in many ways. It may be the utterance of wisdom or knowledge (1 Cor 12:8). Women have been allowed to practice this gift, although in some settings they have not been allowed to prophesy from the same place as a man. The gift opens up avenues for women to take leadership through their service.

Evangelical communities may hold different views about the roles that male and female prophets play in the church. This calls for a broader community process of discernment. When I (Elizabeth Conde-Frazier) was the first female pastor in a community, many purportedly prophetic messages were uttered about my being out of order. I invited the people from the different congregations to a gathering of discernment, and as they listened to my spiritual story of calling, they discussed the matter publicly. After sitting through much deliberation and a barrage of Bible verses, a female elder exclaimed, "You shall know them by the fruits they bear."[26] On the basis of this Bible verse it was decided that I was to be given three years to show the fruit of my ministry. During that time there were to be no arguments or comments about the controversy. At the fulfillment of the specified time, I sent out letters inviting all the people back to assess my ministry. They responded unanimously to my call to serve as pastor. As a result, and in affirmation of my ministry, I was invited without incident to preach at the other congregations who had opposed my pastoral ministry as a woman. Prophecy as a communal invitation to reexamine the tradition allows for the tradition to be reformed as it is weighed against new truth claims in new times (1 Cor 14:29).

This notion of the prophet as visionary and advocate for justice is becoming strong in the *evangélica* community. Prophecy is a word that reimagines and remakes the world. As such, it refashions the mind, imagination, and the life of the prophet. It also informs her work in the community.

26. This was a paraphrase of the Matt 7:16 passage, which speaks about how one tells the difference between a false prophet and a true prophet.

Healing

The emphasis on healing gifts is plural. Just as there are many types of ill-nesses—mental, physical, and spiritual—there are many kinds of healings. The abuses of these gifts as well as the mystery surrounding them have made them controversial and suspect. *Evangélicas* are open to them even as they exercise their gifts of discernment. It is important to note that neither Jesus nor his disciples healed everyone in their midst. When visiting the pool at Bethesda in Jerusalem where there were many who were blind, lame, and paralyzed, Jesus healed only one man (John 5:2–9). Paul addressed Timo-thy's gastric complaint with the advice to take wine as medicine (1 Tim 5:23). Paul himself was not healed of his thorn in the flesh but given the strength to bear it (2 Cor 12:7–9). The gift of healing is not an exercise of supernatural power but the channeling of love and compassion.

When she became shut in by her rheumatoid arthritis, my grandmoth-er would spend the later hours of the night interceding on behalf of the sick. She would keep a list and pray diligently for hours every night. She would then check off the list those whom she had seen Jesus come to as she prayed or would say, "Tell her to allow the doctors and medicine to take its course." On occasion, she would sadly ask my grandfather to have the church pray for the strength for the family because the person on the list was about to finish their journey on earth. She would argue with God as she advocated for someone's healing while realizing that she was not the one to make the determination. She saw herself as one who summoned all her faith, wisdom, and compassion to practice her call through intercessory prayer.

Other members of the body of Christ are sensitive to inner healing needs and have the ability to name the secrets of a person's life that are blocking vitality in them. They are able to pull up roots of bitterness and unforgiveness and to close deep wounds from childhood trauma through their words of truth and prayer.

Healings include not only a miraculous event at the altar call. They are the work of restoring community, social relationships, and the dignity of life wherever people find themselves. They integrate body and soul and restore the disruptions of life. Second- and third- generation *evangélicas* who have become educated carry out healing through their professions: as therapists, doctors, nurses, counselors, community organizers, teachers, businesswomen, and social workers, for instance. They work alongside in-tercessory ministries of women like my grandmother, valuing and encour-aging all works of the Spirit in the work of the church.

Discernment (Martell-Otero and Conde-Frazier)

As fully Person and fully present, the Holy Spirit can be experienced in a number of ways. The dominant culture has been deeply skeptical of Latina/o spirituality, often rejecting it as syncretistic, animistic, superstitious, ignorant, and even as naturalistic. The dominant culture typically cannot understand a spirituality that has deep roots in African and Amerindian beliefs and that sees no contradictions in claiming that *pueden sentir la presencia* of Spirit in the blowing of the wind, in the singing of the *coquí* (tree frog), or in the deep silences of a communal gathering. Yet *evangélica* belief is not naïve. It realizes that just as there is Spirit that blows in their midst, there are other spirits that are not Holy Spirit. Therefore *discernimiento* (discernment) is of utmost importance.

Discernment could be defined as the ability to perceive, distinguish, or recognize the truth from among many conflicting opinions or truth claims. From a biblical standpoint, it can be defined as making a distinction between what comes from God and what does not. On occasion we see the Pharisees accuse Jesus of healing by the power of Beelzebub (Matt 12:24). Jesus' response helps his hearers make the distinction between Beelzebub and God.

Discernment begins when *evangélicas* learn to trust themselves, the gifts of God, and the power of their personhood. Christian vocalist Jaci Velasquez sings a song about the little voice inside that whispers, calls, and guides.[27] This voice is affirmed and enhanced by the Holy Spirit. Those gifts are directed by the voice, with the goal that one unite with a broader purpose and meaning than just self-fulfillment since the work of the Spirit is to interconnect in accordance with the work of the *basileia* (Eph 2:10).

Discernment may express itself as critical thinking, which is a higher order of thinking that questions assumptions and decides whether a claim is true or false, or that discerns the force behind a motive. *Evangélicas* have unmasked injustices. For example, Episcopal priest Altagracia Pérez of the Holy Faith Episcopal Church in Inglewood, California, was a leader of the coalition that blocked a super-chain store from building a new store in their neighborhood. They did this by unmasking the injustices and unraveling the lies of the company.[28]

27. Velasquez, "Little Voice Inside."
28. Greenwald, *Walmart*.

Discernment is for a woman to know the truth of the difference between what the culture, the theology, and what her gifts and the Holy Spirit are telling her. It grounds her in the truth about herself. Discernment is the clarity and peace that allows her to confidently and courageously express her living in Spirit and in truth so that her life as a woman is her spiritual worship (John 4:23–24).

The critical question that arises then is, how *does* one discern Spirit from spirits? If Spirit is a wild child, then one is in danger of committing the mistake of objectifying and once again possessing her by developing a fixed set of criteria that determines what is and is not "Holy Spirit." To do so would be to close the door on the eschatological possibility of dreams and visions of which Scripture claims Spirit to be *arrabon* (pledge) and *aparche* (down payment). Nevertheless, to have no criteria puts one at risk of falling prey to the malevolent spirits who oppress and take life, and who too often do it in the name of God. How often have we witnessed that in human history! Some would claim that the locus of discernment lies within the community of faith.[29] However, what if the community of faith has lost sight of Spirit and fallen prey to unholy spirits? These vexing questions have led Kirsten Kim to declare the issue of discernment to be a "complex problem." Citing Amos Yong, she cautions that discernment must always be concrete, contextual, and therefore provisional.[30]

Evangélicas do not consider discernment a "complex" issue, though it is never an isolated one. Discernment is a communal endeavor: it is always to be done in the community of faith but also looking to the larger community. Scripture is a foundational tool and guide to help us in the process of discernment. Knowing and experiencing this wild child is indispensable. It is the repeated and intimate encounter with Spirit that ultimately aids in recognizing her presence in their midst. Thus discernment always has an intuitive as well as a cognitive or epistemological component. Ultimately, as Jesus was wont to remind us, one discerns the Spirit by her fruit. The *presencia* and *danza* of Spirit never leave in her wake destruction, death, exclusion, oppression, dehumanization, loss, and invisibility. Such would be anathema to the Spirit's very being as *ruach*, Creator, and Life-giver. Rather, where there is Spirit, there is healing: that which is broken, sick, and mangled by the powers and principalities of sin is resisted and overcome when the Spirit moves in our midst. Spirit transforms. "Behold all things

29. "Word and Spirit," 18.
30. Kim, "Spirit and 'Spirits,'" 360.

are made new!" cried out the Apostle Paul (2 Cor 5:17). Spirit is freedom. Therefore, we experience her wherever there are just movements for liberation of people. Spirit is wild child, but she is also Wisdom. Therefore we must question impulsive acts that lead to destructive consequences. Spirit pours out gifts of seeing, hoping, and charisms that give voice; whereas spirits that are not necessarily holy silence, exclude, and reject. Above all, Spirit is life itself: eternal and abundant life poured out, especially in the spaces where sin would construct idols of death. Thus in order to discern when and where the Spirit that blows in our midst is the Holy wild child that invites us to the *bachata*, we must engage fully and know intimately the God from whence this Spirit comes and to which this Spirit leads.

THE SUBVERSIVE ONE ALWAYS GOES NATIVE: A TESTIMONIAL (MALDONADO PÉREZ)

God has always gone native. The incarnation is God's great and resounding "shout out" to a creation that has lost sight of its Creator and, in the process, of its own humanity. Having forgotten God, we had forgotten also what it means to be made in God's image. Through the incarnation God becomes one of us (except without sin). In Christ, God addresses humanity in and through what is familiar, common, *de la casa*. He connects with the masses and, in the process challenges what is, offering instead what can and ought to be. The Holy Spirit, one in mission and purpose with the Godhead, continues the work of connecting us to our God by always and everywhere going native. In this sense it is possible to say that God, through the Holy Spirit is still becoming incarnate.[31]

The book of Acts provides many examples of the Holy Spirit's work at contextualizing the gospel, at making it go native. Indeed, we are quickly made aware of this in the second chapter of the book of Acts, when the Holy Spirit makes her entrance, first as a "sound like a mighty rushing wind," then as "tongues of fire" and, finally, as the One who, having filled all who were present, inspires them to speak "in other tongues as the Spirit gave them utterance" (Acts 2). Consequently, those present from "every nation under heaven" are able to hear the Gospel in their native tongue.[32] The Holy Spirit

31. God the Holy Spirit is present in a way that does not also supersede God's own revelation in Jesus Christ. Second-century Montanists were accused of this.

32. Acts 2:9–11 reports that there were "Parthians, Medes and Elamites; residents of Mesopotamia, Judea and Cappadocia, Pontus and Asia, Phrygia and Pamphylia, Egypt

went native! John Wesley, commenting on Acts 2:4, underscores the power and purpose of this divine manifestation by stating that "the miracle was not in the ears of the hearers, (as some have unaccountably supposed) but in the mouth of the speakers. And this family praising God together, with the tongues of all the world, was an earnest that the whole world should in due time praise God in their various tongues"[33]

My own encounter with the divine also began with the manifestation of a God gone native. I've known the presence of the Holy Spirit since I was very young. It was through this sense of presence in me and in the persons and ministry of the church that I attended that I experienced the Godhead. But it was the Holy Spirit that made the Trinity real. The Scriptures talked about God's love for us through the Son, but the Holy Spirit made it palpable. Phillip Schaff got it right when he said, "The historical manifestation of the Trinity is the condition of the knowledge of the Trinity."[34] God is a God of history. God broke through time to become incarnate and, in as much as the Spirit now lives within us, God also continues to exist in history (although not delimited to us or to creation). The Godhead becomes static, something to study, without the person and work of the Holy Spirit. This is why a chapter on the Holy Spirit must be more witness and testimony to the Spirit's work in and through us than merely a theological, intellectual exposition on what we believe. It must be lived, reflective experience; it must be story.

It is, therefore, not surprising that what we know of the Holy Spirit we know through the stories of its witness through the Scriptures. My own story, not unlike many others in our communities, finds its redemptive edge in the throngs of the Holy Subversive One we call *Espíritu Santo*. I grew up *puertorriqueña* (known to others as a *spic*) and Pentecostal ("Holy Roller") in a context where these were, and still are for some, curious, if not unwelcome, anomalies.[35] The outsider status that relegated curiosities like us to the unscenic part of town became an important lens through which I viewed and experienced my world, indeed my faith. Made up mostly of

---

and the parts of Libya near Cyrene; visitors from Rome (both Jews and converts to Judaism); Cretans and Arabs—we hear them declaring the wonders of God in our own tongues!" (NIV).

33. Wesley, "Notes on the Acts of the Apostles," in "Notes on the Bible," 285. Acts 2 too is a poignant warning against elevating any culture above another or equating it with God's gospel.

34. Schaff, "The Holy Trinity," §149.

35. *Spic* is a derogatory term used for Puerto Ricans and other Latinas/os. The memory of when I was first called that name in school is still vivid.

women, the *cultos* or church services, held almost every weeknight, were a time to let our spiritual and cultural hair down. In this holy gathering, the *Espíritu Santo* that spoke through the sisters was distinctively Latino/a, and God's first language was Spanish. The Holy Subversive One reminded us that we were not only known by God; we were also God's vessels, called and sanctified for divine purposes. Because of this, and despite our trials, we reveled then (and still do now) in the worship of the triune God whose *Espíritu* fills us with holy and hope-filled expectation. At those daily worship services, God was ¡*presente!*, and therefore anything was (and is!) possible. In the freedom of the Spirit, we felt God moving with and through our curvy bodies to the rhythm of the *bongó*. With and through us, God swayed, *merengue* style, to the beat of hands that slapped the tambourines as furiously as if they were slapping out the demons that had oppressed them during the day. Before this God we were and are not outsiders, *ilegales* or *indocumentadas* (undocumented ones). We were, and are, children of the "I Am That I Am" who calls us to stand tall and claim our status as God's "we are who we are" because of the "I Am" that is in us and claims us as God's own. For *evangélicas*, this knowledge was and continues to be cause for *fiesta*, celebration, Holy Ghost and Latina/o style.

Today it continues to be the cause for the kind of mobilization that has been working for change in and outside church walls. This is an important difference for *evangélicas*, who understand that the work of the Holy Spirit is about more than an inward scrutiny—though of course we are called to sanctified lives, to "be holy as God is holy."[36] But, while we must face and exorcise our inner demons, the Holy Spirit also calls us to exorcise those powers and principalities that would have us believe that God is dead or, worse, apathetic to our cries. Eldin Villafañe refers to the systems that transgress the humanity of others as "principalities and powers."[37] These principalities and powers plague our daily lives through direct and indirect—intended or unintended—forms of discrimination; through self-fulfilling prophecies that fuel our alarming number of high-school and college dropouts;[38]

36. Lev 11:44, 20:26; I Thess. 4:3,7; 1 Pet 1: 15, 16 et al.

37. Villafañe talks about "'spiritual power encounters.'" The "community of the Spirit," he says, "struggles with the forces of sin and death, with the demonic powers that-be, whether individually or institutionally manifested and whether morally, physically or spiritually expressed. The church can depend on the *Parakletos* as it brings the charismatic renewal of the church *in* and *for* the world" (Villafañe, *Liberating Spirit*, 187).

38. While the 1989–2009 status dropout rate for Latin@ sixteen- to twenty-four-year-olds not enrolled in school and who have not earned a high school credential (e.g.

through the rate of suicide attempts among Latina/o adolescents;[39] through teen pregnancies; through drugs, gangs, despair, and apathy; through a me-centered culture with a "cool factor" that elevates the acquisition of things and being entertained to the highest good; and a *machismo* that kills our women and maims our men's humanity. All these sins attack the work of the many *evangélica* mothers and daughters who strive to live and model the hope that only the God of light can give. This countercultural living, because it goes against the grain and does not preserve the status quo, is considered wild and even subversive. *Evangélicas* know that the wild child of the Trinity, the Holy Subversive One, calls us to stir things up, to become "devoted tongues" of fire that will dare to proclaim truth to power so that we can get from the question, what does this mean? to the question, what shall we do?, which will change our churches, our communities, and the world.[40] For, at the beginning, in the middle, and in the end, the Holy Spirit is about God's mission and the benefits of God's grace are for *all* of God's children, indeed, for all creation.

That God is grace to us so that we can be grace to others is not an *evangélica* distinctive but a biblical principle that permeates the Judeo-Christian scriptures. God blesses us so that we can bless the neighbor, the stranger, the friend and even the foe, to God's glory Luke 6:29; 10:25–37; Hebrews 13:1–2).[41]

---

a diploma or an equivalent credential) has shown a decrease, the statistics from the In-stitute of Education Sciences show that "in each year during that [1989–2009] period, the status dropout rate was lower for Whites and Blacks than for Hispanics." The Insti-tute showed Latinas/os at a 17.6 dropout rate in 2009, compared, for instance, to 5.2 for Whites, 9.3 for Blacks. For statistical reference comparing ethnicities in the US, see the National Center for Education Statistics, "Fast Facts."

39. According to the Centers for Disease Control and Prevention's 2011 report, suicide was "the third-leading cause of death for Hispanic males 15 to 34 at a rate of 11.51/100,000" (Suicide Prevention Resource Center, "Suicide among Ethnic/Racial Populations in the US: Hispanics"). The Suicide Prevention Resource Center reports that in the 12 months preceding 2009 "more Hispanic female students reported suicidal thoughts and behaviors than Hispanic males compared to 16.1% of White females and 10.7% of Hispanic males." Among Hispanic ethnic subgroups, Puerto Rican adults are reported to have "the highest rates of suicide attempts." See Suicide Prevention Resource Center, "Suicide among Ethnic/Racial Populations in the US: Hispanics."

40. In relation to preaching, Wesley asked for a "devoted tongue." This too is our quest. Such a request needs the inspiration, guidance, wisdom, and empowerment of the Holy Spirit.

41. This point has been especially evident in Feminist, Womanist and *mujerista* the-ologies. Men who treat us condescendingly, intentionally or not, muzzle the voice and

What may be distinctive is that we do not engage in this struggle out of a sense of entitlement. *Evangélicas* are well aware of our own sinfulness. We claim no special dispensation or honors on the basis of gender or ethnicity. We are redeemed, loved, and called because of God's mercy. Not to acknowledge this is to succumb to the sin of entitlement that some of our male counterparts express when they claim their "right" to the priesthood or other service in God's reign through gender (or a reading of Scripture that equates calling to priesthood, for example, with gender). *Evangélicas* know all too well that gender has nothing to do with whether we can or cannot fulfill a call. And for this knowledge we thank the Holy Spirit's constant rumblings in us. For they give witness to our spirit that *any* and *all* gifts have their source in God who works, not on the basis of gender or status, but by and through God's own will and purpose. To claim anything else is to claim entitlement and to deny the veracity of what unmerited grace really means. As vessels of the Holy Spirit, evangélicas have experienced God's unmerited grace as a transforming agent who would have us be in the world as holy sacrament, a visible sign of God's abounding grace for the whole world.

QUESTIONS

1. Why might *evangélicas* envision the Holy Spirit as the wild child of the Trinity? Can you give some examples of *presencia* for *evangélicas*? How is God described as present in your own community?

2. What is *charism*? Name some of the ways they are envisioned by evangélicas.

3. In what ways are *prophet* and *prophecy* understood among *evangélicas*? How are these terms understood in your community of faith? Why?

4. In what ways does discernment affirm our gifts?

5. How do you see the Holy Spirit "going native" in your community?

---

freedom of women to follow God's call. The Bible says that where the Spirit of God is, there is liberty (see 2 Cor 3:17). This liberty is everyone's blessing to encounter God in ways "eyes have not seen nor ears heard." We must not limit, outrage, nor grieve the Holy Spirit, on whom we are dependant and through whom we enabled to live after God (Rom 2:11; Gal 5:22; Phil 4:30; Heb 10:29).

three

From *Satas* to *Santas*: *Sobrajas* No More

Salvation in the Spaces of the Everyday

LOIDA I. MARTELL-OTERO

I GREW UP IN the church. My earliest memories centered on the life of the church and Scripture at home. Religion established the patterns and rhythms of my early childhood through my adolescence, marked by the activities surrounding Sunday school, church services, visiting the sick, and evangelistic forays into the streets of Spanish Harlem and beyond, and even summer camp. My initial theological formation was forged not only by the sermons I heard, but more importantly by the extraordinary women of my childhood congregation. Through their teaching of the Bible, prayers, and *testimonios* (witnessing), as well as through hymns and *coritos* (the short, repeated refrains often based on scriptural texts), I learned about the identity of the God who inhabited our *vida cotidiana* (daily lives). The common theme throughout these teachings was that in Jesus Christ and through the power of the Spirit, God was a saving God. These early teachings left a permanent imprint on my notion of an *evangélica* soteriology. These are not the only influences upon my theology. I often turn to the language afforded to me by my medico-theological background as well as the cultural terminology particular to my Puerto Rican bicoastal background. Such varied influences have helped me to perceive that for many *evangélicas* salvation is an embodied event that brings about *santidad* (vocation), *sanidad* (holistic healing), and *liberación*. To emphasize salvation as a historically concrete event experienced in the spaces of the everyday does not deny its transcendental dimension. I believe that it deepens and enriches its meaning for *evangélic@s* in particular, and the Christian church in general.

OUTSIDE OF CHRIST?—CHRISTIAN TRADITION AND THE MEANING OF SALVATION

Traditionally soteriology has been defined in ways that links it closely with the doctrine of Jesus Christ; that is, with Christology. For example, Daniel L. Migliore defines soteriology as the "doctrine of the saving work of Jesus Christ."[1] William C. Placher promotes a similar understanding when he defines soteriology as "the study of how Jesus acts as *sōter*, or Savior."[2] The meanings of *soteriology* are varied because there is no single definition for the term *salvation*. In other words, whereas the church experienced controversy around the doctrines about Jesus Christ, the Holy Spirit, and Trinity, the early church did not undergo a soteriological controversy that led to a definitive creedal statement defining salvation in specific ways.

Furthermore, a cursory examination reveals that "salvation" has meant different things at different times in the Judeo-Christian tradition. For example, in the First Testament, salvation is understood as God's intervention in concrete and historical events: God saved humanity from hunger, illness, famine, military incursions, and political oppression. Above all, salvation was *shalom*— God's outpouring of peace, well-being, and rich blessings so that the community as a whole could flourish in harmony with God, creation, and each other. The Second Testament maintains this understanding, albeit within an eschatological framework that understands Jesus Christ to be the embodiment of the reign of God. God's reign is by no means simply a transcendental event. As in the First Testament, the reign represents justice, mercy, and communal wholeness for all of creation within human history.

By the patristic era, the understanding of salvation had shifted. It was *theosis* or divinization—Jesus Christ was God become human so that we could be like God: incorruptible and in eternal communion with God. The incarnation was crucial for this view of salvation: what was not assumed

1. Migliore, *Faith Seeking Understanding*, 140.
2. Placher, *Essentials of Christian Theology*, 188.

could not be saved.[3] The Western church eventually became deeply influenced by Anselm of Canterbury's satisfaction theory of the atonement and by later Protestant notions of sin. Salvation took on juridical connotations. Humankind violated the divine law and consequently became indebted to God. Jesus' vicarious death was the means to pay this debt. Jesus' crucifixion, rather than the incarnation, took center stage in what came to be known as atonement soteriologies. In the wake of Pietism and Holiness movements, salvation lost its communal implications. As salvation became an increasingly interiorized, individualistic, and privatized event, greater emphasis was placed on its transcendental dimension: Jesus died "for *me*" so that I could "go to heaven."[4]

An *evangélica* soteriology differs from more traditional approaches because the sociohistorical location and context from which Latinas do theology—that is to say, the *locus theologicus*—is different. Latinas theologize from peripheralized places of powerlessness and voicelessness. An *evangélica* understanding of salvation tends to be functionally Trinitarian rather than solely christocentric because of the prominent role accorded to the Holy Spirit in *evangélica* theology. Further, unlike many traditional atonement soteriologies (with their emphasis on Christ's suffering at the cross and death as a means to satisfy a debt of sin to appease what is at times depicted as a wrathful God), an *evangélica* understanding is more incarnational. That is to say, Jesus' life and ministry and the Spirit's outpouring save in very concrete ways *en lo cotidiano* (in the spaces of the everyday).[5] This historical concreteness implies that salvation must include an inherent ethical imperative that leads to the holistic humanization of the oppressed and disenfranchised. To paraphrase a famous dictum: without justice there can be no salvation.

3. Gregory of Nazianzus, "To Cledonius against Apollinaris," 218.

4. For a summary of the differing notions of salvation see Brondos, *Salvation and the Cross.* Also Fiddes, *Past Event and Present Salvation.*

5. In *evangélica* theology, "incarnational" applies to the Holy Spirit as well as to Jesus Christ through the notion of *presencia*/presence. For more, see chapters 2 and 4 of this book, as well as Martell-Otero, "Liberating News: An Emerging US Hispanic/Latina Soteriology of the Crossroads," 340–42. See also Martell-Otero, "My GPS Does Not Work in Puerto Rico."

EVANGÉLICAS AS *SATAS*: STANDING AT THE PERIPHERY AS *SOBRAJA*

Latin@s in general and Latinas in particular are perennial outsiders, treated as nonbodies within racist, classist, and sexist structures that permeate US society.[6] Most Latinas live in neighborhoods where one must daily struggle for the basic staples of life: fresh and sanitary food, quality education, safe homes, heat and hot water, and myriad other details that contribute to a decent quality of life. Women in my congregation have shared how they sought to shield their babies from rats in dilapidated buildings, or how they covered up broken windows with cardboard in the dead of winter, fearing for the health of their children. Many deal with domestic as well as institutional violence. Adequate medical care is often beyond reach. Life is a perennial struggle. They struggle not just for themselves, but also for their families and communities.

Thus Latinas exist at the periphery of US society as "other." They are dehumanized, treated as *satas*. In Puerto Rico, *sat@* is slang for "mongrel." *Sat@s* teem the streets and byways. They seem to lurk in alleyways. Tourists are scandalized by their presence. People shoo them away, throw stones at them, consider them to be ugly and carriers of vermin, tainted by the very fact of being mixed breeds. In contemporary Puerto Rican society, the meaning of *sat@* has expanded. It denotes an unsavory character, a person of low morals, or someone who has behaved indecently. "¡*No seas tan sato!*" is spit out like an epithet. Many Latinas, particularly immigrant and poor women residing in the US understand this experience having been called "spics," "illegals," and "wetbacks." I use *sat@* as a theological metaphor to connote the existential pluriform and peripheral experience of Latinas. It underscores their status as *sobraja*—a people who are treated as if they have no inherent worth—who are consequently relegated to the bottom rungs of society. These women are as rejected in the United States as *sat@* dogs are in Puerto Rican society. Latinas are the nobodies and are shooed away: dehumanized, stereotyped, exploited, and marginalized.

---

6. See Abalos, *Latinos in the United States*, 61, 185–98. See also Machado, "Voices from *Nepantla*"; Barndt, *Understanding and Dismantling Racism*; Omi and Winant, *Racial Formation in the United States*.

JESÚS JÍBARO ENTRE SAT@S: STANDING OUTSIDE THE GATE[7]

Since the 1970s, insights from both Virgilio Elizondo and Orlando E. Costas led Latin@ theologies to mine the Galilean motif apparently emphasized in the Synoptic Gospels, and particularly in the book of Mark. While Elizondo explored the theological implications of Jesus as *mestizo*, Costas referred to him as *jíbaro*—a distinctively Puerto Rican term for peasant or country bumpkin—emphasizing Jesus' location at the periphery.[8] These motifs of *mestizaje* and periphery have, in turn, allowed Latin@ theologies to approach Christology from a holistically incarnational perspective. Jesus' historical and social locations at the periphery of Galilee are part of this approach. An incarnational Christology is not unique to this tradition, of course. However, for many traditions, an incarnational approach is more about asking ontological questions, i.e., *what* is Christ rather than *who* is Jesus. Perhaps this is why so many traditional soteriologies that purport to regard highly the event of the incarnation ironically have said so little about Jesus' attention to the bodily afflictions of the oppressed of his time. Perhaps this also explains why most contemporary theologians from the center have been blind to or silent about the constant disregard, abuse, and misuse of marginalized bodies. In contradistinction, the shift to a more holistically incarnational Christology in Latin@ theologies has led to the articulation of praxeological soteriologies that address real issues facing Latinas. From such a perspective, Jesus is saving because in him God has come to reside as a marginalized cosmological and human *sato*. That is to say, Jesus is a vehicle of God's salvation because he lived, and continues to live, at the periphery, challenging those who wish to follow him to "go outside the gate."[9]

Thus to refer to him as *"Jesús sato"* is to acknowledge that Jesus is a historical peripherally placed person who faces the struggles of his very humanity in the midst of a colonized and peripherally placed people. This is no idealized or disembodied Messiah. This person, who *evangélica* tradition readily acknowledges as God become human, weeps, gets angry, chastises, and tires. He is a *sato* because of his questionable parental lineage: he is an illegal by birth! He is marginalized because of his cultural

---

7. Translation: The peasant Jesus among *sat@s*. Unless otherwise noted, all Spanish translations in this chapter are mine.

8. Elizondo, *Galilean Journey*. Costas, "Hispanic Theology in North America," 72. Cf. Costas, "Evangelism from the Periphery," 52–54.

9. Heb 13:12–13, NRSV. See Costas, *Christ Outside the Gate*, 188–94.

and religious background, as well as because of his geographical location in Galilee. Jesus is *sobraja*, and ultimately considered an *estorbo* (public nuisance) by those in power.

El evangelio (the good news) that *evangélicas* can claim is that in this *Jesús sato*, who is truly Immanu-el, God has intentionally chosen to be with the *sat@s* and *sobrajas* of the world. In this Jesus, they encounter the one who is present in *sus vidas cotidianas* (their daily lives) and in *sus sufrimientos* (their sufferings). He is the one who begins his ministry empowered by the Holy Spirit: "The Spirit of the Lord is upon me because he has anointed me to bring good news to the poor. He has sent me to proclaim release to the captives and recovery of sight to the blind, to let the oppressed go free, to proclaim the year of the Lord's favor."[10] *Evangélicas* know this Jesus and many have experienced the liberating power of this Spirit. His fundamental vocation is to be with "the least of these"—those considered to be *sobrajas* and *sat@s*, such as women, children, prostitutes, tax collectors, publicans, lepers, and Samaritans. Jesus heard and knew the needs of those in the periphery of his time, and *evangélicas* believe that he knows them today. Jesus' foundational good news was not that they would go to heaven, but rather that "the reign of God is in the midst of you."[11]

For *evangélicas*, then, *Jesús sato* is not an appeasement for a wrathful God. Rather, he is the embodied evidence that God knows them and loves them, because like them God in Jesus has experienced and confronted the sinful structures of the world. They recognize that through Jesus, God understands what it means to be wounded and to suffer. Like them, *Jesús jíbaro* suffered death and abandonment. Like them, he was dehumanized, *tratado como un perro* (treated like a dog). The good news for *evangélicas* is that God faced the worst of the world, but was not overcome by the sin of the world. Suffering, abandonment, cruelty, and death do not have dominion over God. The resurrection is God's no to the *sat@s* of the world being rejected. It is God's resounding no to death-dealing institutional forces—whether social, political, economic, religious, or familial—that destroy bodies and communities. The resurrection of *Jesús sato* is evidence of the faithfulness of God, who sends the Spirit to bring life, and life abundant. The resurrection is evidence that in the eyes of God, those whom the world rejects as *sat@s*, God considers *sant@s* (saints). They are not *sobrajas* but

10. Luke 4:18–19 (NRSV).

11. Mark 1:15; Luke 17: 21. For more on the eschatological meaning of the reign from an *evangélica* perspective, see chapter 7 of this book.

children of the Living God. For those who "stand outside the gate" of hope and justice, this is good news indeed.

HOLY SPIRIT: SALVATION AS PRESENCE AND PERSONHOOD

Jesus' salvific ministry did not end with his resurrection. *Evangélicas* continue to affirm his presence in their midst. They also believe that God, who is present in Jesus, continues to save through the Holy Spirit. In contradistinction to more traditional pneumatologies, *evangélica* pneumatology does not perceive the Spirit to be a force, an energy, or a "bond of love," but a Person, God made palpably present in all the spaces of the daily lives of *evangélicas*. *Evangélica* lay leader Linda Castro testified before her congregation that the Spirit's presence allowed her to affirm that "God is not on a throne but by my side" when she faced a potentially catastrophic illness.[12] This abiding presence of God is a powerfully salvific event in the lives of those who are treated as *sobraja*, abandoned by spouses, family, or community, and left with no visible means of societal support. To assert that God is with us when others have discounted our very humanity is prophetically subversive *euangelion* (good news) for the abandoned. For *evangélico* theologian Samuel Solivan: "The personalization of the Spirit is important to Hispanic American pneumatology because of the relationship of the Spirit to persons, in this case Latinas and Latinos who daily experience treatment as nonpersons, can provide a transformative model of personhood and self-esteem . . . The Holy Spirit as the one sent by the Father and promised by the Son re-presents the wholeness of Christ in relation to us."[13]

The Spirit who is Person affirms our personhood and showers upon us the bounty of God's grace and *hesed* (faithful love). In the Spirit we experience *santidad* (holiness), *sanidad* (healing), and *liberación* (liberation). In the Spirit we receive *shalom* and joy. The voiceless speak in tongues and prophecy. We dream dreams of a better life. We can envision a better world. Anointed by the Spirit we go forth with a mandate to transform our lives, communities, and world. As the Spirit empowered *Jesús sato*, so we are given courage to go into marginalized, poor, and dangerous areas too often eschewed by those from the centers of power. Empowered, *evangélicas* resist

12. "Dios no está en un trono, sino a mi lado." *Testimonio* by Linda Castro, First Baptist Church of Caguas, Puerto Rico, September 26, 2010.

13. Solivan, "The Holy Spirit," 53.

the ecclesial structures that reject their calling simply based on their gender or ethnicity. When they sing *"Dios está aquí"* ("God is here"), they are affirming the palpable presence of *Jesús sato* and the Spirit. This experience of the Spirit's saving presence prevents an *evangélica* understanding of salvation from being solely Christocentric. It is a functionally Trinitarian event.

READING OUR TEXTS: *SANTIDAD, SANIDAD, Y LIBERACIÓN* IN THE SPACES OF THE EVERYDAY

In contradistinction to *mujerista* claims, Scripture is an important theological tool for *evangélicas*.[14] Other authoritative texts such as *testimonios, coritos,* and prayers provide *evangélicas* with a sense of self and agency.[15] When biblical texts are read by those who reside in marginalized social locations, themes come to light that are not normally highlighted by theologians from the center. Stories about healing, feeding, and restoration—often interpreted by many scholars as metaphors—are considered historical by grassroots *evangélicas*. These narratives provide hope for them: as God acted then, so God continues to save today.

Evangélicas read and share these narratives, interweaving them with *testimonios* of their encounters of God. This interweaving produces a holistic communal narrative that provides a counternarrative to what I call "normatizing myths," which often are part of a public discourse arising from centers of power and privilege.[16] These myths include, for example, oft-repeated phrases that picture Latinas as submissive, that describe them as welfare mothers, or that dismiss them as ignorant illegals who rob the deserving of needed resources. Like the bodies of other women of color, the bodies of Latinas are eroticized. These dehumanizing myths rob Latinas of voice and power, relegating them to the peripheral spaces of their communities, churches, and the world; these myths facilitate the justification of violence perpetrated against them. *Testimonios* bring to light the falsehood of these myths, even as they affirm "Dios está aquí" because they are *hijas de Dios* and therefore *familia de Dios*.[17]

14. Isasi Díaz, *En La Lucha/In the Struggle*, 46.

15. Conde-Frazier, "Latina Women and Immigration," 62.

16. Machado has referred to these myths as "historical imagination," or "how those in the dominant group of a nation who have power to tell its history perceive the other" in "Voices from *Nepantla*," 93.

17. Daughters of God . . . family of God.

Elizondo has noted that the indigenous people of Mesoamerica believed that the proper way to speak of the divine was not through metaphysical or philosophical assertions, but rather through *flor y canto* (flower and song).[18] Thus I am not surprised to witness *evangélicas* turning to *coritos* when they have exhausted the means for expressing their pain as well as their joy. *Coritos* can be lamentations or expressions of joy.[19] They are *testimonios* expressed through music. Often, they are a more effective means for *evangélicas* to communicate the depth of their encounters with God.

Interweaving Scripture, stories, and songs, *evangélicas* share their experiences of God's salvation in *lo cotidiano*. *Lo cotidiano* is the space in which the powerless and marginalized seek meaning for and control of their lives.[20] Given the fact that religious faith is foundational to the lives and identities of *evangélicas*, one can define *lo cotidiano* as the space where God is encountered, the *locus theologicus* for *evangélica* theology. Paradoxically, it is also the space where one can most clearly see the impact of structural sin in the lives of Latin@ communities, in general, and Latinas in particular. It is here that they can discern "the grace, justice, presence, and love of God manifested in the everyday occurrences" as they share insights about their experiences of *el Jesús sato* and the power of the Spirit.[21]

Given the importance of Scripture, and its interplay with *testimonios* and *coritos* for the articulation of an *evangélica* soteriology, I have chosen three biblical pericopes that I believe demonstrate that *santidad, sanidad,* and *liberación* are integral to an *evangélica* understanding of salvation. All three texts involve nameless women about whom little is known. In the case of the hemorrhagic woman, not even her ethnicity is entirely certain.[22] Nevertheless, biblical interpreters have speculated much about them. Their relation to the larger community has been questioned, their socioeconomic status assumed, and, in the case of the Samaritan, their morals impugned. Latinas resonate with their stories because they see in them echoes of their

18. Elizondo, *Guadalupe.*

19. I am grateful to Ms. Cynthia Román for her insights about the use effective means of laments in Latina experiences of God, as well as to Dr. Melween Martínez, Rev. Inés Figueroa Jiménez, and Ms. Carla Varelo Martínez for sharing their *testimonios* and songs with me.

20. For more on this important theological-epistemological category in Latina theologies, see Levine, *Popular Voices.* Also Isasi-Díaz, *Mujerista Theology.* Aquino, "Theological Method," 38.

21. Conde-Frazer, "Latina Women," 60, 62.

22. Rosenblatt, "Gender, Ethnicity, and Legal Considerations," 138, 141.

own contemporary experiences—not only of mistreatment, rejection, defamation, but also of grace, love, and salvation.

Satas Called to be Santas

When preached from *evangélico* pulpits, sermons about the Samaritan woman at the well are often replete with warnings about the dangers of women with loose morals, shunned by "respectable women" for prostituting themselves. In contrast, Jesus is painted as a saint for daring to "contaminate" himself by being in her company. His dialogue is often interpreted to be a judgment upon her sinful life. While I have heard many male preachers question her morals, I have heard few criticize the morals of the men who seem to have exploited this woman, using her for their own means without extending the societal protections that were her right. Such sermons are probably more often the result of patriarchal and colonized readings of the text. I concur with Luise Schotroff and other scholars who argue that the text does not support such interpretations. Rather the story can be considered a critique of an unjust distortion of levirate marriage. The Samaritan woman's current partner has failed to fulfill the contractual obligation of marriage and extend to her the rights and benefits owed her.[23] In the patriarchal world of first-century Palestine, this would imply that she is left exposed and defenseless.

Her encounter with Jesus leads to a rich theological conversation. Along its course, Jesus conveys an implied criticism of a system that has not only failed her, but also exploited and demeaned her. As a Samaritan she belongs to a people who "seem to have been hated because of their mixed race."[24] She is a *sata* who faces discrimination precisely because she is a Samaritan and a woman. She is treated as *sobraja*. She is as invisible to contemporary preachers and exegetes as she was to her peers. While those from the center refuse to see her, *Jesús sato*, acknowledges her personhood and engages her in *teología en conjunto*. She is one who worships "in Spirit and in truth." The world may reject her as *sata*, but Jesus sees in her one who is called by God. She is neither *sata* nor *sobraja*, but rather *santa*, a saint called, touched, and transformed by God. As *santa*, she goes forth with a deep sense of vocation: she embodies and declares *euangelion* (good news) to those considered *sat@s* by the world. As *llamada* (one called), she

23. Schotroff, "The Samaritan Woman." See also O'Day, *Gospel of John*.
24. Durber, "Political Readings," 72–73. Also, Haacker, "Samaritan."

leaves the heavy water pitcher she carried, even as she leaves behind a life of exploitation. The woman heretofore treated as *sobraja* is now *santa*; the one "heavy laden" is now given rest.

The story of *la Samaritana* is the story of so many Latinas, particularly undocumented migrants. They too are rejected as impure *satas*. Invisible, faceless, and voiceless, they reside at the periphery of a society that knows how to exploit them and to deny them their human rights. Those from the centers of power often impose their distorted views on these women, accusing them of wantonness, criminal actions, and a number of other sins. Latinas are modern-day *Samaritanas* who struggle against almost insurmountable odds to provide for their families. To do so they too must at times engage in "levirate marriages" with common-law spouses who exploit them, abuse them, or abandon them. Thus they are exploited in the domestic spheres of their existence as well as in the larger society. Daisy L. Machado points out that "En todo el mundo hay mujeres que cosen, mujeres que limpian, mujeres que cuidan niños, mujeres que cocinan, mujeres que son cajeras, mujeres que trabajan en 'las piscas.'"[25] They have no recourse, no rest, and no one to defend them. No one knows their true stories, and most do not care, except *el Jesús sato*.

This Jesus is the one who goes out to find them. He sees them, values them, and gives them purpose. Through him they encounter a God who is not like the *maridos* who take what they can without providing either safe haven or legitimacy. God is the one who meets them on the way, by the wells and in the spaces where they seek the well-being of their families. God is the one who provides fountains of living waters—providing for their food, clothing, and shelter, as well as *dignidad y esperanza* (dignity and hope). In the eyes of God, they are not *sobraja*, ignorant, superstitious, uneducated women who can be scoffed at or ignored. Rather, they are deeply religious and astutely theological women who have much to contribute.

Just as this *Samaritana sata* was *llamada*, so Latinas' encounters with God provide them with a sense of vocation. *Las satas son santas* (the impure are truly saints), women called by God. The Spirit of the Lord has been poured out upon them, restoring their sense of personhood and granting them the charism of "tongues"—empowered to speak on behalf of the poor and oppressed who for so long have been voiceless. *Las sobrajas son siervas/*

25. Machado, "Abre Mis Ojos," 38: "Throughout the world there are women who sew, women who clean, women who take care of children, women who cook, women who are cashiers, women who work in 'the pickings' [or, "work in the fields" often as migrant workers hired to harvest vegetables or other crops under dismal working conditions]."

the "surplus" are servants of God, yet not exploited. As the *Samaritana* left behind her pitcher, so Latinas can come to the Lord and find rest. The ministry and contributions of Latinas cannot be fully appreciated unless one can understand that vocation and rest are integral to their notions of being saved. On Sunday mornings, they gather and joyfully sing:

> Venid a mi todo el que estáis trabajados, todo el que esté cansado
> Os haré descansar, os haré descansar, os haré, os haré descansar
> Toma mi yugo sobre vosotros y aprended de mi que soy manso
> y os haré descansar, os haré os haré descansar
> Porque mi yugo es fácil y ligera mi carga
> y os haré os haré descansar.[26]

El Toque de Sanidad: Salvation as Wholeness[27]

I knew Ellie as a child, playing alongside her brothers.[28] She was now a mother herself, showing the weariness that is too often the visage of those whose life is a constant struggle for survival for themselves and their children. One evening as she leaned against the pillar that separated her apartment building from mine, she told me that she had gone to visit her doctor to remove a recurrent cyst that reappeared on her breast. On the day of her appointment, her regular doctor was on vacation and another examined her. Upon being told that the cyst had to be drained again, she began to weep.

Rather than comfort her, the new doctor reprimanded her: why is a grown woman crying over such simple procedure?

She explained her resistance to undergo such a painful procedure again. He was incredulous: "What pain?" he asked.

It was the first time she had learned that she would be given a local anesthetic. Her regular doctor had always drained the cyst without anesthetic, and consequently Ellie assumed that was how it was always done.

Unfortunately, Ellie's story is not an anomaly. I have heard Latinas' stories of medical misuse and abuse, doctors who scold instead of comfort, or who laugh instead of respecting cultural mores. The inherent racism

---

26. Based on Matt 11:28–30 (NRSV): "Come to me all you that are weary and are carrying heavy burdens, and I will give you rest. Take my yoke upon you, and learn from me; for I am gentle and humble in heart and you will find rest for your souls. For my yoke is easy, and my burden is light."

27. "The Healing Touch."

28. I changed her name to protect her identity.

and failures of the health care system have been well documented.[29] In Puerto Rico, until the 1970s, women were routinely sterilized without their knowledge or consent, ostensibly to control the population growth on the island.[30] Latinas are not strangers to physical abuse by many in the medical field. Conde-Frazier explains: "Women's bodies are constantly distorted and destroyed both physically and morally by society. Our bodies are objectified and labeled 'temptation.' We are forced to accept projections of lustful desires and the resulting shame and guilt."[31] In light of these realities, Latinas turn to the one who does not look at them with lust, does not scoff or scorn, and does not abuse or misuse. The God of *Jesús sato* is creator and healer, the one who pours out a healing Spirit to provide *katartizō* (Eph 4:11–13), mending the complex fractures that rend not only their bodies but also their communities.[32] So they sing:

> Oye o Dios me clamor, y a mi oración atiende
> Desde el cabo de la tierra clamaré a ti cuando mi corazón desmaye
> Llévame a la roca que es más alta que yo,
> Porque tú has sido mi refugio, Señor,
> Porque tú has sido mi refugio.[33]

Evangélicas resonate with biblical stories of healing, and in particular that of the hemorrhagic woman. Nameless and faceless, she too is the object of much speculation of contemporary scholarship.[34] Yet little is known other than that she "had been suffering from hemorrhages for twelve years" and "had endured much under many physicians, and had spent all that she had."[35] Like many *evangélicas* who could claim this woman's story as

29. See, for example, Rodríguez Trías, *Health Disparities*; Council of Scientific Affairs, "Hispanic Health," 248–52; Lillie-Blanton and Lillie, "Equitable Access to Health Care"; Lavastide, *Health Care*, 58–60, 71–76. Peek, et al, "Racism in Health Care," 13–17.

30. Rodríguez Trías, *Women and the Health Care System*. Also Ramírez de Arrellano and Seipp, *Colonialism, Catholicism, and Contraception*. For abuses in Peru, see Reverby, "'Normal Exposure' and Innoculation Syphilis."

31. Conde-Frazier, "Hispanic Protestant Spirituality," 139.

32. Martell-Otero, "Of Satos and Saints," 16–17. Wood, *Ephesians*. Also Barth, *Ephesians 4–6*, 439.

33. Ps 61:1–3 (Versión Reina Valera [VLV]); "Hear my cry, O God; listen to my prayer. From the ends of the earth I will call on you, when my heart is faint. Lead me to the rock that is higher than I/ For you are my refuge [O Lord/ for you are my refuge]" (NRSV).

34. See, for example, Marcus, *Mark 1–8*, 357. For a different reading, see Rosenblatt, "Gender, Ethnicity, and Legal Considerations," 138, 141.

35. Mark 5:25–26 (NRSV).

their own, she had no one to intercede on her own behalf. She had to seek relief for her chronic condition on her own. She approaches Jesus with fear and trembling, as so many in the Latin@ community, particularly undocumented workers, approach hospitals and health care facilities. She tries to remain hidden. Like so many abused women, she hopes that his touch will not harm but heal: "If I but touch his clothes, I will be made well."[36]

Thich Naht Hanh believes that transformative action takes place when we stop to look deeply into the lives and situations of those who surround us.[37] This is what Jesus did. He was touched by this woman. While pressed by others to continue, he stops for her and then declares that her faith had saved or healed her. Thus salvation is *sanidad* or *sōzein*—deliverance from chronic or life-threatening illness.[38] Ultimately, it is *shalom* (peace). Irene Foulkes identifies *shalom* with social justice, a manifestation of God's "solidarity with persons who lack power and who, therefore, suffer violence at the hands of individuals and institutions that organize the world for their benefit."[39]

In her encounter with *Jesús sato*, the woman gains her voice and tells her story. She moves from being ill, victimized, silenced, and invisible to being made whole. She is humanized. "She did not have a curse. She was not a walking curse. She could touch others. She could be beautiful and touch others with her beauty. She could have faith in her body again, in her own spirit, and in her womanhood."[40] This woman is no longer *sobraja*. Rather, Jesus declares her to be "daughter"—she is part of a community; she is *familia*. In his words to her, *evangélicas* hear a word of promise and hope for them and for their communities. The world cannot heal us or make us whole, but God is able.

Liberación: Freedom from Oppression, Freedom for Living

One of the more common *coritos* I grew up hearing was

> Libre, Tú me hiciste libre,
> Tú me hiciste libre, libre, O Señor.
> Rotas fueron las cadenas que estaban atando mi corazón.[41]

36. Mark 5:28 (NRSV). See also Sales, "Somebody Touched Me," 10.

37. Nhat Hanh, *Living Buddha*, 82. Sales, "Somebody Touched Me," 12.

38. Marcus, *Mark 1–8*, 356.

39. Foulkes, "Desde la Mujer Centroaméricana," 16.

40. Conde-Frazier, "Latina Women," 73.

41. "Free, You have made me free / You have made me free, free, Lord. / Broken were the chains that bound my heart."

God is the One who has sent Jesus to set us free, not just from our personal sins, but from all that oppresses and robs us of our very personhood. Jesus' ministry was marked by his defense of "the least of these," including poor women. As *evangélicas*, we trust in this *Jesús sato*—God incarnate *quien hace acta de presencia* (who is present today) to bring justice to the many nameless women who have been exploited, violated, silenced, and destroyed.

> Tu fidelidad es grande.
> . . . incomparable es.[42]

This God of justice who hears the cries of the suffering has sent the Holy Spirit, whose very life we experience in the spaces of the everyday. We experience God's liberation *from* that which binds us, but we also experience it when God gives us evidence that we are created *for* life, love, joy, peace, community, and wholeness. This salvific experience leads *evangélicas* to sing joyfully, *Dad gracias con el corazón . . . porque Él ha dado a Jesús, el Salvador* who has saved them precisely because they are a poor and marginalized people.[43]

Machado underscores that Latinas find themselves in the midst of an unwelcoming environment, surrounded by those who oppress them not only as women, but also especially as Latinas. They are *menospreciadas*—rejected, disrespected, and devalued.[44]

> ¿Debe tener una cultura el poder y el derecho de matar las ilusiones de las mujeres porque considera estas ilusiones menos importantes que las de los hombres? ¿Debe tener una sociedad la capacidad de tratar como inferior a un ser humano solamente porque su género biológico es femenino? ¿Cómo es posible que la iglesia no levante una voz de protesta contra esta injusticia que viola la dignidad de la mujer?[45]

It is from these "peripheralized" spaces of suffering and oblivion that *evangélicas* read the story of the perennially stooped woman as narrated

---

42. "Your faithfulness is great / . . . [it] is incomparable." Witt, "Tu Fidelidad."

43. Smith, "Give Thanks," copyright Integrity's Hosanna! Music, 1978, trans. Alberto Merubia: "Give thanks with all of your heart . . . [God] has given Jesus, the Savior."

44. Machado, "Abre Mis Ojos," 40.

45. Ibid., 38: "Should a culture have the power and right to destroy [lit. murder] the illusions [or, dreams] of women because they consider these dreams less important than those of men? Should a society have the capacity to treat as inferior a human being simply because their biological gender is female? How is it possible that the church does not raise a voice of protest against this injustice that violates the dignity of a woman?"

in Luke 13:10–17. While Latinas may not necessarily be physically fused in such a position, they often spend many hours of each day bending over sewing machines, gathering the harvest as migrant workers, caring for children (whether theirs or others'), cleaning houses and public facilities, or performing menial labor for less than living wages.

According to the Gospel of Luke, this woman had attended this particular synagogue for eighteen years, during which she suffered from "a spirit of infirmity" (*astheneia*) that made her "stooped." That is to say, her condition is attributed to spiritual forces that oppress her as well as to her "socially disvalued" state.[46] "She is one of the 'others' whose existence has been ignored. Even though she is there, nobody notices her. Nobody dares to see her. Nobody cares about her even if they do see her. She is left in complete indifference. She is there in silence. She is virtually anonymous."[47] Her presence seems to be an anomaly: she is in a sacred space where she does not belong. Perhaps that is why no one acknowledges her except Jesus. Seeing her, he approaches her proclaiming the "necessity" to set her "loose" (*lyein*), whereupon he lays hands upon her and she is "straightened." While she may be *sobraja* to others, to him she is a "daughter of Abraham." Until he sets her free, she is powerless to combat her affliction and others' indifference to it. Once free, she is able to claim her identity and give voice to her faith in God. For her, then, salvation is "liberation." According to Luke this is a *kairos* time (13:1)—God *hace acta de presencia* (is present to act in decisive ways) in human history to "set the captive free."[48] Liberation is thus a profound aspect of God's salvation for the oppressed (4:18).

Many Latinas know what it is to be treated with disrespect in supposed sacred places where they are not wanted. They know what it feels to be invisible, with very few caring what happens to them or to their communities. This is why *evangélicas* profess faith in *Jesús sato*, who sees them, frees them, and accords them the dignity that others refuse to grant. It is through the saving power of the Spirit that they can stand straight, and through God's charisms that they are empowered to speak and praise God with loud voices. Latinas, particularly the poor, have also experienced the swift vituperation of those, like the synagogue leader in this story, who

46. Torgerson, "The Healing of the Bent Woman," 180. Also Culpepper, "The Stooped Woman," 273.

47. Kinukawa, "The Bent-over Woman," 297.

48. For a fuller discussion of *kairos*, considering both its locative and temporal meanings, see chapter 7 of this book.

protest when they perceive that their sacred spaces of privilege have been invaded. The response is often violent: death at the hands of minutemen or border patrols, or *macanazos* at the hands of police.[49] Sometimes the reaction is less visibly violent, though no less damaging because it is institutional in character: for example, in the strengthening of English-only laws or the passage of anti-immigrant legislation. Yet, like the once-stooped and now-straightened woman, *evangélicas* know that in the eyes of God they are *hijas de Dios* (God's daughters) and therefore *mujeres digna*—women deserving respect.[50] Salvation as liberation is thus a reversal of unjust conditions. Places that once functioned as sites of exclusion can and do become sacred loci of celebration where God's *shalom* is poured out. This is truly a Sabbath moment and time of good news.

CONCLUSION

The evangelical understanding of salvation as transcendent event is reflected in its traditional Sunday-service altar call: accept Jesus Christ as personal Lord and savior, and God will forgive our debts and allow us entry into heaven. To reject Jesus leads to condemnation and hell. This overemphasis on the transcendent permits a notion of Christianity that can minimize its ethical imperative: one does not need to undergo a conversion that demands that one "turn [one's] back on the existing order . . . and accept a correspondingly new style of life" in which "no area of life could be left out." To go to heaven one need only trust that Christ paid the debt, without acknowledging the "privileged place . . . [of] the weak and outcast, the poor, the oppressed, the sick, children, women," or those who are "the most obvious victims of human sin."[51] Yet any soteriology that does not incorporate its radical call to serve those at the periphery is, in Dietrich Bonhoeffer's words, "cheap grace."[52] It is a disincarnate Christianity that allows its adherents to exploit the poor, ignore the suffering, and smugly await a heavenly reward at no cost to them. Only a soteriology of the privileged can ignore God's call to go "outside the gate." This is why the locus of salvation is never

---

49. *Macana* is a police baton. Harmful blows with such a baton are *macanazos*. For more on the institutional violence experienced at the border, see De La Torre, *Trails of Hope and Terror*.

50. Otaño, "La Mujer Encorvada," 129–30.

51. Costas, "A Radical Evangelical Contribution," 137–38.

52. Bonhoeffer, "Costly Grace," 45–47.

at the centers of power, which are blind to their inherent sin of injustice. To truly experience God's salvation, one must begin at the periphery, where *Jesús sato* beckons us to follow.

A Latina *evangélica* soteriology challenges soteriologies from the center. When seen through the lens of liminal spaces of survival, salvation must by necessity become an incarnational event that responds to the daily suffering of forgotten people. From such a perspective one can only ask: how can theologians speak about metaphorical heaven and rewards, crosses and sacrifice, with such disincarnate passion when faced with the reality of so many whose bodies are literally abused, exploited, and disfigured? How can we so glibly take the cup and bread of Eucharist on Sunday mornings while excluding so many from the table that is God's grace to the excluded? How can the Western church place so much emphasis on the forgiveness of debt through Jesus Christ, and be complicit with economic institutions that demand exorbitant fees from the poor? In light of the scope of dehumanization that takes place, how can Christians "go to sleep so peacefully despite the millions around them who live and suffer . . . in the world?"[53]

Evangélicas have faith in the Jesus that knows them and their struggles because he lived as a *sato*. They believe that Scripture is a reliable *testimonio* of God's faithfulness and saving grace because the Spirit gives witness of the Spirit's working in their lives. Thus a Latina *evangélica* soteriology is a Trinitarian event. A Latina *evangélica* soteriology is not disincarnate, devoid of the concrete day-to-day realities of the poor and suffering, or focused solely on going to heaven. From the spaces of the everyday, salvation is life in the face of death-dealing powers and principalities. The themes of *santidad, sanidad,* and *liberación* are a reminder that salvation is about the triune God's reign, and thus about incarnational justice. Salvation *is* an ethical imperative precisely because it is a gracious gift of God. It is grace, but costly grace. We are reminded of its cost when Scripture witnesses to the death of *Jesús sato*, whose body was broken by the religious and political powers of his day because he resisted the violence done to the bodies of the suffering poor. It is this Jesus who knew the brokenness of his people wrought by colonization and military occupation, and who touched the broken bodies of the infirm, the excluded, and the abused. This is the Jesus who reaches out to the broken ones of contemporary society through the power of the Spirit to bring *katartismos* or *sanidad*. Salvation as integral wholeness means the healing of not just persons but whole communities

53. Costas, *Liberating News,* 69.

that have been fractured by complex socioeconomic, religious, political, and cultural factors. To claim this salvation also means to confess our complicity in the breaking of bodies, and to struggle for the holistic healing of those destroyed by our greed, indifference, xenophobia, and hatred of those we deem "other."

Salvation is the outpouring of God's Spirit, and therefore of abundant life that gives hope to those without hope, and frees those bound and made powerless by the powers and principalities of our day. The triune God who is community-in-Godself is palpably present among the excluded and rejected, and calls them to be community: they are sons and daughters of God, inhabitants of God's reign. While the early church envisioned salvation as divinization, a Latina *evangélica* emphasizes that it is, above all, humanization. *Las sobrajas son santas e hijas de Dios*. Those considered nobodies are now somebodies because they are re-formed as community and *familia*. The Spirit's anointing of new life is witnessed through the gracious gift of God's charisms: the voiceless now speak and sing, glorifying God. They are prophets, "heralds of God's promise" and incarnate *arrabons* (signs) that God's justice will prevail.[54] In Christ and through the Spirit, they are an affirmation that what the world has rejected, God has loved and called. *Las satas ya no son sobrajas, sino santas*, a people called by God.

QUESTIONS

1. What is your church's predominant doctrine of salvation as shown in its preaching, Bible classes, and worship?

2. What role, if any, does the Holy Spirit play in the doctrine of salvation of your tradition?

3. What is the relationship between "personal" and "social" salvation?

4. What is Pelagianism? Does the notion of "ethical imperative" lead to a Pelagian soteriology?

54. See Elizondo, *Guadalupe*, 10.

four

The Trinity *Es* and *Son Familia*

ZAIDA MALDONADO PÉREZ

INTRODUCTION

From the day whereon I renounced the things of the world to consecrate my soul to luminous and heavenly contemplation, when the supreme intelligence carried me hence to set me down far from all that pertains to the flesh, to hide me in the secret places of the heavenly tabernacle; from that day my eyes have been blinded by the light of the Trinity, whose brightness surpasses all that the mind can conceive. —Gregory of Nazianzus[1]

THE MYSTERY OF THE Trinity has proved baffling throughout the centuries. Explaining how God is three in one and one in three has given rise to many analogies, all of which fall short of capturing the essence of the Godhead that, in Rudolf Otto's words, inspires both fear and awe. Yet this has not stopped the church from trying to explain the Trinity. Indeed, the need to counter emerging ideas that questioned Christian monotheism and threatened traditional understanding of the saving work of God in Christ led to the creation of conceptual formulas for determining and safeguarding burgeoning orthodox faith. These formulas, important as they were then and are now, nevertheless do not begin to plumb the depths of an otherwise

1. Quoted in Lossky, "God in Trinity," 44.

inscrutable Godhead whose light leaves us blinded, "whose brightness surpasses all that the mind can conceive." Truly, as it relates to attempts at defining God "in se," God remains eternally "wholly other."[2]

But tradition and our experience of this God reveal that evasion is not an essence of God's character. This *unknown* mystery that is the Trinity is also the *known* God of history; the One that searches us out to make the divine known, familiar, present, and palpable. Latina *evangélicas* have experienced this presence variously. It is not my intention here to homogenize experiences that, at their core, remain very *de nosotras*. My aim is, rather, to explore some basic language, metaphors, and motifs for understanding an emerging *evangélica* theology of the Trinity. One such motif is the language of *familia*. The Trinity *es* and *son familia* to each other and is *familia* to all God's children. Therefore God is not only *familia*; God is *familial*. As *familia*, God is ¡*presente!*—Emmanuel, "God with us." Trinity is a *familia* that is reconstituted and that reconstitutes itself to include its adopted children. The experience of reconstituted Latina families at the familial, religious, and social levels, coupled with an understanding of the reconstitution of the Trinity upon Jesus' resurrection by the Father through the power of the Holy Spirit (in a nonontological sense since the Trinity did not diminish itself upon the death of Jesus), deepen our experience of the triune God in ways not only comforting but, above all, redemptive.

In this chapter, I will explore *evangélica* theology on the Trinity from the perspective of *familia* as a biblically and contextually viable expression for understanding and relating to the God that *es* and *son familia* to each other and to us.[3] Because the idea of family is a social construct, its definition will vary from context to context and from time to time. For our purposes, I will define *familia* first as unity amid otherness where the unity that binds an otherwise disparate group of people is not necessarily blood ties but simply a movement toward the other, a mutual self-rendering expressed through being-for-the-other. It is the act of being-for-the-other,

---

2. See Otto, *The Idea of the Holy*, 26. He refers to "that which is mysterious" as "wholly other." This he defines as "that which is quite beyond the sphere of the usual, the intelligible, and the familiar, which therefore falls quite outside the limits of the 'canny', and is contrasted with it, filling the mind with blank wonder and astonishment." Still, for Otto, as for *evangélicas* God is not "*wholly* 'wholly other'" (e.g. see translator preface xviii) or we would not be able to know this God. Emphasis on *how* this God is primarily known, however, has differed throughout history.

3. I elaborate on the notion of the Trinity as *familia* in Maldonado Pérez, "The Trinity," in *Handbook of Latina/o Theologies*, 32–39.

exemplified best through the economic Trinity—God's activity in the world—that is at the heart of what it means to be *familia*. Second, *familia* for most Latinas (and Latinos) serves as a dynamic, meaning, and identity-forming center. More than an integrative motif or a definition, *familia* is an on-going, existential event.

I am aware that the use of *familia* as a heuristic tool for understanding the Trinity has its advantages and disadvantages. Like other analogies used throughout the history of the church to understand the Godhead, this one also falls short.[4] We will consider some of the pitfalls related to the use of the concept of *familia* below.

"I Believe in One God"; The Three that Manifest as One[5]

It was only when I attended seminary that I noticed that some non-Spanish-speaking believers made a concerted effort to refer to the persons of the Trinity by their functions. By referring to God as Creator, Redeemer, and Sanctifier they not only focused on the economic Trinity, but they emphasized the threeness. The distinctions had nothing to do with tritheistic tendencies on their part. They were not praying to a divided Godhead. As Gregory of Nazianzus so eloquently stated it in his Orations, we all understood well enough that the division in the Trinity "is of Persons, not of Godhead."[6] I realized soon that it had more to do with finding orthodox ways for recovering nonsexist language and metaphors for a God that has been reified as male. Because the Spanish language (and all Romance languages) has no neuter forms for persons and things, hearing God referred to as Creator, Redeemer, and Sanctifier did not, at least for me, achieve its

4. It is not my intention to idealize or romanticize the concept and experience(s) of *familia* in our communities. While there is evidence that the concept and experience of *familia* among Latinas/os in the U.S. is changing (I wouldn't say it is disappearing) it is still a powerful, and thus, viable concept among Latinas. Diane Kendall, for instance, refers to the work of sociologist Norma Williams to point to ensuing disappearance of extended family networks especially among economically advantaged Mexican Americans in urban centers and among Puerto Rican families. However, she also cites poet Cherrié Morriaga who describes *familia* as much more than blood ties. See Kendall, "Families and Intimate Relationships," 505.

5. From the *Quicumque vult*, otherwise attributed to Athanasius (c. 296–373), bishop of Alexandria. See Schaff, "The Athanasian Creed," §132. It is also quoted fully in Boff, *Trinity and Society*, 69.

6. Gregory of Nazianzus (trans. Schaff), "The Third Theological Oration," §2: "Though numerically distinct there is no severance of Essence."

intentions: God was still male. What stood out for me in the prayers was an emphasis on the distinctions between the persons by their functions.

This emphasis was alien to me. My own experience as an *evangélica* was that we do not focus on distinguishing or defining the persons of the Trinity through traditional formularies that assign particular functions to each. That is, while we understand that God is Creator, Redeemer, and Sanctifier, for instance, and that these functions are normally attributed to the Father, Son and Holy Spirit respectively, we do not tend to relate to the Trinity, nor address, praise, or pray to the Godhead specifically through these distinctions.[7] This is due in large part to our emphasis on the unity of the Godhead versus what to us may seem to be an overemphasis on the distinctions. As one *evangélica* expressed it, "I pray to all three [persons] as one, using the different 'names' at one point or another."[8] That is, our focus is not so much on *how* or *that* the One God is and functions as Three, but that the God that is Three also *is*, *functions*, and *interrelates* and relates to its creation as the One God. What stands out, then, is the unity of the Godhead's diversity and work. God is, above all, the Three that works and loves as One.[9] Indeed, "we worship one God in the Trinity and the Trinity in unity"[10]

Emphasis on the triune God who comes to us as One is not to be mistaken for a monarchian understanding of the Trinity. Monarchianism, whether in its dynamic (i.e. adoptionist) or modalist form, erases all distinctions in the Trinity.[11] *Evangélicas* affirm the distinct, essential, and eternal subsistences of the Trinity especially through the language of praise and worship. Yet we do not lay emphasis on who within the Trinity proceeds

7. Emphasis on prayer to the Trinity by identifying the Persons with their functions reflects concerns for recovering nonsexist language and metaphors for a God that has been all too often reified as male.

8. I asked if she prays to each of the Persons of the Trinity and whether she felt closer to one than another.

9. The economic Trinity helps us understand the immanent Trinity, both of which form and inform our understanding of the Godhead.

10. See the *Quicumque vultus* creed as quoted in Boff, *Trinity and Society*, 69.

11. In dynamic monarchianism, the human Jesus is adopted by the Father through the power of his Spirit (*dynamis*), which comes to rest on him. In *Against Praxeas*, and against modalist monarchianism, Tertullian says of Praxeas that "he maintains that there is only one Lord, the Almighty Creator of the world, in order that out of this *doctrine of the* unity he may fabricate a heresy. He says that the Father Himself came down into the Virgin, was Himself born of her, Himself suffered, indeed was Himself Jesus Christ." See Tertullian, *Against Prseas* §1. The doctrine of patripassionism stems from this view and means that God the Father suffered the passion, that the Father died on the cross.

or is generated from whom. Indeed, the distinctions among these (that the Father is unbegotten, that the Son is begotten eternally from the Father, and that the Holy Spirit proceeds—or spirates—from the Father and the Son) is reminiscent of the centuries-old Trinitarian debate over the unity of God.[12] Early Christian attempts at conceptualizing the unity of God while maintaining "divine filiation" was a necessary response to evolving theories that threatened this unity by diminishing the Son's deity. Gnostics made him into a demiurge and the Arians into a created being before time. This devaluation, in turn, also endangered the means of redemption.[13] *Evangélicas* affirm the full divinity of Christ and, as regards the Holy Spirit, we also stand firm against any Macedonianism (the view that denies the Godhead of the Holy Spirit). We affirm that none of the Persons of the Trinity "should be understood to be even a little less than another, in whatsoever way one thing can be less than another, in order that there may be neither a confusion of persons, nor such a distinction as that there should be any inequality."[14] With the Nicene-Constantinopolitan Creed we confess a God that is One in Three Persons and One Substance. And with the *Quicumque vult* (the creed attributed to Saint Athanasius), we affirm that we "worship one God in the Trinity and the Trinity in unity; we distinguish among the persons, but we do not divide the substance."[15]

It follows, then, that we would not focus on distinguishing the persons of the Trinity by their attributes. The God that *es y son* share equally in the appellations eternal, all powerful, holy, loving, and just.[16] Indeed, because we do not emphasize functional distinctions though we acknowledge them, we use such attributes to praise the persons of the Trinity indistinctively.[17]

12. I know of no controversy from *evangélicas* over the double procession called the *filioque* clause. Our religious language references a double procession.

13. If Christ is not truly God—"true God from true God"—then the church has been worshiping something other than God (a creature!), and we have not been reconciled to God.

14. Augustine, *On the Trinity* 7.6.12

15. Boff, *Trinity and Society*, 69. This emphasis on the Trinity as the Three that manifest as One affirms, with some degree of gravitas, early church insistence that the external operations of the Trinity are indivisible (*opera trinitatis ad extra indivisa sunt*). That is, none of the Persons is excluded from any of the operations of the Trinity.

16. "But in God it is not so; for the Father, the Son, and the Holy Spirit together is not a greater essence than the Father alone or the Son alone; but these three substances or persons, if they must be so called, together are equal to each singly" (Augustine, *On the Trinity* 7.6.11).

17. I should say that one of the Persons of the Trinity, the Holy Spirit is especially

This means that our language about God is foundationally doxological. The Trinity is the subject of our praise and the essence of our purpose for life and living. The Good News proceeds from God through the Holy Spirit, not as information but as very God incarnate; as *Jesucristo*. Through his incarnation, life, and resurrection, the other-centered, compassionate power of the Godhead is revealed in history and we, who are otherwise estranged from our Creator, become the bearers of the Spirit's invitation to an intimate, relational knowledge of *el Dios trino*.

The Trinity as Being-in-otherness and Being-for-the-other

Evangélicas see no sequence of persons in the Trinity. God is not "first one and then three"[18] as God has always been the same "I Am," the one who is "the same yesterday, today and forever" (Exodus 3:14; Hebrews 13:8). Second, a unity of *different* Persons of the Trinity means, on the other hand, that we also see *difference* in the Trinity as absolute. For *evangélicas*, a unity without difference is a theological oxymoron. Unity necessarily implies difference or "otherness."[19] This Trinity relates to each other as One—they are One in all that they share—but other in that which distinguishes them.[20] Trinitarian interrelations of the One to the Other is not to be confused with human tolerance of the other, however. Toleration implies a normative center from which the other deviates. It suggests a value judgment over the other. Thus, it also signifies power over the one being tolerated. There is no unity in toleration, only an agreement to bear the other until such time as it may no longer be to one's advantage. Thus, toleration is self-serving. The persons of the Trinity do not tolerate their difference or otherness. Their unity lies in their mutual self-affirmation without which they are not the one-plurality of three.

---

called upon for the gift of "speaking in tongues." However, even then, some find themselves calling out to the three persons "Jesus, lléname de tu Santo Espíritu" or, as the one chorus goes, "Dios, manda tu gran poder" ("God send your great power"), referring to the power of the Holy Spirit.

18. Zizioulas, "Communion and Otherness," 53.

19. Ibid., 347–61.

20. Per the Cappadocians (Basil the Great, Gregory of Nyssa, and Gregory of Nazianzus) and others, the alterity or otherness is to be found in the difference in the Persons of the Trinity. The Father is not the Son, the Son is not the Father, and so on. See also the *Quicumque vult*, also called the Athanasian Creed.

Referring to the Trinity's "otherness" as ontological (and therefore not moral or psychological), John Zizioulas reminds us that the "Holy Trinity is different not by way of difference of qualities or attributes, but by way of simple self-affirmation of being who [God] is." The Trinity is at its core eternal Being-in-affirmation: "God is love because [God] is Trinity."[21] Another way of expressing this affirmation is to speak of the Trinity as *ad alium*. The Persons engage in a "complete turn to the other two [persons by each]." They are in an eternal act of *entrega* or mutual self-rendering.[22] The Spanish word *entregarse*, which translates "self-rendering," helps to shed more light on the activity of the Trinity as One that is *ad alium*. Whereas in English, the word *self-render* implies a brokenness or in some sense a depletion of the other, the Spanish word *entrega*, on the other hand, has no such connotation. Indeed, the root of the word implies reciprocity in this self-giving (the word *entrega* itself includes the word *entre*, which means "between" or "among"). There is no *ad alium* or *entrega* without this dynamic reciprocity and otherness.[23]

Evangélica Trinitarian theology espouses a tripersonal God that is dynamic in its intrapersonal relationship and in the way it engages the world. The love between the Persons of the Trinity—this Being-in-Otherness—is, at the same time, Being-for-the-Other. It is vibrant, perichoretic (interpenetrating) movement that reaches out to one another and to its creation so that nothing is left untouched by the divine.

In *Liberating News: A Theology of Contextual Evangelization*, evangelical scholar Orlando E. Costas argues for a Trinitarian model that expresses this Being-for-the-other through a dynamic, missionally orchestrated, constant back-and forth movement perhaps better captured in Spanish as a missional *va y ven*: "The gospel presupposes a Trinitarian model of God as missions" that Costas describes as a "two-fold movement: from God to the world and from the world back to God."[24] He refers to this descending, ascending Trinitarian *va y ven* as "God as mission" and "God as uniting

---

21. Zizioulas, *Communion and Otherness*, 358. Augustine says it thus: "but you see the Trinity if you see love." See Augustine, *On the Trinity*, 7.8.12.

22. Lacueva, *Curso de Formación Teológica Evangélica*, 133.

23. Leonardo Boff, referring to Augustine's work on the unity of the Trinity, differentiates between Being as "being-for-itself" and person, as meaning "being in relation to others or with others." He further defines "relationship" as "an ordering of one Person to another, a connection between each of the divine three" (Boff, *Trinity and Society*, 6, 91).

24. See Costas, *Liberating Spirit*, 73, 174n3, wherein Costas refers to "God as mission" or "the holy and loving Father of Jesus," "God as uniting Spirit," 73.

Spirit."[25] The first movement ("God as mission") is disclosed in the gospels as "the holy and loving Father of Jesus, and as the loving and obedient Son of the Father." This movement sends "the Son by the Father in the power of the Spirit for the salvation of the world."[26] The second movement reveals "God as uniting Spirit" or God as unity.[27] Through the Holy Spirit, the world is reconciled "through the Son for the glory of the Father."[28] Citing the difference between him, Karl Rahner, and Vincent Martin—the last two of whom "locate the oneness of God in the Father," Costas sides with Jürgen Moltmann in locating that oneness or unity of God "in the eternal Trinitarian community of love, or the communal event of Father, Son and Spirit."[29] Costas goes so far as to cite preference for a "medieval notion" of God as "pure act."[30]

An *evangélica* Trinitarian theology might find the description of God as "pure act" less appealing than the more personal expression of "God as missions" and "God as uniting Spirit." Indeed, pushed too far, God as "pure act" may seem to obfuscate the distinctions in the Trinity. The "communal event," this Trinitarian *va y ven* that is at once united in mission and also missional in its uniting activity resonates, however, with an *evangélica* theology because it resonates with the gospel call to redemption through relationship with a loving God.[31]

For *evangélicas,* a loving God is, to borrow Moltmann's descriptor, a "bearing" God. This means that God is not only sending and uniting as an outside agent but that God is bearing Godself to us in Christ who, through

25. Ibid.

26. Ibid.

27. Ibid.

28. Ibid.

29. Costas, *Liberating Spirit,*174n3. Note, he also admits that Martin's "reciprocal relations" model, with its "proposal of 'one consciousness, one freedom, one creativity,' also "allows for the notion of 'one in community,' especially in relation to the world."

30. Ibid.

31. I find Moltmann's depiction of a "bearing" God at the heart of what God in Christ did for us on the cross. God bore our sins and also our suffering. The imagery of God bearing the weight of our sins helps us penetrate the depths of God's love for the victim and sinner in a more vivid and dynamic sense than *atonement* (a more forensic, static, and less personal term than *bearer*). However, the concept of "bearing" for *evangélicas* must also go beyond this to include the life-giving, birthing aspect of "bearing." The above reference to the "bearing God" is from a lecture titled "The Crucified God: A Modern Theology of the Cross" that Moltmann delivered at the Seattle University School of Theology and Ministry as part of its Great Lecture Series in 2007.

the power of the Holy Spirit, bears our sin in order to bear life for God's creation. Thus, God is not only one who bears sins but one who births.[32] To bear is thus not only to carry, but also to bring to life. God bears the joy, the hope, and the promise of renewal for those who wait upon the Lord. It is no wonder then, that *evangélicas* have always been the heart, soul, and muscle of our churches. Followers of the bearing God, they know what it is to bear the weight of the needs of a church who has always looked to them for the resolve, the stamina, and the Holy Ghost–imbued charge to dare to kick up their heels and get the job done. While pastors have come and gone, it has been *evangélicas*—the *madres de la iglesia*—who have borne the pain of being forsaken by those who found it much easier to move on than to "fight the good fight" with and for those who have little or no battle left in them. They very easily identify with a God who "bears" the pain of being ostracized, criticized, doubted, and left to die, because they dare to make the claim that the Spirit of the Lord is upon them because the Lord has anointed them to "proclaim the good news to the poor . . . and the year of the Lord's favor."[33] As instruments of the bearing, "womb God," they also know what it is to be used to "bear"—to give birth to—*hijas* and *hijos en el espíritu* (spiritual daughters and sons) that form a community that becomes the event through which God makes miracles happen. This means that these *evangélicas, madres de la iglesia* (mothers of the church), also intimately know the joy, the hope, and the difference that keeps them proclaiming the miracle-bearing God. The Trinitarian "communal event" as a model is ever so vivid, so powerfully expressed through these *evangélica* women. Without them, we would lack a powerful witness of this strong, relentless, and miracle-bearing love called Trinity.[34]

In short, these *madres de la iglesia* remind us that as a redeemed body or *familia* we are to be in motion toward the other (*ad alium*)—a *va y ven familia*—that is missional in spirit and character. In this we are to be especially bold, especially Trinitarian.

This being-in-community also calls for the essentialism of the other without whom we are bereft of what it means to be created in the image of God. Without the difference of otherness, we are unable to fathom the meaning of being-in-common union at the heart of what it means to be

---

32. Deut 32:18, refers to God as one who births.

33. Luke 4:18–19.

34. It is significant to me that the word *Trinity*, in Spanish, is feminine, if only grammatically.

saved. We are *familia* by virtue of the work of the Trinity, by whom we are one with Christ through and in whom we are united to God and to each other as brothers and sisters.

Let us remember, however, that we are also *familia* to non-Christians by virtue of being created by God and by virtue of our sinful condition. We boast then not of a "difference" that makes us better than our fellow human beings—for we have all sinned and come short of the glory of God (Rom 3:23)—but of the One who, despite our condition, calls us all to relationship, to *familia à la Trinidad*.

Thus, while *evangélicas* focus on the unity of the Godhead, it is the difference-in-relationship, this being-in-affirmation of each other's personhood and this miracle-bearing expectation that keeps us turning to the Trinitarian source that becomes the locus for language about who we are as the people of God. Leonardo Boff states it beautifully in his summary of the three Cappadocians' reflections on the relationship between the Persons: "The communion between the three is full, since the Father does everything by the Word in the Holy Spirit. The Trinity can only be conceived of as an interplay of mutual relations of truth and love."[35] Such is the Trinity; such too is our call.

The Three That Work as One Are Our Provision

This emphasis on the economic Trinity, the God *ad extra*, is especially evident in our more popular songs known as *coritos*. *Coritos* are normally not expositions about God; they are not theological treatises put to music.[36] Rather, they are very personal, colloquial reflections of a relational theology based on Scripture's reference to us as *familia*—"sons and daughters of God," heirs of all the privileges that come to those who are *de la casa*. The Spirit's confirmation of our status as daughters (and sons) and of a God who is in and for us empowers us to approach God boldly. This we do in the name of *Jesús*, through the power of *el Espíritu Santo* sent to us by *el Padre*.

Our ability to confess and approach the God who exists in community is itself a revelation of what we referred to earlier as the "missional" work of the Trinity. This self-giving and uniting missional movement encompasses

---

35. Boff, *Trinity and Society*, 54.

36. This does not mean that we do not understand the value of such hymns for our instruction and edification, but that in general we do not use them solely to teach but also to engage the Godhead and divine mercy, power, and justice.

and directs our own mission as *evangélicas* and our reason for praise. Our praises are heartfelt expressions that confess and profess a preference for the Trinity that comes to us fully, *Padre, Hijo, y Espíritu Santo*, through the liberating and empowering presence of the Spirit. The God-in-Christ-through-the-power-of-the-Spirit, this God in community unites us fully to the Godhead and to each other as the Christian *familia*, the body of Christ. The divine Three are the One who is *¡presente!* in the everydayness of life. Thus, we confess, as one popular song says, that "Dios, tú eres mi sustento, a mi vida, da aliento. Tu Espíritu se deja sentir como el viento."[37]

This very popular *corito* brings together several metaphors for God and is especially reminiscent of stories in the Hebrew Scriptures. Here Trinity is "Dios, tan solo Dios" ("God, God alone"—meaning that God is the only one able to accomplish the feats to which the song refers and thus also the only true God).[38] In it the singer uses the very personal and familial form of address, *tú*, to speak to God as one who "knows" God in a profoundly intimate, relational way. This also explains the *corito*'s use of the first-person singular throughout. It is a confessional *corito* filled with the poetry of one who is deeply in love with God and wholly trusts God's love for the beloved in the midst of the storms and trials of life. Thus, this God is *sustento*, the one who sustains. In Spanish, this word implies the kind of provision that is nurturing. It conjures up the image of the mother who *sustenta* (sustains, nurtures) her child at her breast. The deeper meaning of this claim is expressed in the next metaphor for God as *aliento*. Although translated into English as "encourager," in Spanish it means much more: it means peace, comfort and, above all, God's very breath animating an otherwise lifeless person to live and hope fully. This oxygen-giving God is the *Espíritu* that makes presence known as the blowing wind or *viento*. God is the needed strength and power that *me lleva a luchar* (rouses me), even as God's Spirit accompanies me (*llevar* also means "to carry") to fight against *el tiempo*, or the (dire) times. Like our weeping, our *luchas* are for a "time": they are not without the promised "joy that comes in the morning" (Ps 30:5). The *corito* affirms this by referring to God as the *provisión* that comes *to* us *del cielo* (from heaven), meeting and providing for us where we

37. Burgos, "Dios de Mi Sustento," *Hay Motivos* CD 1990.

38. For more on the role of *coritos* from an *evangélica* perspective, see also Martell-Otero, "Encuentro con el Jesús Sato: An *Evangélica Soter*-ology," 74–91. For a nuanced and general view on *coritos* in the Caribbean and Latin America, see Cardoza-Orlandi, "*Qué Lindo Es Mi Cristo*: The Erotic Jesus/Christ in the Caribbean, Latin America and Latino/a Protestant Christian Music," 157–70.

are. To speak of *provision del cielo* is to remember that even in the desert God provided a hungry people with *el maná*, food for their bodies, a witness to God's present supply for all their needs.[39] And God becomes our *provisión del cielo* through God's ultimate Provision, God incarnate. Christ, our spiritual manna, is sent to us from the heavens, and through the Holy Spirit becomes our ever-present God.

But reference to God as the Provision that comes from above or *el cielo* also sets up a binary opposition that calls for further elaboration. Here *cielo* is set against an earthly existence wherein struggles to do more than survive are often met with insurmountable odds, the pain of dead ends, subliminal or explicit aggression, or indifference. Against such circumstances and in the absence of any earthly assistance, our only succor must come from *el cielo*.[40] Transcending the heavens to become our provision in and against worldly powers and our own inner "demons" (spiritual battles), our *Socorro-God* reminds us that God's arm "no se ha cortado" ("has not shortened"; Isa 59:1). God is our liberator, *El Dios que me desata*, the one who literally unties us from that which constrains us to move forward.[41]

Finally, as the *corito* above and so many others profess, God is the one who refreshes our souls, calms the tempestuous storm as we call upon his name. Indeed, the language is not philosophical; it is metaphorically rich language about the triune God that comes through as our One God who is

---

39. Reference to *provisión* can also relate to Christ as God's provision through his incarnation, life, death, and resurrection. In addition, one could argue for a sacramental reference here. However, this may be reading too much into what *evangélicas* would understand (the main issue) since the sacrament of the Eucharist, although important, for most *evangélicas* does not carry the theological weight it does for, say, Roman Catholics or Orthodox. *Evangélicas* who do tend to practice weekly communion are found within the Iglesia Cristiana, Discípulos de Cristo.

40. *"Mi socorro viene de Jehová* who made the heavens and the earth" (Ps 121:2), is an often quoted Bible verse. *Socorro* is a popular name in the Spanish language, and is used as a tribute, as well as a plea, to the God who is our provision, our *socorro del cielo* (succor, help, or relief from heaven).

41. Another very popular *corito*, "Alaba a tu Dios" (Praise Your God), written c. eighteen years after this one, by Danny Berríos, also highlights this popular motif in our *coritos* by referring to God as the one who goes before us clearing the path and destroying or breaking chains. As the *corito* states, God is the one who sends his angels to fight with us and opens doors that none can close. The specific lyrics to which I am referring follow: "Dios va al frente abriendo caminos, quebrando cadenas, sacando espinas, manda a sus ángeles contigo a luchar, él abre puertas nadie puede cerrar" ("God goes before us clearing the way, breaking the chains, pulling out thorns, sending his angels with you to fight. He opens doors that no person can close"; translation mine).

sustento, aliento, Espíritu, fuerza, provisión del cielo, and libertador (nurturer/sustainer, breath/encourager, power/strength, provision from heaven, and liberator). There is in this *corito* no distinction of Trinitarian persons by their particular functions. It is rather an invocation and testimony, a pithy but deeply passionate love song, celebrating, even as it invokes, God for making the divine self known in the life of the one for whom the greatest tribute is to call this divine *Presente, Dios, tan solo Dios. ¡Dios!*[42] (God, God alone, God!)

Jesús, el Padre, and *Espiritu Santo* receive praise for being the God whose attributes are *for us* because *all* of God is *for us*.[43]

Evangélicas' focus on the Trinity mainly as subject and object of praise and imitation rather than as the object for philosophical or metaphysical scrutiny should not by any means be understood as a reflection of a lack of theological ability. Certainly much is written, taught, and preached by *evangélicas* that would counter this perception. It is to say, however, that *evangélica* thoughts on the Trinity reflect a reading of Scripture that is more in tune with a Hebrew expression of the God of history than the philosophical, speculative, metaphysical expressions of God common in the centuries after the New Testament. This more concrete vision is thus a choice informed by the Scripture stories of a people who struggled against sin and the God who never abandoned them.

An *evangélica* focus on the immanence of God, however, does not preclude an understanding of God's transcendence. "'Am I only a God nearby,' declares the LORD, 'and not a God far away?'" (Jer 23:23). While we profess a God of history, a God among us, we also understand that God is beyond us. God is *el Dios de lo alto* (God from on high).[44] This God with us is with us through the Holy Spirit. *Evangélica* Trinitarian theology is pneumatologically nuanced in contrast to other traditions or expressions with a more christological focus. Our pneumatological nuance (I prefer *nuance* to *emphasis*), however, does not diminish the role of Christ; rather, the Holy

---

42. In some ways, it is also a reminder to self and to God of God's promises of faithfulness.

43. God is the God in relation who, as another very popular *corito* puts it, "camina contigo de noche y de día" ("walks with you day and night") and because of the powerful One who accompanies us, we are encouraged in the same *corito*: "levanta tus manos tu victoria llegó, comienza a cantar y alaba a Dios!" ("raise your hands, your victory has arrived; begin to sing and praise God"; translation mine). Berríos, "Alaba a Dios"

44. Orlando Costas refers to this point as well. I have reversed his statement "God is above and beyond us but also among us" (Costas, *Liberating Spirit,* 72).

Spirit intensifies the significance and work of Christ through its witness to our spirit. And it does so without minimizing the self-giving event of the One who sent the Son to express Trinitarian love. Because of Christ, we are given the Paraclete (John 15:26) the "Spirit of Christ" (1 Pet 1:11; see also Rom 8:9; Phil 1:19) and of the Parent (Matt 3:16–17; Rom 8:14; Eph 4:30). For this reason, a pneumatological penchant is also important for underscoring a view of the Trinity as an "eternal communal event." An immanent God should not be equated with the omnipotent and impassible God of the Greek philosophers. The God who is ¡presente! is fully so not only through the power to lift burdens or stop oppression. Such an understanding gravely curtails the work, grandeur, and sovereignty of God. It hides the complexity of the God who is also mystery and confuses a call for discipleship with an invitation to earthly bliss. Evangélicas know that this is far from the truth. Our theology of the Trinity cannot but stand squarely on the gospel witness of a God who, moved by divine love for God's own creation, became incarnate, walked among us, and suffered the invective and cruelty of a people blinded by sin. The crucifixion is not only a stark reflection of this; it is also a paradoxical expression of the magnanimity of God's love—that the One who knew no sin should die on our behalf on a sinner's cross (2 Cor 5:21). There is no more ultimate expression of this presence, none equal among other gods, than that our God would become flesh, live among us, and suffer violence from us for our sake. We understand then, that the experience of suffering is not outside of the Trinity, but that it is part of following the "crucified God."[45] Struggle, and the suffering that it often engenders, is now and shall be until Christ returns an integral part of experiencing life in a sinful world.

Yet it is neither God's nor our intention to make suffering the center of our theology. Although a reality for all, suffering is a result of sin, and sin and its effects are outside of the will of God for us and for God's good creation. The possibility for and work of redemption through Christ for his creation would affirm this. In the words of Heiko Oberman, it is not that "in the midst of life we are surrounded by death," for that would be fatalistic. Instead, and quoting Luther, Oberman reminds us that, "in the midst

---

45. Gerald McDermott, referring to the Heidelberg Disputation of 1518, notes Martin Luther's distinction between "theologians of glory who base their views of God on created things that can be seen, and theologians of the cross, who say God best reveals himself 'through the passion of the cross" (Mc Dermott, *Martin Luther*, 89). See also Grimm and Lehmann, *Luther's Works*, 39–58.

of death[,] we are surrounded by life."[46] The Transcendent Trinity is also the God who is *¡presente!* not only as One who bears the pain of suffering with us but, especially, as One who calls and empowers us to *luchar contra el tiempo*. The presence and work of the Trinity imbues us with hope, even when hope seems to elude us.

THE TRINITY AS RECONSTITUTED *FAMILIA*

The *familia* motif for understanding the Trinity has its disadvantages. I elaborate on some of these in a prior work.[47] For our purposes, some important limitations include exclusivist tendencies based on social or religious markers that express themselves through pressure to conform to family standards, norms, values, and expectations. Such tendencies may carry over to the way we live out our understanding of what it means to be the church. The motif also conjures up patriarchal and thus also hierarchical proclivities that serve to control outcome and exclude unconformity.

Nevertheless, while the motif possesses some significant challenges, it also brings to the task at hand many virtues.[48] These merit our attention for what we can learn about *evangélicas* and a Trinitarian theology. First among these is the significance we place on the importance and experience of *familia* as a dynamic, meaning, and identity-forming center. Eldin Villafañe quotes the renowned sociologist on Puerto Rican migration to the US, Joseph P. Fitzpatrick, who states plainly, "The world to a Latin consists of a pattern of intimate personal relationships, and the basic relationships are those of this family."[49] Furthermore, Latina/o "confidence, [her] sense of security and identity are perceived in [her] relationship to others who are family."[50] For Latinas/os in the US this becomes especially true when we allow for a kind of hybrid and fluid understanding of who constitutes *familia* and who gets to define it.

---

46. Heiko Oberman, writing on Luther, ends his book by quoting a medieval song: "in the midst of life we are surrounded by death" (see Oberman, *Luther*, 330).

47. Maldonado Pérez, "The Trinity," 32–39.

48. I elaborate further on some of the challenges for Latinas/os in my chapter on "The Trinity," in *Handbook of Latina/o Theologies*, 32–39.

49. Fitzpatrick, *Puerto Rican Americans: The Meaning of Migration to the Mainland*, 78. Quoted in Villafañe, *The Liberating Spirit*, 13.

50. Ibid.

For first and second generation Latinas/os in the US and the notable present influx of immigrants, the experience of *familia* becomes especially critical for the emotional and other kinds of support it provides. *Familia* becomes essential for helping the newcomer-turned-outsider adjust to and survive very different and sometimes hostile environments intent on shutting out the stranger and the disparate one. The work and expectation of *familia* as a support system or *provisión* (financial and so on) reinforces the importance of this network for daily living. This means, at least, that for Latinas/os in the US and other places where they may not have blood ties to family members, *familia* are those who take them in, affirm their full identity as a person and sister or fellow struggler, and give them a sense of belonging.[51] In this new *hermandad* the outsider becomes an insider, one of the *familia.* [52]

This forging of new ties that undercuts the dominant cultural paradigm of what constitutes a family is concretely subversive.[53] *Familia* become those who, by choice or circumstance, are "no longer foreigners but friends"—to expand upon Ephesians 2:19. They are *familia* by virtue of that which unites them. Being and living as *familia* is thus central to our survival and to how we make sense of the world.

Because of its strong role in informing and forming our worldview, the *familia* motif, then, surfaces first as an important lens through which we understand the Trinity.[54] Second, it is also especially significant because it permeates the Scriptures through which we gauge, challenge, and inform that worldview. God, the loving and chastising parent, is especially

51. "The individual in Latin America has a deep consciousness of his membership in a family. [She or he] thinks of his importance in terms of his family membership . . . it is as strong among the families of the very poor as it is among those of the very wealthy." Quoted in Villafañe, *The Liberating Spirit: Toward and Hispanic American Pentecostal Social Ethic,* 13.

52. *Hermandad* in Spanish has no gender connotation as do "fellowship," "brotherhood," "fraternity," or "sisterhood," all translations of *hermandad.*

53. Atkinson, *The Oldest Vocation,* 19, refers to the role that persecution and martyrdom played in the development of a new kind of community. "This community or *communitas,*" she argues, "undercut the values of the dominant culture, breaking traditional bonds and forging new ones." Latinas (and Latinos) have learned to forge new communities that undercut the traditional understanding of "family" as those who are connected through blood ties. Quoted in Maldonado Pérez, *The Subversive Role of Visions in Early Christian Martyrs,* 85.

54. Although I use *worldview* in the singular, it is not my intention to say that all Latinas/os have the same worldview, only that the notion and value of *familia* play an important role in that worldview.

vibrantly portrayed in the Hebrew Scriptures (Exod 4:22; Isa 63:16; 64:8; Deut 1:30–31; 8:5; 32:6; Hos 1:10; 11:1). Common terms used to identify members of a family are used in the New Testament writings where Jesus refers to God as "Father" or "Abba" and the Father refers to Jesus as "Son." Paul also emphasizes the familial motif in his writings (Rom 8:15, 19; Gal 3:26–27;[55] see also 1 John 3:1–2). Other references in the New Testament to "children of God," "sons and daughters," and, therefore also to "sisters and brothers" in Christ are pervasive (Matt 5: 44–45; Heb 13:1; 1 Pet 1:22; et al.). Both Testaments express poignantly what this means for how we are to treat each other[56] (Lev 19:18; 1 John 3:16–18). The Apostles', Pseudo-Athanasian, and Nicene-Constantinopolitan Creeds also following the Scriptures, engage familial terms to refer to the persons of the Trinity. In short, all of these affirm the interrelations in the Trinity as *familial.*

Third, the *familia motif,* at its very core, is a theologically laden expression for what it means to be called a child of God. It is soteriological in its essence. Through the work of the Trinity, we are made brothers and sisters of our brother Christ, children of the One God. It is also eschatological in that to which it points—that present-future "day" when we will truly live as the one *familia* of God, brothers and sisters, "children of the resurrection" under and with the one holy family of the Trinity, Father, Son, and Holy Spirit.[57] Jesus expressed this future-present hope that we "may all be one" with each other and with God—"just as you Father, are in me and I in you," in his prayer before his crucifixion (John 17:21, NRSV). It is a prayer that calls for a countercultural expression of what it means to be part of God's family living out of a "dis-order" that witnesses to and critiques existing mores and values. It is a call to live out of the reign that is and is yet to come.[58]

Theologically and culturally speaking then, the *familia* motif is rich. But, for *evangélicas* in the US, language about *familia* is, in many ways, really language about a *reconstituted* family that breaks with social and religious norms. Examples for this cut across the religious, cultural, and sociological realms. Space will not allow us to include all the instances in which we see *familia* as one that is reconstituted. However, among the examples

---

55. I am assuming, I think with the majority of Bible scholars, Pauline authorship of Galatians.

56. Scripture is also especially revealing about how we are to treat the alien and oppressed among us (Isa 58:1–12; Luke 10:25–27; Matt 25- 31–44; among many others).

57. Luke 20:34–36.

58. See also chapter 7, below, on eschatology and the reign of God.

that often lead to our sense of *familia* as reconstituted is the experience of being ostracized for religious reasons. In a highly Roman Catholic religious culture, many, upon becoming *evangélicas*, have experienced some degree of disowning by their family members, some of whom associate being Latina/o with being Roman Catholic.[59] Emphasis on a piety and holiness that frowns upon previous religious activities that included *fiestas patronales, quinceañeros, fiestas* for *primera communion* (often involving alcohol and dancing) leads to antisocial perceptions against the one leaving the *madre iglesia* (mother church). Pained by subtle or blatant rejection (on both sides!), the *evangélica* outsiders are taken in, adopted, and nurtured by the new *reconstituted* family into which they have been invited.

I referred earlier to the new *familia* that is reconstituted out of the need for solidarity against pressures insurmountable if faced alone. This is another example of where the new *hermandad* becomes critical for the support and inside knowledge about pending challenges and ways to overcome them. Immigrants to the US can speak firsthand about the role of this *hermandad* through reconstituted *familias*.[60]

I am also reminded of our *abuelitas* and *madres* who forged new families through the taking in, literally or by way of special attention, of forsaken or despondent children of the barrio.[61] The children were called *hijas* or *hijos de crianza* (daughters or sons by virtue of being reared). The term was not meant to differentiate birth children from the others but to emphasize their status as daughters or as sons, part of the *familia*. My mother talks about how my *abuelita Perfecta* (her name) made sure she always cooked plenty to accommodate the children who stopped by at dinnertime.[62] In a sense, those children were hers too. Once homeless herself, she bore their pain and made sure that they knew they were welcome at her table. These *hijos/as de crianza* are also the spiritual children of bold *evangélicas* whose compassion has witnessed to the grace of the loving God who calls society's unredeemable to their home in the divine bosom. One such example is now the deceased "mamá Leo." Mamá Leo, as Eldin Villafañe recounts,

59. For more on this see Maldonado, *Protestantes,* 13–16, 131–32.

60. I do not want to romanticize this reconstituted *familia.* While the family is important to their survival, nevertheless as fallen human beings, members of a family will display inconsistencies and betrayal.

61. This may be something that we are losing as our jobs take us from one place to another and as we take on the more Anglo notion of *familia* as nuclear.

62. My mother too was instrumental in taking in one of my childhood friends to live with us in times of need.

"is what all the hundreds of ex-addicts, prostitutes, alcoholics, and street people call Rev. Leoncia Rosado. These are the social outcasts no one cared for; sad to say, even the church." Such *abuelitas* and *madres* in the faith not only taught us what it means to follow the outcast Christ. They taught us that *familia* is not about who we are by way of blood—Pérez, López, Maldonado, Smith, Cho, Marquez—it is about whose we are by way of grace. This grace not only compels us to heed God's call to relationship with the divine One, but it equips us for the charge to love others as God loved us (Mark 12:28–31; John 3:15).

Theologically speaking, the notion of a *reconstituted* family is especially useful for the nuance that it provides for understanding the Trinity and our role as "children" of the one God. It provides an insight into the familial life of the Trinity as one that is also *reconstituted*. The Trinity, although never diminished in its Being upon the descent of the Son and his death on the cross, is in a sense reconstituted upon Jesus' resurrection by the Father through the power of the Holy Spirit. Jesus, having suffered and borne the cruelty of our sin, is lifted up and brought home. There, he "sits at the right hand of the Father" with a glorified body, a constant witness to us of the hope that awaits our own bodies.[63] Reunited after the Father's grief and the Son's sense of abandonment (Matt 27:46; Mark 15:34), the suffering of the Trinity is mitigated by the Holy Spirit's raising the Son, who takes his rightful place at the Father's side.[64] And, there, as our advocate, the Spirit provides a model for our own call and work—we are called to love, to serve, and to advocate for those in need of advocacy. This means, then, that the hope we await reveals itself through that advocacy in the present. The triune God reconstitutes not only our sense of *familia* but also our present.

But the Trinity is also reconstituted upon loving and receiving its adopted children (Matt 12:48–50; Rom 8:15).[65] This calling forth of a new bond that undercuts preexisting ties and loyalties based on bloodlines or

63. The glorified body has no gender. As a member of the Godhead, which is Spirit, the Son has no gender. While the human Jesus Christ was male, the second Person of the Trinity has no gender. *Son* is a filial title. This does not imply that our resurrection is only of the spirit, as in gnostic heresies. See John 20:19–20, for instance.

64. See Moltmann's lecture, "The Crucified God," Seattle University, SMT's Great Lecture Series, 2007.

65. If we believe that God's will is eternal, we can say that even if only figuratively, this "reconstitution" is an eternal event in the mind or heart of God. Otherwise, it is also possible to talk about a reconstitution at the time of creation. All this, we are reminded, is an analogy for what we experience is happening when we are invited to "be one" with the Trinity (John 17:21).

other cultural values runs through the Scripture narratives as divine sub-version.[66] From Genesis to Revelation, God invites "whosoever will" to join this new, subversive *familia*, a reconstituted family, a *hermandad* of equals, called to imitate the life and work of our Triune God.

CONCLUDING REMARKS

Although God is mystery, as Gregory of Nazianzus reminds us in our open-ing quotation, God also desires to be known. God's general and special revelation through Christ is an expression of this. Scriptures uses anthro-pological expressions to talk about God as Father and Son. The Holy Spirit also is referred to as a One who grieves and loves (Rom 15:30; Eph 4:30). Familial language for God is especially attractive to *evangélicas*.[67] Its attrac-tion, however, is not at all connected to cultural mores about a woman's place in the home and her role in bearing children. Scriptural expressions of what constitutes a *familia* have nothing to do with gender expectations or blood ties. In this, it is highly subversive, calling anyone who will follow Jesus his brother or sister and the child of the One tripersonal God.

The Trinity is also a model for how we are to treat one another. God is the Being-in-Otherness who affirms each of the Trinitarian Persons. This self-affirmation is something that *evangélicas* find fully in God. It is not always or most often, however, something they find in the family of God, who lives more in conformity with sociocultural norms and expectations. Such *familias* would do well to consider the subversive nature of the family of the Trinitarian God who bears our pain and births hope, for all.

QUESTIONS

1. How is *familia* a biblically and contextually viable expression for un-derstanding God and what God requires of us? What challenges does this metaphor also pose?

---

66. By this too, the suffering of the Son and the grieving of the Father, as shared also by the Holy Spirit, is mitigated.

67. We regret, however, that we do not hear more of the many feminine metaphors for God. This paucity creates a false image of God as male that, in its own way, becomes idolatrous.

2. What might be a useful metaphor for your community? How do scriptural references to the Trinity enlighten and challenge your metaphor?

3. What hymn or song in your tradition captures the significance of the Trinity? Can you identify a song from another community and compare these? (For instance, you can use the one in this chapter and in the chapter on eschatology.)

five

Evangélicas Reading Scriptures

Readings from within and beyond the Tradition

ELIZABETH CONDE-FRAZIER

INTRODUCTION

THIS CHAPTER DESCRIBES HOW the *evangélico* community and particularly
the women of that community have read the Scriptures. I begin by reviewing the theological frameworks that have guided Protestants' readings of
Scripture and that have defined the locus of authority. I then discuss the
insights of biblical scholars in the Latino/a community who over the years
have described how Latino/as read Scripture and have suggested ways to
get at liberative readings. These voices have brought a necessary critique
to the so-called authoritative methods and interpretations that have kept a
silencing grip over the interpreters of the word in the Latino/a community.
Biblical scholars have revealed the reasons for this authoritative control,
and have shown the difference between it and the authority of the Spirit
that the people claim. These scholars have also identified and helped to
name the approaches to reading the Scriptures that already exist in the
community so as to affirm the practices that have brought life to the community. In particular we will look at some of the approaches of Latina *evangélica* scholars to the Scriptures. I will end with the voices of the Latinas

in the church (of both laypersons and clergy) who study, read and preach the Scriptures. We will glimpse how their interpretations of sacred writings help build their lives.

THE BIBLE AND COLONIZATION

The Bible is not a neutral book. It was used to colonize the peoples of Latin America. The Spanish colonization of Latin America and the Caribbean and then the second colonization by the United States each employed religion, first Catholicism and then Protestantism, to bring its way of life and its gods to create a new identity in the peoples. Such an identity made them in the image of the colonizer who used the teachings of the sacred text to enforce this new identity as the one that is pleasing to the new god. The colonizer used the text and his interpretation of the text to control the colonized.

However, even before the Bible came to Latin America, the Bible in Spain had represented sentiments and movements of dissent against the crown of Spain under Isabel and Fernando, who used the religion of Catholicism to fortify their empire and its conquests: "España por la gracia de Dios" ("Spain by the grace of God").[1] In particular, Muslims, Jews, and the intelligentsia used the Bible in Spain to affirm ideals and identities squelched by the crown. These groups and their literature, including sacred texts, were prohibited and condemned by the Inquisition.[2] What these sacred texts have represented for the peoples who have claimed and used them has been a dialectic between the powers of conquest and liberation across the years.[3] *Evangélica* feminists today add to this history of struggle.

HERMENEUTICAL INFLUENCES IN THE *EVANGÉLICA* CHURCH

The Bible has always held special authority in the *evangélica* community. The nature and theological implications of that authority are understood in different ways. Various doctrines of authority and inspiration of the Bible

1. See González, *Luces Bajo el Almud*, chapter 1.

2. In his work on "Proto-Evangélico Geneologies," Daniel Ramirez summarizes how Erasmian humanism in early sixteenth-century Spain was seen as a flirtation with the new ways of feeling and thinking. See Ramirez, "Migrating Faiths." See also Bataillon, *Erasmo y España*; and Revuelta Sañudo and Morón Arroyo, *El eramismo en España*.

3. Agosto, "Reading the Word in America."

in modern times have shaped the Protestant theology that, beginning in the late nineteenth century, missionaries brought to our countries of origin, and that they continue to bring today.

Believers define the Bible as the word of God and use the concept of inspiration to account for the sacred character of the biblical writings. This notion of inspiration soon developed further into "a variety of claims about the nature and content of the text."[4] However, authority also speaks to the trust that a faith or community of faith will give to the text. What is it then that through the years has brought the *evangélica* community to give authority to the biblical text? How is authority defined, and what is the response to the text because of this authority?

Different questions come from the construction of this authority: Who reads and/or interprets this text? Does the interpretation hold equal authority to other interpretations? With what purpose and in what context are the Scriptures read? Are there any checks and balances for the interpretive process? How has the text been a part of the meaning making of the community that reads it? How can this word from the past, read in contemporary times, bring understanding for one's life in the present and for the future? If the Bible is the word of God or divine communication with finite humans, how can human thought apprehend divine thought?

To answer these questions the *evangélica* community reaches into the resources of the Protestant Reformation, particularly to Martin Luther's notion of *sola scriptura*. For Luther the word of God was much more than Scripture. According to the Bible itself, the word of God is none other than God (John 1:11).[5] For Luther, the authority of Scripture was not based on the inerrancy of the text but on the fact that God's word is also God's creative and redemptive action that comes to us in Jesus and throughout history. Based on this understanding the text could contain errors, and different methods of scholarship could be applied to it without taking away any of its authority.

The practice of pietistic traditions in the US, part of the Great Awakenings has also influenced *evangélicas/os*. Within these traditions the goal of Bible reading was to gain illumination for one's life. The Bible was read prayerfully and in a context of devotion so that one's life could become more Christ-like. When the daily time to read Scripture came, one would pray for God to illumine both the Scripture and one's mind in order to understand

---

4. Bird, "The Authority of the Bible," 35.

5. González, "How the Bible Has Been Interpreted," 101–2.

and then open one's heart so that one's will would not resist obedience to the will of God found in the text. One read examining oneself and searching for guidance not only into the life of faith but also along the path of life in a new country as immigrants.[6]

Even today Protestants say a prayer for illumination before reading and preaching the Scripture in church services. It is through illumination that the Holy Spirit enlightens the mind of the receiver of the word so that the meaning for one's life may be clear. In this way, the word not only informs and instructs but also addresses a person. In the moment of illumination the word of God, which is God, and the reader are in dialogue with one another. The dialogue is based on the relationship that the two have with one another through Jesus. The Holy Spirit makes understanding possible. For some, the knowledge of the Spirit is beyond academic degrees or classes and is accessible to all. An academic degree may make historical-critical study accessible, and this can situate the text historically and culturally and also make accessible the original languages. However, this is not enough to render the meaning of the text to the hearers in this moment. It does not take into account the questions readers may bring to the text or an understanding of the text's response and questions to the reader. Academic training may also create distance between readers and text rather than engagement of readers with text, since without academic knowledge one cannot understand the context and content of the text.

Illumination is for connecting the God of the Scripture with the reader in a communicative moment of intimacy not in the past but in the here and now. Gonzalez insists that it is in this communication that both hearer and text speak to and question each other and demand responses in genuine dialogue.[7] Illumination opens the hearer's spiritual understanding so that the divine oracles become intelligible to the human mind and heart. These influences working together maintain belief in the divine character of the Bible.

While the influence of the historical-critical method has brought exegesis to the sermon, the focus of the Latino/a community had not been on the original authors' intended meaning but on the significance that a text has for the persons and congregations who read and study or receive it today. The genius of the *evangélica* community has been the way that it has integrated the two.

---

6. This resembles John Wesley's approach to Scripture. See Wesley, "Preface to the Old Testament," 20.

7. Gonzalez, *Santa Biblia*, 13–14.

Moisés Silva asserts that "asking for a meaning is asking for an application of scripture to a need; we are also asking scripture to remedy our inability to use the passage."[8] An important prerequisite in the faith community upon reading the text is to value it. One demonstrates appreciation by approaching the text with commitment. This commitment is part of the relational quality of the text.[9] The commitment goes both ways. It is part of a dialectic between the one who is the Word and the one who reads the word seeking answers and/or purpose. It is the commitment of the God who becomes the enfleshed Word, Jesus, which makes possible interpretation beyond our human understanding and weaknesses: our subjectivities or the ambiguities of culture and language. It is God who makes the reading fruitful: "For as the rain and the snow come down from heaven, and do not return there until they have watered the earth, making it bring forth and sprout, giving seed to the sower and bread to the eater, so shall my word be that goes out from my mouth it shall not return to me empty, but it shall accomplish that which I purpose, and succeed in the thing for which I sent it" (Isa 55:10–11, NRSV). With this assurance in Jesus, who makes the illumination of the word possible through the work of the Holy Spirit, *evangélicas/os* interpret, teach, preach, and act in accordance with the word.

Is there a way to check on human subjectivity within the dialectic of interpretation? It is Christian theology that provides a framework within which human experience may be interpreted. This implies that experience must be interpreted and not that it can interpret itself. This is Luther's position: that experience itself is not a reliable theological resource but must be corrected by theology, and that theology is empty without experience.[10] If one experiences something that is contradictory to Christian theology, one must see it as only temporary and flawed. It does not represent Christian truth.[11] This teaches women not to trust their own experience and fails to give a corrective to theology itself. Theology has been based on the Bible. This leaves women without an authoritative resource to challenge the patriarchal and discriminatory elements of theology. *Evangélicas* have claimed that the interpreters have been flawed and that the Holy Spirit, through the agreement of both text and experience, has given a fresh

---

8. Silva, "Contemporary Theories of Biblical Interpretation," 120.

9. Ibid.

10. McGrath, *Christian Theology*, 228.

11. Ibid.

interpretation that poses a corrective to the traditional understandings reflected in (patriarchal Western) theology.

BIBLICAL HERMENEUTICS IN THE LATINO/A *EVANGÉLICO/A* COMMUNITY

Biblical hermeneutics became important as Hispanic and Latino/a theology emerged. Out of the Protestant tradition Orlando E. Costas, a contextual missiologist, turned his focus upon the experience of Latinos learning to accept and live the experience of making the Unites States their permanent place of residence. The image of the "Galilean became central to his theology . . . as a peripheral region."[12] Costas compared Galilee to the periphery of the centers of power where Hispanics live. He suggested that Hispanics' marginal experience in the United States is similar to that of Jesus, who was crucified outside the gate of Jerusalem where there was no justice. (Gates were symbolic of the place where one's case was heard and judged justly.)[13] Costas expanded the tradition and brought a new understanding to texts by reading them in a new context.

This theme of marginality has taken contextualized expressions. These can be seen in a survey of the sermon topics of Latino/a preachers discussed in *Santa Biblia: The Bible through Hispanic Eyes*.[14] Emerging themes in that volume are marginality, poverty, *mestizaje* and *mulatez*, exiles and aliens, and solidarity. The concepts of identity and socioeconomic power become lenses through which to see liberating strategies. This reflects how the Bible is read from lived reality, with the purpose of interpreting and finding both meaning and God in the midst of it. Finding God is important, not because God is considered absent, but because God is the refuge of the poor when evildoers frustrate their plans (Ps 14:6), and God has not despised or disdained the suffering of the afflicted or hidden his face from them but has listened to their cry (Ps 22:24). Strength is a part of empowerment but does not fully define it.

Hispanic/Latina theologians will further explore and expand the themes of empowerment. *Mujerista* and Latina Feminist theology speak of

---

12. Gonzalez and Jimenez, *Púlpito*, 40. Also see Costas, "Universality of Galilee," 16–23.

13. See Costas, *Christ Outside the Gate*.

14. González, *Santa Biblia*.

the woman's moral agency and relations of power.[15] These theologians recognize the liberating potential of the Bible while also pointing out how the message has been dressed in patriarchal garb. María Pilar Aquino uses the framework of *lo cotidiano* to move beyond it. *Lo cotidiano* refers to the thinking and doing of our routines. It encompasses the aesthetic, the celebratory, the tedious, and the mundane. For Aquino it is a source for theology.[16]

Protestant women preachers who do biblical interpretation in relationship to the church and its theological framework have entered the pulpit not only to speak a liberating word that points out and confronts patriarchal interpretations. In the very act of placing their bodies in the pulpit (at times in resistance to the doctrines that would keep them from the pulpit), they have incarnated a liberating word.

The patriarchal doctrines that have been a part of our congregations are a result of the cultural norms and, more powerfully, the theology that North Atlantic and US missionaries spread when they introduced Protestantism to Latin America and the Caribbean. In spreading this gospel, these missionaries became complicit in a colonizing agenda. For this reason, Hispanic and Latino/a theological scholars have engaged a postcolonial critique and reading of the Scriptures. Kwok Pui-Lan describes this as "a reading strategy and discursive practice that seeks to unmask colonial epistemological frameworks, unravel Eurocentric logics, and interrogate stereotypical cultural representations."[17] It involves examining the colonial aspects in the text at the time it was written as well as the history of interpretation of the text up until the present.[18] This reading is one that seeks to disengage from a colonial interpretation. Fernando F. Segovia advances a postcolonial reading of Scripture among Latino/a theologians using the framework of diaspora to interpret the condition of Latino/as in the United States and to establish correlation between diaspora and the biblical images of exile and otherness.[19]

How do *evangélicas* interpret the Bible? How do they approach the text? How do they define their role as biblical critics? What is their relationship

15. See Isasi-Díaz, *En La Lucha*. Also see Aquino, et al., *A Reader in Latina Feminist Theology*.

16. See Aquino, "Theological Method," 39.

17. Kwok Pui-Lan, *Postcolonial Imagination*, 2.

18. Latino/a theologians realize that many of us come from countries that do not live a post colonial reality but under neocolonialism.

19. See Segovia, "Toward a Hermeneutic of the Diaspora," 57–73.

to the church and its tradition, to their cultural and gender interpretations, and to society as a whole? What does the conversation between *evangélicas* and the biblical text reveal? How do they interact with the cultural world of the text and intersect it with the world today? What hermeneutical space do we create for ourselves and what is the spirit in this space? My purpose is not to discuss all these questions fully but to begin such a consideration from an *evangélica* feminist perspective. To do this I will engage the biblical interpretative work of *evangélica* Latina feminist scholars. I will also focus on the grassroots preaching and hermeneutics of Latina clergy and laity as they have preached and taught the text in the context of the *evangélica* church. The hermeneutical frameworks already mentioned will serve as ways to define the analysis of the women's interpretations and struggles.

READINGS BY *EVANGÉLICA* SCHOLARS

In this section I show how three *evangélica* scholars use different interpretive frameworks to approach scriptural text. In each one we will observe how the readings become liberative for women.

Aida Besançon-Spencer is an *evangélica* New Testament scholar who uses historical-critical method to bring justice to power relations of men and women in the church. She uses her scholarship to address the topic of women called to ministry. In the preface to her book *Beyond the Curse: Women Called to Ministry* she states that she writes with the purpose of bringing justice and vindication to women.[20] She writes to point to things in the text that we have not known to look for previously, particularly insights about women's roles, including leadership roles in the church. She carefully researches the text in its original language and examines the historical situations behind the texts. She shows how the biblical metaphor "head" "does not limit women in ministry, and how Jesus and Paul place ministry in higher priority over homemaking for a woman.[21] For Besançon-Spencer "the discussion of the relationship between men and women in the church is personal and subjective."[22]

She begins her discussion by examining the Genesis passage about the creation of the woman in the image of God, and places parameters around the understanding of the curse of Eve such that her interpretation of the

20. Besançon Spencer, *Beyond the Curse*.
21. Ibid.
22. Ibid., 14.

woman's creation as well as of what takes place after her conversation with the serpent becomes liberating. Besançon-Spencer notes the differences between liberating messages of the text and the oppressive interpretation of the traditions of male readers across the history of biblical interpretation. She concludes with examples of how a liberating understanding of the texts can shape marriage and church life differently.

While Besançon Spencer stays within the interpretive frameworks of the theological tradition, she clearly expands and deepens that tradition by using the very language that male interpreters use to give a fresh and liberative reading. She also gives continuity to the commitment with which female readers approach the text, offering new tools with which to defend their liberative living.

In her writing titled "Reading from Ourselves: Identity and Hermeneutics among Mexican-American Feminists," Leticia Guardiola-Saenz evaluates identity as a hermeneutical lens for rereading a biblical story in order to "explore its role in the process of liberation."[23] The framework she uses is cultural studies. She defines the concept of culture within this framework as the political dimensions of the texts and the practices of everyday life.[24] The notions of race, identity, and difference are some of the central elements in cultural studies used to contest the dominant structures.[25] From this understanding Guardiola-Saenz uses identity as a hermeneutical lens through which to view the construction of reading strategies that will support a practice for historical change and social transformation.[26]

She offers an example of this by rereading the story of the Canaanite woman's encounter with Jesus (Matt 15:21–28; Mark 7:25–30). From the perspective of postcolonial readers she raises *what-if* questions: "What if I recast the story? Would that attempt change the history of exploitation and destruction that the ideology of chosenness endorsed?"[27] She then recasts the Canaanite woman as one who confronts the oppressor (Jesus) by asking him to heal her daughter and in the process vindicates herself as other and her oppressor as her equal, as other.[28] She sees the woman as giving Jesus a lesson in human courage and love for life. She posits that when we read

23. Guardiola-Saenz, "Reading from Ourselves," 81–82.

24. Ibid., 85.

25. Ibid., 86.

26. Ibid., 93.

27. Ibid., 95.

28. Ibid.

from our own reality "with a clear awareness of the power relations we need to defy, it will empower us to cross the borders that we need to challenge in order to bring about transformation through the agency of our self-defined identity.[29] In this reading Guardiola-Saenz goes beyond a Christology that presents Jesus as perfect and thus places upon the Canaanite woman the burden for the reason Jesus answers her as he does— with an answer uncharacteristic of our image of Jesus' perfection.

Daisy L. Machado has long been a pastor in the US Latina context, as well as a scholar and activist. She reads the text by making correlations between the biblical narrative and our own present realities. When the two engage each other, a liberative discourse takes place, and the reader encounters new challenges.

In her chapter titled "The Unnamed Woman: Justice, Feminists and the Undocumented Woman," Machado chooses the concubine of Judges 19 and correlates the violence that this woman suffers with the violence experienced by an immigrant woman whom she meets in a South Texas shelter.[30] The status of both women, concubine and undocumented immigrant, leaves them unprotected. The way that neither is valued leaves them unnamed in their respective societies. In both stories the women are seen as objects; their bodies are used, abused, and tortured, and no one comes to their aid. The men and forces of their time that act against them are beyond the women's control.

Machado points out to us that the biblical story "concludes with three imperatives[:] consider what you have seen, take counsel on what action to take[,] and speak."[31] The passage challenges us in our time and situation to a courageous and just action, to a similar response against violence toward and disempowerment of immigrant women. Where the stories have shown us the depths of death, the biblical imperative urges us to actions that bring life. We can understand by this that the story of the anonymous concubine is not an example of what to do but of what not to do. Readers are to find guidance beyond the passage to consider a corrective, a more just action.

By using correlation between text and present reality Machado shows how the biblical horrors are alive in the present-day story of the immigrant woman. The challenge of the text becomes the imperative for readers today. To respond to the imperative is to become a skilled interpreter of the text.

29. Ibid., 96.

30. Machado, "The Unnamed Woman," 161–76.

31. Ibid., 165.

We have examined the handling of the text of *evangélica* scholars. Now let us look at different groups of *evangélica* clergy and laywomen. The first example of biblical interpretation is the sermon of a young immigrant woman, a student of a Bible institute.

TEXT AND LIFE EXPERIENCE: READING BEYOND THE TRADITION

The following is a sermon written by an alternatively documented young woman as a part of a class assignment. It is a unique version of Jesus' encounter with the blind beggar (Luke 18:35–43).

> Others sermons put the spotlight on Jesus and his power to heal and save others. However, I as a Hispanic, I see the social status of the blind man. I think Luke wants to show the social apathy toward the poor on the part of Jesus and the crowd.
>
> I think the blind beggar represents those people sitting at the margin with no name, no identity, no legal papers, IDs, depersonalized, in hospitals, emergency rooms, streets maybe homeless or waiting for a job. They are begging for a little bit of the abundance of others. They are begging, not asking—begging for mercy. They are begging for compassion, help, and any type of caring love. They can't see their oppressors but can feel the oppression. They don't exist to society. Society passes by them, even those that are going to celebrate the Passover. They are part of society but are ignored and rejected. Society deliberately chooses to overshadow them with their laws and regulations.
>
> The blind man initiates his acknowledgement by asking what is happening to his fellow outcasts who have the ability to see. I believe they represent those that even though they are at the margin with him have more advantage over him. They can see and feel their oppressors. They have given a face to their hurt and pain. Therefore, they have lost hope in everyone especially Jesus from Nazareth. What good can come from Nazareth? They represent those that cannot see beyond their hurts, cannot hope for anything good in their lives. They have given up. They have no hope for a better life so they remain quiet. It's not that they don't believe in Jesus but [that] they have lost faith in all people. They have given up! (They had seen so many injustices [that they] have lost hope!)
>
> But deep inside, the blind man wants to see. More than seeing, he wants to change his social status. He wants to have access to the temple. He wants security. He wants to be *somebody* in society.

Even though immigrants do not have an identity in America, they have a voice. The blind man cried out twice in order to be heard[,] and immigrants need to keep crying out for help. Some of course have lost hope in the governments or even God and therefore choose to ignore the injustices around them. However, the blind man was one man[,] and he was able to get Jesus' attention and eventually all people's. He made himself known in the environment. He was heard.

Latino immigrants have a voice. They can be heard. We cry out for mercy and Jesus does not always hear us like the blind man whom he did not listen to immediately. Rather than beg, we must stand up knowing that we cry out for what is ours—human dignity—until God listens to us.

The miracle is not that Jesus healed but that the blind man dared to be known in the multitude of people. He took a step further into a world where he did not belong. He took a step to go into the center to speak to those who were there. Eventually, screaming like crazy, he was heard. Crying out changed his status from beggar to believing that he was a person. The undocumented today need that miracle too.[32]

This young woman is a Latina American of Native American descent. Her own hardships and immigrant journey were imprinted in this sermon. She told her classmates that "Yes, God does not always hear and God does not always look upon the poor." She based this on her experience. The question of another student challenged her: "How can you go against the faith that Jesus listens to prayer and answers prayer?" She responded: "That is what they have told you, but you need to test what they have said to you with what is the reality that you are living. The Bible has authority not by itself but along with the reality of our lives. It is in dialogue with our lives and together they are the authority. The Bible alone is not the authority but the experience of our lives."[33]

This was clearly outside the tradition of the teaching of this Bible institute and of the other students in the class. The dialogue between text and life experience is how this student defined the locus of the authority of the sacred text. This allowed her to stand firm in her interpretation of the text even when it was challenged. She followed her hermeneutic of the reality

32. Sermon by Latin American Bible Institute student in April 2008. Used with her permission. Name withheld for privacy.

33. Conversation, documented April 2008, Latin American Bible Institute, La Puente, CA.

of life. The Jesus she presents is different, and the image of him parts ways with the traditional definitions and understandings of Christology. There isn't the mystification of trust in God but the need to bring out and trust one's inner power, given to us by the creator God, as a way of bringing about change in one's life. It is her experience of suffering that dialogues with the text and signifies both text and tradition. Hers is a hermeneutics of experience that has an intercultural, intertextual exchange between the ancient text and the modern experience. Reflection on the exchange between Scriptures and experience produces an authority all its own.

The authority of the interpreter is one that we have not defined yet. When the interpreter is a woman, what is her authority made of? How has it been constructed and how does she have agency in the fashioning of her own authority?

The interpreter interprets the biblical text in light of her present life. She uses the preaching moment to tell her story as the story of many others like her. She dares to say that which is untenable for their faith. This is a meaning-making moment of the people, who together are seeking and sharing a process of understanding God's mystery and grace (or lack thereof) in their lives.

In this case the very realities of being alternatively documented confront the hearers of the sermon with the limits of the tradition of faith. The interpreter has concluded that the Jesus of the tradition has limited her, and that she needs to cry out instead. She sees the crying out as a moment in which Jesus, as well as the other bystanders, is brought to consciousness about the plight of the one suffering. Pointing to the limits of the authority of the tradition, which is based on a believed truth about Jesus, changes the balance between the authority of the tradition and the authority of one's life and meaning making in the moment of the interpretation.

The process encompasses a discontinuity and a continuity of the tradition. The continuity entails handing on or transmitting the tradition. At the same time, the very nature of the tradition requires that we critique it in order to reactualize it. To reactualize is to use the tradition not to invoke the past but to see what it reveals about the present and the future. The tradition then interprets present experience, "the past speaks to the present for the sake of the future,"[34] thus creating a dialectic between the three. The tradition then becomes a living tradition that fosters liberation

---

34. Boys, *Educating in Faith*, 20.

or oppression. If the tradition fosters oppression, then the tradition must be reformed before it is reactualized.

In this case, the crying out of those who suffer sparks the salvific presence of Christ. This cry is not a powerless plea, but one that reawakens in others a sense of the common worth of all humanity. Hence the salvific act comprises the actions of God plus the actions of the faithful. This cry has its own authority to redefine those who have been ignored as full persons and to restore their full rights to all that sustains life. The balance between the authority of readers and the tradition is the dialectic. Nonetheless in this dialectic the Scriptures facilitate a dialogue of intimacy between God and readers, where the scripture itself models the possibility for God and the women to enter a conversation that allows the women to challenge God as much as God challenges them. This type of dialogue holds the agency of both in a mutual and reciprocal tension, thus allowing for both to be transformed, and transforming not only each other but also the world in which they are co-creators.[35]

WHY THE WOMAN BLED: A COMMUNAL NARRATIVE[36]

The story that follows was told to me by a group of women at a retreat. As we discussed issues of sexuality and how these are informed by our understanding that a woman is created in the image of God, the women offered this story. The story is a rereading of the narrative of the woman with the issue of blood (Mark 5:21–34) from the experience of sexual abuse. It weaves the sacred stories of the women with the biblical story as the women in both texts struggle to find meaning in their suffering.

In a Pentecostal church in New England a group of women went to the bathroom of the church after the Sunday worship service to repreach the sermon in ways that would be relevant to their lives. They chose the bathroom as a private space where the male keepers of the "sound doctrine" of the church could not enter. This gave them the freedom to interpret the

---

35. This is not unlike the nature of the dialogue between Abraham and God or between Moses and God in the biblical account.

36. The women allowed me to retell their story in a fictionalized form that maintains their interpretation of the passage. For the full story see Conde-Frazier, "Latina Women and Immigration," 67–74.

Scriptures. They explained: "That little picture of a woman on the door is the best thing in the world. It makes this a holy tent."[37]

The women began the group preaching dynamic by asking questions. They paid attention to Scripture words or phrases that caught their attention. Some of the women had taken Bible courses at their Bible institute and they used that knowledge to help them exegete the passage. They used their intellect, faith, and critical thinking to look at the story from many angles until they saw something new that spoke deeply to their lives.

This time they read the story from the experience of sexual abuse. Some of the women had undergone this experience, and reading the story led them to see both Jesus and their experience differently. They created a dialectic between the story and their own lives. The moment allowed two of the women to tell their stories to the others while interpreting the passage. From their own experience the women understood that the woman described in Mark's gospel account bled in order to protect herself from being touched since during her menstruation she was considered impure. The interpreters saw the doctors that the biblical woman visited as those gynecologists in the community who did not understand their culture or womanness, and who instead treated their patients with disdain and with a lack of ethical understanding. The comments, care, and medical advice of these gynecologists aggravated women's situations.

However, when the woman in the biblical story saw Jesus, she decided that she would touch the hem of his garment because she saw that he was a different man who could bring good instead of evil into her life, and because there was light in his eye. Nonetheless, because she had been sexually abused, she could not bear him touching her. One of the present-day interpreters described the healing moment this way: "The woman came from behind, she touched his hem and was healed. She felt it in her body in every place where the curse had touched her. The shame began to subside and she started to feel relieved. She held her breasts without fear and closed her eyes and saw a beautiful woman looking at herself in the mirror wearing a white and gold dress. Meanwhile, Jesus was asking who touched him."[38]

The telling of the story led to the women's healing. To symbolize this the women turned on the water faucet and poured water upon those who were being healed. A cleansing ritual was taking place at the altar of the

---

37. Ibid., 68.
38. Ibid., 71.

sink. It was like a second baptism in which they died to their past sufferings and were resurrected to a new life.

However, the healing was not yet complete. Only the symptoms had been healed. It was now necessary to break the silence by telling the truth so that the fear, helplessness, and shame would be healed. This is why it was important for them to address in their own lives Jesus' question: "Who touched me?" The answer would break the silence and tell the truth. The women saw this truth as the only medicine for casting out the curse of the sickness.

In the gospel account, Jesus believes and accepts the woman's truth because he is truth. He answers: "Daughter, your faith has made you well" (Mark 5:34). The present-day women interpreted this faith as the biblical woman's renewed faith in herself.

"And how about the faith? He told her that her faith had healed her. What did he mean by that?"

"It was that she was able to trust a man once more." Jesus brought out the faith in herself. She did not have a curse. She was not a walking curse. She could touch others. She could be beautiful and touch others with her beauty. She could have faith in her body again, in her own spirit and in her womanhood."[39]

As the women defined the different situations in which men, even in marriage, abuse the body of a woman, the commitment they made was to condemn the acts against women by breaking the silence and telling the truth so that peace and healing would come. This is how they defined the way of justice: "La verdad trae justicia. Truth brings justice."[40]

LIBERATIVE MEANINGS

Elsa Tamez points out that liberative meanings come when a reading of the Scripture responds to the situation that has motivated the reading.[41] In this rereading of the Scriptures, liberative meaning has the power to affect not only the individual lives of Latinas but the lives of their communities as the women receive the challenge to change the way the community fails to respond to the suffering of women who are sexually abused.

39. Ibid., 73.

40. Ibid., 74.

41. Tamez, "Women's Rereading of the Bible," 190.

CONCLUSION

While using the resources available to them as scholars, clergy, or laity, the women read for liberation. Some women define the source of their liberative approach as a hermeneutical key while others call it the illumination of the Holy Spirit. The women read the text from the context of their lives so that they establish a dialogue between the sacred text and the text of their lives. Liberation is not only in the reading but in the action that takes place after the reading. The reading is not finished until the readers respond to the challenge it presents. This is the purpose for which the word was given. The action is still the reading as it reflects the commitment to Jesus, the enfleshed word, and we become a community that also gives flesh to the word by our actions. In this way the hermeneutical space births a word that becomes a liberating event in the community. Thus it becomes an enfleshed or incarnated word. In this way the women are faithful to the one who is the Word. It is with this belief and intent that evangélicas read the Scriptures.

STUDY QUESTIONS

1. How can we read the Scriptures so that a new meaning comes to us and touches our lives as it did the lives of the women preaching in the bathroom?

2. How do I understand the authority of the Scriptures in my life?

3. How does my theology of Scripture function in my faith?

4. What other hermeneutical tools influence my reading of the biblical text?

six

Being the Gospel Together

The Marks of an Evangélica *Ecclesiology*

ELIZABETH CONDE-FRAZIER

How can one approach the writing of an *evangélica* ecclesiology? There exists a great diversity among the different *evangélica* churches and the *pastoras* of those congregations that are giving shape to an ecclesiology. The churches represent a range of cultures, denominations, theologies, and generations. It is a huge task simply to describe what they are all doing (since their realities are so diverse), let alone to establish commonalities.

For congregations shaped by the realities of immigration, the congregation is a place to remake *familia* and a sense of stability and community in one's life. Because we are *familia*, the same gifts and limitations of *familia* are reflected in the new extended *familia* of choice. We learn to live and journey through these. Divisions are sometimes a part of the family dynamic and the life in the Spirit calls us to learn to forgive and to continue the journey towards maturation. The congregation is where we preserve culture and language while interpreting a new cultural space. For those most at risk in the new culture because of their status, the congregation becomes sanctuary on an ongoing basis as well as when there is crisis. One common thread ties these different realities: Latinas give shape to the church from many different spaces and the variety of roles they occupy in the congregation. As Martell-Otero points out in her chapter on eschatology, women are aware of the spaces they inhabit and the relation to the world around them so that they have learned to negotiate their space in the church.[1] Yet even these directions and roles are expanding rapidly as a 1992 study by sociologist María Pérez y González entitled *Latinas in Ministry: A Study on Pioneering Women Ministers, Educators and Students of Theology* shows.[2] It identified 673 women in ministry along the northeast corridor of the United States. Two years later the number had increased by over 150.[3] The definition of Latinas in ministry employed by the study was, "women who are in community-based organizations, church-based service and educational programs, and in lay leadership positions whose motivation for these is rooted in their Christian convictions. They view their particular work as ministry."[4] Women have expanded the understanding of the mission of the church to include social justice or "holistic ministry," meaning "serving the spiritual and social needs of others— taking care of the whole person, not just the salvation of the soul."[5] Such women are refashioning the understanding of the nature of the church and of its structure.

Evangélica ecclesiology happens from the margins of the church. Women often carry out their work without the same remuneration that men receive and at times without an official role or the permission of the ecclesial structures. The women's responses to this lack of recognition has been varied: some have continued to fight from within the structures, others have left them to join other more embracing structures, and still others have created their own ecclesial, parachurch, and non-profit organizations in order to more effectively and freely continue their work.

To capture the common patterns of practice and theological reflection that informs the women's ecclesiology, I will begin from their three starting points: the biblical account, the place of call and the charisms of the Holy Spirit, and the life experiences of the women.

---

1. See p. 119.

2. Pérez y González, *Latinas in Ministry*, 4–6, commissioned by The New York Mission Society.

3. Pérez y González, "The Heresy of Social Justice," 2.

4. Ibid., 3.

5. Ibid., 5.

THE BIBLICAL FOUNDATION: THE DEFINITION OF THE PURPOSE OF THE CHURCH

"The love of Christ compels us . . . And he died for all so that those who live may live no longer for themselves, but for him who dies and was raised for them . . . All this is from God, who reconciled us to himself through Christ, and has given us the ministry of reconciliation; that is, in Christ God was reconciling the world to himself, not counting their trespasses against them and entrusting the message of reconciliation to us. So we are ambassadors for Christ since God is making his appeal through us, we entreat you on behalf of Christ, be reconciled to God (2 Cor 5:14, 18–20, NRSV).

Reconciliation (Greek: *katallage*) is to change or to make otherwise. In Greek social and political spheres the term denoted a change in relationships between individuals, groups, or nations.[6] It is to change a hostile, broken, or apathetic relationship to one of favor or friendship. For the church, the central point of this reconciliation is Christ's death on the cross. Through his death, reconciliation with God and others and among others is now possible (Rom 5:10). God is portrayed in the above passage as the one always reconciling the world to Godself in Christ. Reconciliation is made possible because our trespasses or misdeeds are not counted against us. Now that God has reconciled us to Godself, God commits to us the message of reconciliation. Having been entrusted with this message, we, like Paul, understand ourselves to be ambassadors, those who represent the interests of God.[7]

"Christ's love compels us." This can be taken to mean the love Christ has for us, or the love we have for Christ. For *evangélicas* it means both, for the meanings are intertwined. The verb compel (*synechō*) is "to hold together," "to surround, not to allow to escape, and to hold together so that it does not fall apart."[8] In receiving Christ's love, Latinas in ministry consider themselves to be held together by that love no matter the external pressures. Such a love surrounds them as if to keep them from being crushed, and it drives them to carry out this work of reconciliation.

What form does such work of reconciliation take for the women? They see reconciliation with Christ first as entering into a relationship with Christ. Second, they understand reconciliation to oneself to be a work of

6. Belleville, "A Ministry of Reconciliation."

7. Ibid.

8. Ibid.

healing one's view of oneself and of coming into the fullness of who they are. They see discrimination, racism, gender discrimination, and poverty as the things that cause one to become alienated from oneself. Reconciliation occurs by becoming involved in health, education, economic empowerment, and politics. Unlike their male counterparts in the leadership of the church, Latina women in ministry have even entered the political arena, running for office and organizing communities. They do not consider such activities to be personal ventures but the mission of the church. Because these areas are all connected to the broader umbrella of reconciliation, the women understand them to be part of announcing the gospel. They are ambassadors declaring the good news of reconciliation. The church is devoted to these acts of service and social justice. However what motivates them are not humanistic understandings of justice or human rights per se. What separates the church from other individuals and bodies doing similar work is the spirit in which they do it—the compelling love of Christ.

The love of Christ compels women to enter into coalitions and partnerships with those who may not recognize Christ, to proclaim reconciliation as ambassadors of Christ, and to create with Christ a new creation (2 Cor 5:17). It also makes them heretics in some circles. Pérez y González explains how many Protestant or Pentecostal church leaders "have long preached and believed that the church should only deal with matters of the soul and how they fear becoming involved in acts of social justice because believers are not to be of this world but to be pilgrims passing by."[9] For these reasons, "Latinas engaging in acts of social justice within the barrios are in a sense engaging in 'heretical' acts. They are occasionally accused of acting in opposition to the norms of the church and condoning and engaging in the lifestyles and 'wrongdoings' of those they assist."[10] These differences in understanding the mission of the church have caused some women to practice their ministries apart from their denominations.[11]

An *evangélica* ecclesiology does not focus so much on the church as the keeper of proper belief but as a proper or right action in the world that changes the person and society. Proper belief is the work of Christ in the believer, which is facilitated through worship. Persons experience God's touch through the songs, prayers, and preaching, and also through testimonies or faith stories of the people, which draw others into believing. A *testimonio* is

9. Pérez and González, "The Heresy of Social Justice," 5.

10. Ibid., 7.

11. Ibid.

the story of the places where the divine has touched our lives. It depicts the transcendent in the immanent. The church follows up the work through its teachings. These teachings, however, need to be incarnated—in us.

The purpose of teaching is to come to a relational knowledge of God. In the Bible, the Hebrew word for this kind of knowledge is *yada*. It is a knowledge in which the totality of one's being is engaged, not only one's mind. It therefore also includes an emotional response. Knowledge of God implies our knowledge of ourselves related to God so that we assume our religious obligations. In the Scriptures, the grammatical object of "to know" is frequently to know God's ways or precepts, not just to know the reality of God (Pss 25:4, 12; 119:104).[12] For the church, the reality of God is experienced in the acts of social action and justice.

Social action and justice are expressions of God's redemptive work. "In the New Testament the realization of God's redemptive work modifies what it is to know God thus bringing it to new levels. The subject matter of knowledge is the mystery of the basileia of God."[13] The *basileia* of God is understood in terms of peace among the nations, justice for the poor, universal education and human rights and dignity for all. It calls on the church to work for justice, peace and the integrity of creation.[14] This work begins in the congregation in its everyday activities of loving the neighbor. Living this way fashions a new consciousness, a neighbor consciousness in keeping with the values of the *basileia* and which makes possible the work of the church at a broader level. This consciousness leads us to compassion in all its expressions, including social justice, and it is an integral dimension of the spiritual life. It is the Holy Spirit that empowers humanity into the fullness of relational life.[15] This relational life is embedded in the fabric of the congregation by way of the five tasks of the church: worship, fellowship, proclamation/teaching, service, and prophetic ministry.

To claim the ministry of reconciliation as the central image for an ecclesiology is to claim Jesus as *kyrios* (lord). Jesus' lordship is characterized by his solidarity with those who are marginalized and by his devoted service to them. It has nothing to do with power over others as we know it. The lordship of Jesus was the fundamental confession of the early church. The confession of Jesus as *kyrios* is the recognition of his sovereignty over all of

---

12. See Conde-Frazier et. al., *A Many Colored Kingdom*, 196–97.

13. Ibid., 197.

14. This was the WCC statement at the Vancouver Assembly in 1982.

15. Rogers, "Dancing with Grace," 386.

human life, and his opposition to all that works against that life and creation.[16] Latina ecclesiology is informed by this Christology. It is the reason why *pastoras* do not make distinctions between the ministries that address personal and social needs of the people. Directed by this understanding, Latinas have positioned the church in some of the poorest and most forgotten areas without regard for personal recognition or compensation.

A Christology whose synthesis is the confession of Jesus as Lord is the foundation of an ecclesiology that conceives of the church as a community that proclaims a Jesus who is Lord of the totality of human life and the creation. Without this a proper Christology, we do not have a holistic gospel or mission. To claim Jesus as Lord is to say that his sovereignty extends to the economic, the political, the social, the cultural, the aesthetic, the ecological, the personal, and the communal arenas. Nothing is excluded from his sovereignty. And likewise nothing is excluded from the church's ministry of reconciliation.[17]

CHARISMS OF THE HOLY SPIRIT: CALL, AUTHORITY, AND STRUCTURE

I began by stating that an ecclesiology defined by the women comes from the margins. This is because women are not always allowed to exercise the full authority given to them by the charisms of the Holy Spirit. "Authority is defined as a struggling to be self-defining. It is not found in what others say but in the inner voice of the self, a gift from God."[18] This is the voice in our lives that reflects upon the happenings and the roles we play. This is the voice that lets us know if something is right or wrong about what the other voices or influences tell us. Having this voice is described as having agency. Agency is important in order to develop the spiritual practice of discernment. An agent is a cause or power that produces an effect by its action. The inner voice of a woman should be strong enough to have the power to bring about the action in her life that she desires to produce. In other words, a woman should be able to know herself and to act in ways congruent with who she is in the world. The other voices either confuse or affirm her.[19] If these are domineering voices, they suppress our voice and thus suppress

16. Padilla, "Introduction," 21–26.

17. See Padilla, "Introduction," 27, 49.

18. Conde-Frazier, "Latina Women and Immigration," 62.

19. Ibid., 62–63.

the voice of the Spirit in us. To suppress is to keep down, to keep from appearing, to keep secret. Basically, these voices quench the Spirit. When the Spirit of God is quenched, the Spirit is grieved. The woman's own voice is checked and the flow of Christ's leading and will in her life is restrained because she now learns to hear that voice through the filter of the dominating voices of authority. Even the Scriptures are heard through the filter of those other voices.

A call in a woman's life is the Spirit calling her to bring forth the fullness of her gifts. It is Christ's compelling love. It restores the authority of her voice that God created within her that she might become. We have learned to repress ourselves, or at least to shape ourselves according to the image of another. However, *call* means that the feelings and the gifts that have been hidden are now called forth from their secret places to act for the purposes of God. For we too are God's workmanship, created in Christ Jesus to do good works, which God prepared in advance for us to do (Eph. 2:10). The call in our lives is the Spirit's voice bursting forth within the woman to give birth to her and through her.[20] The call connects her with the fire of the Spirit that creates, redeems, restores, and makes whole— the ministry of reconciliation.

A Latina woman's sense of call is therefore often especially strong because it is authorized by the Holy Spirit, and because women have to hold tenaciously and discerningly to that authority as opposed to the authorities of the church. The Spirit authorizes a woman in her call and gives evidence of that through the gifts and ministries given to each woman.[21] It is also the Spirit therefore, who becomes midwife to the ministries of women as they bear fruit.[22]

At a conference on women in ministry at the Hartford Seminary in 1996, men and women of the Latino Protestant church gathered with the purpose of "doing theology" in relationship to the issue of women in ordained ministry. The method for theological reflection began with the hearing of the *testimonios* of four women in ministry. The first part of the women's stories began with their call. The call is a place that the Latino community recognizes as being replete with the voice of God through the Holy Spirit and therefore a source of authority for the community's theological considerations.

20. Ibid., 63.

21. Martell-Otero, "Women Doing Theology," 77.

22. Elizabeth Conde-Frazier, "Hispanic Protestant Spirituality," 141.

In her *testimonio*, the Reverend Julie Ramírez says, "It was the Holy Spirit who called me and the only one to whom I was responsible for responding boldly to my call."[23] Similarly, Pastor Sandra Cruz states:

> My gifts of leadership had been nurtured and affirmed in the church since I was a little girl. I was encouraged to take part in the different ministries of the church. I was mentored by deacons, deaconesses, Sunday school teachers and by the pastor. I learned not only the skills for serving but the spirit of servanthood. Part of this was how to pray. In prayer I was taught to listen for God's voice. I saw God's voice and the voice of the church align themselves when it came to my call to ministry. However, when it came time to give me the actual position and title, some people left the church . . . The only way I understand that is as a place where the Spirit of God and the traditions of the church didn't seem to agree . . . I felt the call of God to the pastorate even more strongly and the authority of God's voice in me was the one I obeyed. It gave me great power to act without fear[24]

Latina women's call is not only about serving in the church but about changing its structures, for a Latina ecclesiology is more than a theological reflection. Coming from the margins, our ecclesiology must reshape the structures of the ecclesial bodies. So for example, sensing a strong calling in herself and acknowledging that of other women in her denomination, Pastor Ana María Falcon-García acted to reform the traditions of the church, thus bringing them into congruence with the voice of God in her own life as well as in the lives of other women. On May 27, 1987, she introduced and defended an amendment to the constitution of her denomination, the Iglesia Cristiana Pentecostal, that would allow the ordination of women. In her arguments she provided biblical and theological grounding for her amendment as well as the evidence of the voice of the Spirit in the women affirming their calls along with the fruits of their ministries. The amendment passed, and she became the second woman to be ordained in that denomination. With a Master's of Divinity, a certification in addiction counseling and a Doctor of Ministry degree almost finished, she is the most educated clergy in her denomination and has encouraged other women also to become theologically prepared.

---

23. Audiotape of Conference, March 1996, Hartford, CT.

24. Conde-Frazier, "Latina Women and Immigration," 64–65.

When asked about this "voice of the Sprit," the women sharing their *testimonios* and the women listening affirmed that the voice of the Spirit was present in the *testimonios* themselves. These serve as an authoritative source along with the biblical historical sources. When the tradition's patriarchy excluded their voices and the Bible was read through the lens of the culture silencing them, the women found that their ability to hear the Spirit's voice in themselves gave them words to speak and strength to act beyond the systems of domination of the church and culture. *Testimonios* are a first expression of rebellion against domination. *Testimonios* make it possible for the women in the church to act as catalysts in the process of the liberation of women. Liberation theologian José Comblin reminds us that it is clearly the work of the Holy Spirit to produce words where there has been silence.[25]

How do this experience of call and the understanding of the charisms of the Holy Spirit help to shape the working relationships of the female clergy with the other leaders of the congregation? In his book *Ecclesiogenesis: The Base Communities Reinvent the Church*, Leonardo Boff quotes Gotthold Hasenhuttl's definition on the charisms: "Charism is the concrete call, received through the salvific event, exercised in the community, constituting the community in ongoing fashion, building it, and serving human beings in love."[26] The ministry of reconciliation is carried out by all through the gifts that the Holy Spirit pours out upon all without regard for gender or age (Joel 2:28–29; Acts 2:17–18). This means that the task at hand depends on a shared authority exercised in accordance with the grace and function of each charism (Rom 12:6–8; 1 Cor 12; Eph 4:11–13). *Evangélicas* give shape to a structure that recognizes and makes room for the operation of the gifts in an interdependent way. They share their authority in organic ways. They invite others to come alongside them as needs arise in the same way that a woman invites someone into the kitchen to wash and cut the lettuce while she stirs the rice, and they engage in conversation—all this while also watching the children play. There is no hierarchy, only a natural caring for others.

This is problematic for those so used to hierarchical authority that the lack of it causes them to believe that there is an absence of leadership and therefore to resist operating under this style of female leadership. Boff sheds light on the charism of presiding by describing it as the gift that brings "unity

25. Comblin, "The Holy Spirit," 151.

26. Boff, *Ecclesiogenesis*, 238.

of the whole, to the order and harmony of the charisms, in such wise that all things will work together for the upbuilding of the same body . . . This will be the charism of assistance, of direction, of administration (1 Cor 12:28) . . . The specific formality of this charism does not reside in accumulation and absorption, but in integration and coordination. This charism is within the community and not over it but for the good of the community."[27]

While women may keep the existing structures of committees and councils to facilitate the work of the congregation, they run them differently. They appropriate the model of the household along with understandings about good communication and management that they bring from their other professions (since most are bivocational). Each woman brings her expertise and gifts to how she fashions her style of leadership while keeping a vision of the full participation of all as exemplified by the Pentecost experience of the early church. The women live into and reflect upon a clerical body and congregation with a variety of ministries and functions. This is similar to Letty Russell's *Church in the Round*.[28] The work requires all voices and involvement in spiritual discernment, theological reflection, and hermeneutic discussions out of which spring forth worship, service, and prophetic undertakings. This allows for the fertilization of the work by unique expressions and values of the women, such as relationship building, compassion, and nurture, which are traditionally attributed to women. It also gives expression to the value of passion and with it anger and weeping. Anger has been repressed by the church and the culture, but as women practice the ministry of intercession, they feel free to include anger as a gift and spiritual practice for the prophetic work of the church.[29]

Evangélicas do not speak of declericalization. Instead they reflect on the way that their leadership changes the nature and function of the office. Because they represent the poor and because they are women, *evangélicas* see the exercise and claim of the authority of the office as a way to gain voice for representing the issues of the community in arenas that still respect the office. Within the office they do not seek personal privilege but justice for the oppressed.

In the same vein, then, the bread and wine at the communion table come to represent the full participation in the body of Christ with the

---

27. Ibid., 28.

28. Russell, *Church in the Round*.

29. This confirms some of Elisabeth Schüssler Fiorenza's insights. See *Discipleship of Equals*, 3–15.

understanding that the church also gives herself with dedication to the teaching of Christ and in service to the *basileia*. This devotion arises because of the love of Christ that compels us, the love that broke his body and shed his blood in order that we might be reconciled and become reconcilers.

THE LIFE EXPERIENCES OF THE WOMEN: COMPASSION AND THE MINISTRY OF RECONCILIATION

The life experiences of women inform an *evangélica* ecclesiology. We will explore how their experiences as women, *pastoras*, or lay ministers shape the community of faith to which they become so devoted, and thus also shape a theology of the church.

The relational knowledge of God (*yada*) discussed earlier is experienced by *evangélicas* as compassion. In Romans 12, where Paul speaks of the gifts in the body of Christ, each gift has a grace. The grace of compassion is cheerfulness. While compassion calls us to the work of being with others in their suffering, the grace of this togetherness is joy and celebration. An *evangélica* ecclesiology brings together the two. *Koinonia* is "the church as the habitation of God in the Spirit. It is the Christ-bearer, as are its members . . . The church is the alternative community."[30] *Diakonia* is the church as servant. This calls her to discipleship. What is a disciple whose Lord is Jesus? Christian discipleship is a lifestyle that participates actively in the realization of the purposes of God for human life and creation as revealed in Jesus: a new creation. The ministry of reconciliation requires that we recover the priesthood of all believers so that the church may be a community where all of the members encourage one another to discover and to develop their gifts and ministries in the multiple areas of life that need to be transformed by the power of the gospel. They are to create spaces of ministerial freedom and missional love that cover the needs of the people they are called to serve. When a woman lives in the freedom of such love and service, she can become the salt of the earth and the light of the world.[31]

Evangélicas bring to these understandings the strength of their compassion. *Compassion* connotes solidarity and springs from a place of solidarity. It is sharing from a place of weakness. Compassion involves imagination and action. The action is one of laying down one's life for another (John 15:13; 1 John 3:16–17). Compassion includes *hesed*. *Hesed* is

30. Arana-Quiroz, "Integral Mission," 199.
31. See Padilla, "Introduction," 19–49.

the Hebrew word often translated as "compassion" or "mercy." Yet scholars agree that no English word is an adequate translation. It implies the doing of deliverance that justice is about. It requires transcendence of the self: one cannot carry out justice if one has a guarded heart. It is part of the journey of conversion, for it brings us from indifference to care. This is why compassion involves internalizing others. We gain a sense of our common humanity with others who had previously been strangers to us. When we show compassion, we connect with them, and they permeate us and become significant in our lives.[32] This then informs the forms that our service takes in the community. Boff calls this the *diakonia* of reconciliation and asserts that when we live our lives for others then we live our lives beyond the sphere of worship alone and operate in "the global sphere of life—in daily life with the masses."[33]

It is compassion that roots *evangélicas'* sense of community, and through their ministry they lead others into that deep experiential and relational understanding. Compassion entails feeling the very deep emotions of others and extending one's own feelings. It is the knowledge that we need interconnections in order to foster, maintain, and transmit life. This was seen in Mama Leo's ministry to heroin addicts when she would spend endless nights accompanying them as they went through withdrawal. The experience shaped her preaching and understanding of the congregation's ministry in that community since at the time no other church or parachurch organization had undertaken the task of ministering to this population. Compassion draws from heart knowledge, from God's love poured into our hearts through the Holy Spirit (Rom 5:5). It is knowledge that connects the subject with the object, the abstraction with the action. Heart knowledge trains us for community and interdependence, the unity of the new creation. It teaches us to intercede.

Intercession turns compassion into passion. The women express their full emotions during intercession. "Vigorous spirituality welcomes both anger and weeping into the spiritual life."[34] Without anger, apathy sets in. Anger over injustice motivates us to social transformation, for righteous anger comes as the strength and courage to confront and denounce alongside the creativity to redeem relationships or rearrange unrighteousness into justice. In the power of anger, the Spirit calls us into fullness of self to

32. Conde-Frazier, et.al., *A Many Colored Kingdom*, 191–95.

33. Boff, *Ecclesiogenesis*, 91.

34. Ibid., 48.

bring healing and liberation. Esmeralda Collazo didn't speak English, but she was angry at the fact that funds allotted for bilingual education were being mishandled. Her anger gave her the courage to show up at a school district meeting to demand that proper action be taken. Her perseverance at other meetings led to an investigation and funds were redirected appropriately, leading to new programs for children in three schools.

Anger is accompanied by our tears. We weep for the suffering of the world, but it is a weeping that inspires us to action according to our gifts. Hildegard of Bingen points out that tears are the aroma of holy work.[35] They are a deep yearning to do good. Anger and tears create the space for the work of the Spirit. They are the groaning of the Spirit for renewal of creation and an expression of compassion thus revealing a deep spiritual well. To fear our tears or to suppress our anger is to block the power of the spirit springing forth from within our spiritual wells to resist death and to sustain and renew life.[36]

Brixeida Marquez started a ministry for men with AIDS who were being released from prison at the end stages of their illness. Many men had no medical benefits and in many cases were estranged from their families. In tears and in anger against the unjust system, Brixeida struggled with God in prayer while she sought out resources until she found a home for the men and round-the-clock volunteers that cared for them during their last days. Her tears of frustration and anger were turned to strength and creativity.

This passion comes from an understanding and fellowship with the feelings of God. It is a communion with the divine consciousness. This communion takes place not only through prayer but through our fellowship with one another. The passion comes from reflection upon or participation in the divine pathos where God is involved in the life of the greater community. This is what Abraham Heschel calls sympathy with God or feeling the feelings of God.[37] The burden of a prophet is compassion for humanity and sympathy for God. It is a prophetic space, a borderland between divine consciousness and neighbor consciousness.

Passion not only informs our ministries but is also a wisdom to be used for the work of transforming ideologies of oppressive structures. In *Naming the Powers,* Walter Wink explains that powers do not exist independent of the tangible forms that they take in the world: "They are political systems or

---

35. Uhlein, *Meditations with Hildegard of Bingen.*

36. Lakey Hess, *Caretakers of Our Common House,* 49.

37. These insights come from Heschel, *The Prophets: An Introduction,* 26.

appointed officials . . . They are the spirituality of institutions . . . The inner spirit or the driving force that animates, legitimates, and regulates its [the institution's] physical manifestations in the world."[38] Powers express ideologies that can be either controlling or liberating, and manifest themselves in a political party, an economic system, or an educational or ecclesial structure. Ideologies are widely shared beliefs, attitudes, and behaviors that are incorporated in social practices and institutional life. To transform an ideology and its power one needs to generate a new consciousness. Such new thinking creates new critical movements and group practices that seek to change unjust systems. Generating a new consciousness involves becoming aware of one's cultural blinders and the ideological filters through which we have become socialized to interpret the world.

This passion informs the other tasks of the church: worship, fellowship, preaching and teaching. It enhances the church's knowledge of God by embedding new routines into church life that involve the congregation in the daily lives of those who are suffering so that they are our brothers and sisters and not outsiders. These new routines become our spirituality, our communion with God. This communion takes place not only through prayer but through our fellowship with one another. The passion comes from reflection upon or participation in the divine pathos where God is involved in the life of the greater community.

When we reflect on or participate in the divine pathos, we promote God's purposes for sufficiency, solidarity and emancipation. *Sufficiency* is the meeting of basic human needs. This is equated with faithfulness to God in Matthew 25:31–46 because it involves actions and practices that foster the human dignity of others. In the biblical passage mentioned, dignity becomes the norm by which the adequacy of all forms of human behavior is to be judged. It comes from a theology of the person created in the image of God, the imago Dei. The *imago Dei* is what gives the person worthiness as opposed to any other human standard. It is the creation that gives each person intrinsic dignity. To respect the dignity of each person is a form of reverencing God. Rethinking the worthiness of all immigrants along these lines informs the church's ministry and advocacy on behalf of those alternately documented.

As *evangélicas* have been affirmed in their roles in the church, they have moved beyond survival to establishing their mark on the theological reflection and praxis of the church. In more recent years, *pastoras* have

---

38. Wink, *Naming the Powers*, 5.

begun to share the wisdom of self-care with younger women. Living in interdependence is imperative as a way of caring for the quality and health of the relationships of which they are a part. Self-care is an integral part of reconciliation with oneself and others. Through reconciliation, through interconnectivity, the church becomes mediator and reconciler of divergent realities. It becomes the "crucible of the common experience of all human beings," not only of those in the congregation.[39]

The spirituality of the *evangélica* church is marked therefore by a movement from compassion to passion, which in turn creates a "neighbor consciousness" of sufficiency based on the notion of *imago Dei*, and notion of interconnectivity that leads the flourishing of various ministries. This gives the church its prophetic edge that is crucial as it faces a number of issues, particularly those created by globalization. Globalization has created a cultural and political hegemony that pacifies and falsifies human consciousness, its senses, perceptions, conscience, soul, and spirit, while turning cultural activities into commodities for profit: schools, public media, education and training, knowledge, and even religious and spiritual programs have been turned into commodities. The market has created a consumerist culture among people throughout the world and has distorted the sensitivities of persons and their perceptions of beauty and identity.[40]

In light of this, what is the ministry of reconciliation? How do we reconcile persons to themselves, to the aesthetics and wisdom of their cultures? "We need to restore the holistic view of the world in which all living beings flourish in convivial solidarity."[41] We need to restore the economy to services and activities that are life enhancing rather than one big casino for financial speculation that sacrifices nations and peoples. This vision calls for disciple participation in the world orders that now serve the market so that disciples can proclaim the values of the gospel amid these world orders.

The church is where saints are equipped for the work of this ministry (Ephesians 4:17). Our prophetic function is to become the moral and spiritual conscience of the nations. The church is to unmask the ideologies that are the root causes of poverty. The church is the defender of human rights. Love, service, and the cross are the triad of our prophetic and diaconal functions as we propose a new lifestyle in contrast with the lifestyle of consumerism.

39. Boff, *Ecclesiogenesis*, 91.

40. Kim, *Education for the 21st Century in Asia*, 4.

41. Ibid., 5.

An *evangélica* notion of a compassionate church has the spiritual as well as biblical and theological foundations to face these challenges and respond to a prophetic call of transformation.

A *DABAR* CHURCH: THE MARKS OF AN *EVANGÉLICA* ECCLESIOLOGY

"And he died for all, so that those who live might no longer live for themselves, but for him who died and was raised for them (1 Cor 5:15, NRSV). An *evangélica* ecclesiology is incarnational. In a time of many words (many of them counterfeit), only an incarnated word will feed the great spiritual hunger of this generation that cries out for authentic community. The church must proclaim an incarnated word. *Dabar* is a Hebrew word that means "word as event." In an oral culture words have power over things. Our words have the power to bless and to curse, and as soon as they are spoken, they become an action taking place or about to take place among us. Word as event happens when my words become deeds and my deeds become an expression of servanthood. This servanthood gives forth fruit. This fruit may be a small modification, an alteration (however slight) in our world. These variances accumulate until there is a noticeable difference that we can call a renovation, that might capture a semblance of the *basileia* of God. *Dabar* requires integrity and the coordination of our ideals and our practices, of our vision statements and actions, that make a difference. A *dabar* church is a people of the incarnated word. We not only preach the gospel but are the gospel.

An *evangélica* ecclesiology is Pentecostal and communal. As *evangélicas* we are a Pentecost people, for Pentecost was not about the individual gifts. Those gifts are the myriad expressions of God's agapic love poured into God's people. Pentecost is a revolution, the explosion of love among us and through us and released and poured out into the world to redeem, to regain and reclaim life from the clutches of death, to bring light into darkness.

The early church expressed its gifts in her communal life. She exercised ministry not with a vision of success but with a vision to bear fruit. The image of community reflected in the fifteenth chapter of the Gospel of John is a powerful one for me.[42] The gospel presents us with the image of a vine. New Testament scholar Gail O'Day brings fresh insight into this image. She points out that all the branches run together as they grow out of the central vine. The branches encircle each other completely. This is an image

42. For a fuller discussion of this image see O'Day, *The Gospel of John*, 760–61.

of interrelationships, mutuality and indwelling in Christ and each other. None of the branches is free standing. To bear fruit is a decidedly corporate act. Each branch is immersed in the communal work (doing works of love). In the vine image we are known for the acts of love done communally, not as individual persons. We are not building individual accomplishments but a community of justice and righteousness, or *shalom*. We are empowered by the abiding presence of Jesus, and a corporate enactment of the love of God in Jesus takes place through us.

The gift that is emphasized in John 15 is that of bearing communal fruit—the fruit of a praxis of love (John 15:13). This praxis includes the practice of our vocations in communal fashion. Through this praxis, we effect the transformation of society.

Finally, *evangélica* ecclesiology has a vision of the cross of Jesus, of the expression of her radical discipleship in the community. An ecclesiology that centers on the ministry of reconciliation includes a call to self-giving love. Jesus' ultimate service is the gift of his life in love and we are called to love as Jesus loved and this love is our servanthood. The church is called to follow Jesus to his death but also is offered the promise of sharing in Jesus' glorification. There is an eschatological dimension to this ecclesiology. In other words, we die to our life for love of those whom God loves and for whom Jesus died, and then we are honored by God. Sometimes this honor befalls us in our lifetime and sometimes when we enter into our rest.

What is the privilege of the cross? Oscar García-Johnson writes: "It was a sacrament of agony and failure: a demoralizing icon." Then he adds how through his praxis of love and obedience Jesus brings to the cross "a redemptive, humanizing, and renewing power . . . It converted exclusion into inclusion, hatred into love, and deception into hope." [43] The privilege of the cross is the privilege of loss; it is grief and tears because we do feel compassion, and from this compassion flows Latinas' own praxis of obedience and love, of imagination and healing, so that the power of the resurrection is released. *Evangélicas* do not pray to be delivered from these pangs but rejoice because those who suffer with Christ are likewise glorified with him.

Those who take up the cross with Jesus are raised and glorified with Jesus in the end. This last mark of the church is an eschatological one. Glorification is the mark of an *evangélica* ecclesiology. We are branded by the sign of the cross, and from our radical discipleship comes our blessing where God exalts us. We are dressed in the grand beauty of our *kyrios*; we are decorated

43. García-Johnson, *The Mestizo/a Community of the Spirit*, 86–87.

in a display of light that spreads a finer joy, a great brightness and luster. We are the bride of Christ. We become radiant. Radiance happens when we are sent off in rays from the source of light. This radiance begins now, for in our world today Jesus is the light of the world, and the church is sent into the world to be the light of the world. As the Latina church, we are sent off as rays of brightness and love to the brokenness of the world so that our gifts of the Spirit may make a splendid appearance as works of mercy and healing, displaying a brilliant glory.

STUDY QUESTIONS

1. What roles do women play in the church, and how do these define the work of the church?

2. How does a sense of servanthood as defined by *evangélicas* show forth the church as "light of the world"?

3. What is the relationship between the church and the reign of God?

Neither "Left Behind" Nor Deciphering Secret Codes

An Evangélica *Understanding of Eschatology*

LOIDA I. MARTELL-OTERO

ESCHATOLOGY—THE TERM AROSE DURING the 1600s—is the study of the last things. Its root, *eschatos*, can refer to outcomes, but literally means either a spatial or temporal edge or horizon.[1] Unfortunately, this edge often has been interpreted only along its temporal axis. Within this discussion, time itself has been treated as an independent object, something independent of space.[2] Time, more often than not, has been approached as *chronos*, as a measureable and linear phenomenon that takes place within history. From a popular perspective, eschatology has become almost synonymous with Jesus Christ's second coming. The primary concern is focused on the *when* of Jesus' return and who will be left behind. This reductionist approach to eschatology has made it a topic that frightens or confuses people with timelines and secret codes. Unfortunately, it is discussed rarely in our churches, and so misconceptions about it abound.

In this chapter, I argue that eschatology is more than just a temporal event. It is certainly not *chronos*—the historical points of time that we

1. Hellwig, "Eschatology," 349. Keller, *Apocalypse*, xiii.
2. Augustine, *Confessions*, 232. Cf. Moltmann, *The Coming of God*, 264.

measure with watches and calendars. It is not, in fact, solely about a "future." It is more than about Christ's return. In light of the pressing conditions facing our planet and its inhabitants, there is a growing realization among contextual theologians that eschatology is about more than a transcendent reality or a future event. Indeed as Juan B. Libánio puts it, eschatology has "invaded" the very fabric of our daily lives (*la cotidianidad*).[3] It is intimately related to creation and salvation. Eschatology has to do with the reign of God. From an *evangélica* perspective, I argue that eschatology is about the fulfillment of God's vision—one that began at creation. This vision is related to the holistic formation of community and responds to God's command for justice and mercy. Per Keller's insightful definition, if eschatology can be viewed from the perspective of boundary or liminal space, then we can refer to it as a border crossing: the intersection of God space with creation space. Given these considerations, I further argue that the reign is not just an abstract concept or an intangible void but a place—a sacred space where *kairos* time and divine space intersect to permit the flourishing of perichoretic relations: the place where we can live abundantly. Such a motif has salvific resonance for those who are allowed "no place" in the world.

TIME: THE FINAL FRONTIER

Anyone who has ever watched *Star Trek* will recognize the phrase "the final frontier"—applied to space. Yet for much of the Western European post-Enlightenment world, the frontier has been not space but time. Within a linear understanding, time seems to cause anxiety.[4] We seem to race perpetually against time. Everywhere we look, we have timepieces that mark its passage: in our kitchens, cars, rooms, phones, and televisions. Time is apparently an enemy that must be vanquished. Expressions in English such as "running out of time" and "killing time," or even the English word *deadline* reflect modernity's battle with this elusive adversary. Ted Peters notes, "time is both friend and thief . . . As thief . . . time is constantly passing, ever eroding, ever destroying, ever forgetting. Time is merciless. Time steals from every entity its future."[5] Physical and cosmic death is very much a part of this anxiety about time. All things come to an end. The solution

3. Libánio and Bingemer, *Escatología*, 78.

4. Schwarz, *Eschatology*, 7.

5. Peters, "Where Are We Going?," 348. See also Moltmann, *The Coming of God*, 57; and Keller, *Apocalypse*, 85–86.

would seem to lie in God ending the end of time. Subsequently, much of the literature on eschatology, both popular and academic, has focused on time as eschatology's predominant dimension.

Closely related to this understanding of eschatology is the focus on Jesus Christ's *parousia*, or second coming. In some way, that coming is to end all time, to end all death, and give victory to a select few who will live infinitely. This interpretation is most tangible in the various millennial expressions often associated with eschatology, but with none so much as the dispensational premillennial position first espoused by John Darby in the 1830s. Darby's position has become widespread in many contemporary evangelical churches. This position basically posits that Jesus Christ will return to remove a faithful remnant or the "true church" from the earth (an event referred to as "the rapture"). Those remaining on earth will suffer a time of great tribulation instigated by an Antichrist. The time of power of this Antichrist is limited, for Christ will return and institute a thousand-year reign of peace—the millennium. This period is followed by a cosmic battle, which will decide the final fate of the devil and his minions; death will be swallowed up; all found wanting on God's Day of Judgment will be sent to the lake of fire; and those cleansed by the blood of the Lamb will receive everlasting life. While this scenario is primarily based on a literal interpretation of Revelation 20, dispensational premillennialists take seriously various First Testament passages, drawing literal parallels to contemporary historical events.

Such dispensational premillennialism was popularized with its integration into the Scofield Study Bible, which was translated into various languages, including Spanish. It has been further disseminated, and its theological intent distorted, by the Left Behind series of novels.[6] However, whereas many grassroots Christians in *evangélica* churches believe that such a scenario *is* eschatology, its introduction is really "an alien eschatological framework" that undermines the community's hope and faith.[7] Nevertheless, evangelicals as well as *evangélic@s* pore over the book of Revelation and other apocalyptic writings of the Bible. At times some assume that what was originally meant to be metaphorical language is actually a secret code that can be deciphered by those with special spiritual discernment. Adequate discussions from the pulpit and in the Sunday school classroom

6. A number of sources have offered critiques of the Left Behind series including Althouse, "'Left Behind'—Fact or Fiction," 187–205. Byasee, "Enraptured," 18–22.

7. Alfaro, "Se Fue con el Señor," 341.

must take place to clarify these unfortunate theological misconceptions. While it is beyond the scope of this chapter to critically evaluate the differing millennial positions and to effectively differentiate them from Tim LaHaye's fiction, the point I want to make is that all of them emphasize the importance of timelines.[8] They tend to reduce eschatology to chronology: one is urged to examine "the signs of the times" to ensure that one can discern when Jesus will return.

Nonmillennial approaches have broadened the conversation to focus more on the coming reign of God. Nevertheless, futurity and its relation to history is still an important category. Thus, Ernst Jenni defines *eschatology* as "a future in which the circumstances of history are changed to such an extent that one can speak of a new, entirely different state of things," albeit within history.[9] With this emphasis on futurity—on the *when* rather than the *what*—, the category of *chronos* trumps spatiality or presence. At the very least, the *when* impacts and shapes the *what*. A version of this is expressed by Jürgen Moltmann, who argues that God's transcendence is to be understood in terms of futurity: God is the one who comes to us from the future, and this future is what influences and transforms our present.[10] The emphasis on temporality is further evident in the debate among biblical scholars whether Jesus Christ's initial incarnation and subsequent resurrection was the inauguration of the eschatological reign of God, and therefore already "realized," or whether the *parousia* and the subsequent consummation of the reign is a future or "consistent" event. Most leading scholars have accepted a compromised position that we live in the in-between tension of the not-yet and the already.[11]

Time is not irrelevant in the discussion of eschatology. However, the more classical expressions have been responsive to the modernist concerns of those in power, those who express anxiety about time (*chronos*) and finitude. Post-Enlightenment theologians wrestle with issues of "secularism" that produce "meaninglessness."[12] Within such a context, eschatology raises issues of power and judgment, and places in relief the ultimate

8. Grenz claims that "the question of chronology of the end" is a "major point of debate in eschatology" in *The Millennial Maze*, 197. For a further discussion of the various millennial positions, see Clouse, *The Meaning of the Millennium*.

9. Jenni, "Eschatology of the OT," 126.

10. Moltmann, *The Coming of God*, 24–25, 265–66. See also Moltmann, "Liberating and Anticipating the Future," 189, 197–98.

11. Dodd, *Apostolic Preaching*; Kümmel, "Futuristic and Realized Eschatology," 303–14.

12. Pannenberg, "The Task of Christian Eschatology," 1.

powerlessness of those who believe themselves to be in power. However, for the poor and the oppressed, the issue is about articulating an eschatology not for a "world come of age" but for a people threatened with death, whose very existence is questioned in all dimensions at all times. What I find missing in the discussions that focus on time is the concern over the issues of justice. Furthermore, I find in such discussions little that connects the concepts of creation and salvation with eschatological fulfillment. How are these linked, if at all? I believe that more recent contemporary approaches to eschatology respond better to these questions and hold greater promise in the articulation of an *evangélica* eschatology.

BASILEIA TOU THEOU: GOD'S VISION SINCE CREATION

Constructive and contemporary theologies, particularly contextual theologies from the perspectives of people of color and of white women, are less focused on the chronological dimensions of eschatology and rather favor exploring the ramifications in the biblical notion of the reign of God (*basileia tou theou*)—a richly nuanced theological term, mostly in the Synoptic Gospels and used primarily by Jesus. Jesus often spoke of the presence or coming reign, and tended to use metaphors and parables to describe its characteristics. Yet he rarely defined what he meant by this distinctive phrase. Scholars surmise that for his audience in first-century Palestine, it could have been part of a daily lexicon. However, modern-day exegetes are left with the task of extracting what it meant in Jesus' context and what its implications are for us today.

Basileia is a verbal noun that connotes action. Its emphasis in the Second Testament is not so much on "kingdom" (though certainly this is implied) as on the act of reigning.[13] Thus biblical and theological scholars have interpreted the phrase *basileia tou theou* to refer to God's sovereignty or God's power. The biblical evidence does not point to an experience of abusive power. It is not a power over but rather a liberative power imbued with grace, love, and justice.[14] It is an eschatological shorthand that affirms that God's purpose for creation is and will be done "on earth as it is in heaven."

While this particular phrasing is not present throughout the Bible, its primary principle is. It is expressed, for example, when the psalmist sings,

13. I use the terms "First Testament" and "Second Testament" to refer to what older nomenclature called the Hebrew Bible (or Old Testament) and New Testament.

14. Martin, "A Sacred Hope," 210.

"The earth is the Lord's and the fullness thereof" (Ps 24:1). From the beginning of creation, God who is community-in-Godself expressed God's purpose for all of creation: that all humanity should live in community with God and all of creation. There was to be space and a place for all living creatures to thrive fully and in relation to each other. This grace-full relationality in diversity was described as "the image of God."[15] This was God's vision for us all.

The Greeks later used the term *perichoresis* to refer to this intimate joining. According to Karl Barth, God's purpose for creating was so that the divine could be in communion with that which was not God.[16] Molly T. Marshall and others describe this vision in Trinitarian terms as God's invitation to an eternal "perichoretic dance"—an apt metaphor for Latinas, who often express their sense of God's presence in song and musical movement.[17] This intimate joining, this dance is "salvation"—the coming together of God, humanity, and creation. The Greeks used the term *theosis* or *divinization* to describe the joining of humankind with the divine. Eschatology as presence of the reign of God is the fulfillment of the vision of creation and promise of salvation.

BUSCAD PRIMERO EL REINO DE DIOS Y SU JUSTICIA[18]

In light of sin, humanity has damaged God's vision repeatedly. We have tended to resist the Reign for which we claim to wait with such anxiety. We have damaged the earth. We have damaged each other. We exploit the most vulnerable among us. We shatter community. Time and time again, God has reminded us of the vision of God's intent for creation. God instituted the Sabbath and Jubilee, affirming the divine intention of *shalom*. In Spanish we say, "No hay peor ciego que el que no quiera ver."[19] Since the First Testament, the vision of God's promise has not been forgotten because of the insistent words of prophets. When humanity places its sights on timelines and pots of gold, prophets are the ones who shake their fists at the heavens and remind us that God does not demand a *when* but rather

15. Genesis 1:27.

16. Barth, *CD* 3/1:94–95.

17. Marshall, *Joining the Dance*. Cf. Zizioulas, *Lectures on Christian Dogmatics*. For Latina tendency to relate music with the divine, see chapter 3 in this book.

18. Seek first the reign of God and its justice (Matt 6:13).

19. "There is no worse blind person than one who refuses to see."

a *what*: "What does the Lord require of you but to do justice, and to love kindness, and to walk humbly with your God?"[20] Prophets are the ones who can see visions when the rest of us go blind.

Perhaps that is why we are in continuous need of having someone point out to us *where* the reign is. Jesus did it in parables. Eventually the Christian church came to believe that Jesus was himself the embodiment of the reign. Yet rather than listen to Jesus' wise response each time they questioned him about timelines, they chose rather to make of him a timeline. It is interesting that *parousia* does not really mean "second coming" as so many define the term, but rather is a Greek term meaning "presence." The issue is not whether Jesus is coming a second time but that he was and is the embodiment of the reign. In him we are to see again God's vision for humankind. In his ministry, we see again God's affirmation of the "least of these," for those whose lives are discounted as irrelevant by those with power. No life is irrelevant. No one is *sobraja* (leftovers) under God's reign. That is the point of the reign. There is space and a place here for everyone, as "in the beginning." Whenever he was asked about its arrival time, Jesus would wave away the question. The *when* was not the point, but rather the *what*. "In my [Parent's] house there are many dwelling places. If it were not so, would I have told you that I go to prepare a place for you?"[21] The reign is *parousia*, for those who have been told they have no place. There is a place at the table, a place at the inn, a place at the synagogue, a place at the banquet. *Hay fiesta con Jesús.*[22]

In light of our persistent blindness, it is no wonder that contextual theologians of color, particularly women, usually begin their discussions of eschatology not with timelines but rather with the topic of justice. Kwok Pui-lan decries the "erotic violence" perpetrated against women in Southeast Asia—part of the history of conquest, slavery, and colonization to which poor women in the globalized Third World continue to be subjected. For them, eschatological hope is not about going to heaven but rather about resisting and surviving in a hostile world that rejects their right to exist.[23] Joan M. Martin's womanist eschatology entails both prophetic and

---

20. Micah 6:8 (NRSV).

21. John 14:2 (NRSV).

22. *Fiesta* can be translated in one of two ways here: either as "party" or "celebration," or as "feast." Both meanings are found in this phrase. We are invited to celebrate a new and abundant life with Jesus, but we are also invited to the banquet/ feast table to partake of the blessings God has set forth for us. Thus "There is a celebration/feast with Jesus."

23. Kwok, "Mending of Creation," 149–53.

apocalyptic elements that denounce the patriarchal, racist, and imperialist sins of a society that once dared to sell African Americans as property, and that at present continues to treat people of color as less than human. For Martin, the reign of God is liberating justice that brings a new valuation, one that "finds its definition and ground in the God who is free," permitting the oppressed to resist "the falsehood embodied in oppression" and to see themselves as God has meant them to be. It is a humanizing process.[24] When seen from the perspective of the suffering world, the issue of timelines tends to recede in importance. Perhaps that is why Letty M. Russell prefers to define eschatology as "the mending of creation" rather than the doctrine of the end-times or the coming of Christ per se.[25]

When viewed from such perspectives, the reign of God can be understood in more nuanced ways. It is not simply a transcendental hope. It is more than a future event. It is a present challenge to do God's will on this earth *as it is done in heaven*. The reign is God's salvific, grace-full, sovereign, transforming presence in the midst of all creation, such that we live in "reconciliation with God, neighbor and nature."[26] To live under the reign is to experience salvation in the spaces of the everyday. It is to live with hope such that we ourselves begin to reorder our lives and our relationships "in justice, charity, and compassion," and to struggle for the transformation of societal structures that determine "whether people live or starve, whether they can live humanly or are brutalized, whether they can participate in community or are excluded, whether their lives are an experience of gracious goodness of the creator or are lived in torture or constant fear."[27]

To define *eschatology* as "the last things" does not necessarily imply chronology. Given that Jesus' concern was always for "the least of these," and that he continues to "stand outside the gate" among the displaced and forgotten, perhaps it is more accurate to define "the last" as the rejected, the forgotten, the powerless, the voiceless, the dehumanized ones suffering in our society. Eschatology is not the *when* but the *who*.[28]

---

24. Martin, "A Sacred Hope," 211–12, 222–23.

25. Russell, *Household of Freedom*, 71.

26. Costas, *Integrity of Mission*, 6.

27. Hellwig, "Eschatology," 361–62. See also Gutiérrez, *Theology of Liberation*, 135. Libánio and Bingemer, *Escatología*, 109.

28. Hebrews 13:12–13.

ESCHATOLOGICAL HOPE FROM PERIPHERIC PLACES

Latina *evangélica* eschatological beliefs have been derided as being super-stitious, irrelevant, and otherworldly—often by the very colonizing forces that taught them such theologies. Yet Harold Recinos and other *evangélico* theologians do not perceive irrelevance in such schemas but rather a pro-found voice of protest against the death-dealing powers that assault Latin@ communities on a daily basis.

> Latinos in the United States live in subhuman social conditions.
> The theology emerging from the barrio experience is designed
> to make sense of the reality of oppression . . . the otherworldly
> dimension of Latino theology coming out of the ghetto experi-
> ence seeks to describe the transcendent quality of God's king-
> dom, which is above this world's structures of inequality. God's
> kingdom points to a new world based on justice and equality . . .
> God's promise of a new heaven and a new earth calls into ques-
> tion for Latino theology the present structure of dehumanization
> and invisibility that marks the existential experience of the ghetto
> . . . the otherworldliness of Latino theology in the United States
> context reflects a coded language that seeks to keep alive the bar-
> rio's aspirations for social justice.[29]

Injustice against Latinas has been described repeatedly throughout this book, and documented in many other sources. I do not feel the need here to repeat the statistics or to review the myriad conditions that collectively contribute to the dehumanization and disintegration of a people. Suffice it to say that these statistics can be summarized by defining injustice as death.

Death can be defined in various ways. Medical ethicists have written tomes in an attempt to pinpoint what death is, and when it takes place. Such an understanding would encompass a physiological understanding of death: the cessation of our biological existence as we understand it. Yet death is so much more. Eldin Villafañe defines death from a theological perspective as a separation or "absence" of the divine presence from human life.[30] Most Latinas, particularly the poor, know what it is to die. We die small deaths every day. These deaths begin with our dreams as children when we learn that we have no right to have dreams because we are Puerto Rican or Dominican or not white, or for whatever unspoken reason is given to let us know that we are not "them"—those of the dominant culture. We

29. Recinos, *Hear the Cry!*, 135.
30. Villafañe, *Liberating Spirit*, 171.

die when we go to our schools and are treated as ignorant brutes for reasons we cannot fathom—reasons we eventually come to understand are related to our culture, our accent, and our ethnicity. We die when our expressed hopes to become doctors and lawyers are rejected because we are women of color. We die when we encounter violence against our bodies, minds, and spirits in a patriarchal world because we are women, poor, and therefore "things" to be used for the satisfaction of those in power. We die small deaths when we go to doctors and instead of healing receive mistreatment. We die when we see our children die amid a violence we cannot contain, explain, or justify. We die even in our churches when our sense of call is subverted, and we are left to work in the kitchen and in home visitation because allegedly God does not permit us in the sacred space of the pulpit or the baptistery. We who have uprooted ourselves and our families from our native homes to live in a strange and often hostile land have experienced a kind of death in that uprooting, and too often experience physical death in an attempt to cross an equally hostile physical border.[31] For those of us born in the United States but constantly told to "go home," a continuous experiential dissonance echoes the death of uprootedness familiar to our immigrant sisters. In small and large ways, the world lets us know that as Latinas we do not belong, particularly within the borders of this country. There is no place for us. *Brillamos por nuestra ausencia.*[32] There is no room at the inn. For Latinas, injustice is to be dis-placed.

We are a people who reside at the margins of US society. Orlando E. Costas referred to these spaces as "peripheric" places. It was here, he asserted, that Jesus died faithful to the core for those who daily die "outside the gate" of justice, and it is here that Jesus remains, challenging and beckoning those from the center to join him.[33] It is indeed "the last" about which eschatology is so concerned. Justo L. González and Zaida Maldonado Pérez claim that the reign is not another place but another order.[34] I would respectfully modify this assertion: for those who have no place, the room at the inn, the place at the table, the space next to Jesus outside

---

31. Machado, "The Unnamed Woman," 162. See also Martell-Otero, "Creating a Sacred Space," 9–18.

32. We shine by our absence. That is to say, our presence is marked particularly by our absence.

33. Costas, *Christ Outside the Gate,* 188–94.

34. González and Maldonado Pérez, *Christian Theology,* 145.

the gate is precisely the celebration of another "order of place." It is not a circumscribed geographical place, but rather a sacred space.

On a recent trip to Puerto Rico, I experienced a momentary spatial dissonance. The GPS that I had brought from the continental Unites States could not find any of the addresses I requested. Google Maps, MapQuest, and similar online tools were equally ineffective. As the days passed, the sense of dissonance increased as I began to realize that I had to re-remember that spatiality and time were measured differently on the island. The question to ask for directions was not, how long will it to take to get there?, or even a question about distances, but rather where can I find so-and-so?—giving the name of the person for whom I was looking. In answer to the proper question, precise miles and geographical indicators such as road names were not given. Rather I was told about curves in the paths, about schoolhouses and grocery stores along the roadways, and to look out for intersections marked by trees and houses. Although it took a few days, I found myself readjusting and hearkening back to the rhythms of my youth. Relationality rather than precision was the hallmark of finding places. Place is where relations are.

I suspect that the Puerto Rican sense of spatiality is part of our indigenous legacy. While little is known directly about our indigenous or Taíno culture in Puerto Rico, one of the distinctives of some Amerindian worldviews is the precedence given to spatiality over temporality.[35] Such worldviews do not deny the importance of time but subordinate it to space. God is present in sacred spaces, which continue to be holy throughout time.[36] These spaces are the intersection of divine space and *kairos* with creation. They are border crossings, *eschatos* moments, and places in the midst of us.

The sacredness of place was especially underscored when I visited El Yunque, the national rainforest, now under federal mandate on the island and a must-see tourist attraction. For many natives of Puerto Rico,

---

35. Within the first fifty years of the conquest of the Americas, the indigenous people on the island had succumbed to disease, intermarriage, and the violence of the colonizing forces. See Figueroa, *Breve Historia*, 69. The historical writings about Taíno culture has been inferred either from archeological findings, or from the writings of Spanish missionaries who passed on their translated versions of Taíno myths and religious beliefs to their superiors. Even the word *Taíno* is not necessarily what the indigenous people called themselves, but what one missioner translated from their word for "noble," "good," or "wise." For more see Alegría, *Apuntes*, 20–21, 34. For a definition of *Taíno*, see Arrón, "Lengua de los Taínos," 53. For the precedence of spatiality in relation to temporality, see Deloria, *God Is Red*, 120–21.

36. Tinker, *American Indian Liberation*, 7–10.

El Yunque is more than that, however. It is a sacred space. Local lore has it that it was once the home of the Taíno gods. Its holiness is still palpable as one walks its myriad paths and senses the presence of the divine in the midst of its lush and verdant topography. It is interesting to see how those spiritual roots of our Taíno legacy, which senses the sacred in places, have been transmuted through the religious sensibilities of our Puerto Rican Protestant traditions. An *evangélica* confessed to me that she goes there for spiritual renewal, and that her mother-in-law goes there on a yearly trip to dip her feet into its cold-water streams and to eat a meal at the base of its foothills: a very sacramental *kairos* moment in a sacred place. A healing takes place there—a sense of wholeness and rightness is restored. While the US federal government may lay claim to *El Yunque*, Puerto Ricans know the One to whom this holy ground belongs.

Those in the dominant culture often roll their eyes and speak in pejorative terms about people whose cultural values give less importance to time. We, in turn, have learned to blunt the sharp critique of the dominant culture by turning insult into humor. We laughingly call it Puerto Rican time. Justo L. González refers to this different understanding of time in his book *Mañana*. He asserts that when Latin@s say, "mañana," it is not a sign of laziness. Rather it has a deeper meaning. "*Mañana* is much more than 'tomorrow.' It is the radical questioning of today. For those who control the present order of society, today is the time to build for tomorrow, and tomorrow will bring about the fruits of what they sow today. For impoverished Hispanics and others, the real *mañana* is a time unlike today. It is a time of a new reality."[37] Growing up in Puerto Rico, I did not hear the word *mañana* as much as I heard the word *ahorita* (later). Regardless which word one hears, Latinas can ascribe another meaning to either—a meaning deeply connected to the concept of place. Latinas have been socialized to be deeply incarnational. Precisely as women, we always negotiate the spaces we inhabit. We are aware of our social location, including of the concrete places we occupy and our relation to the world around us. We are acutely aware of our beings within, of our bodies, and of the rhythms of our lives. This awareness leads us to focus more on presence than on *chronos*. When we say "ahorita" or "mañana," we are affirming that what we are doing, that the people we are with, and the places where we are at a given moment are more important than someone's pressing agenda or timeline. *Mañana* has no substance, and has no guarantee, which is why we often end our

---

37. González, *Mañana*, 164.

sentences with "Si Dios quiere" ("If God wills"). However, the people we are with do have substance. *¡Presente!* (Present!)

Time is often a commodity for people in power. How often I have heard the phrase, "to get more bang for the buck"! Those in power use time to exploit the labor of the powerless.[38] Latinas know this well. Our bodies have been "stooped over" for a long time (cf. Luke 13:10–17), working inhumane hours for nonliving wages. I believe that when Latinas say "ahorita" or "mañana," they are claiming that one can or should accomplish only so much within a given space of time because people, not things, and certainly not tasks, are important. Relations are important. To be present is important. *Si Dios quiere* reflects an understanding of time as *kairos*, as God-given grace that takes place. *Kairos* is more than just *chronos*, more than just a measurable unit of time. It is more than just a historical event. It has nothing to do with timelines. It is a decisive event—often associated with salvation—permeated with God's presence and God's purpose. While scholars and preachers often define *kairos* as a "decisive time," few mention that *kairos* also includes a spatial dimension. It means "the right spot" or "a suitable place."[39] A *kairos* moment implies the intersection of divine space and time. One has a sense that one is "at the right place at the right time."

Place is the cross-section of time as divine *kairos* and creation space. Place is where we *are*. Relations *take place*. Eschatology deals with sacred space. It is the border crossing of God's eternity with our creation space. We often associate the word *eternity* with the word *infinite*. We confuse it with timelines. I would submit that eternity is what God is. Therefore eternity is not related to *chronos* but to *kairos*, and therefore to God's fullness, presence, and (above all) *koinonia* (relations). To live in God's fullness is to live in the realization that time and space are not independent dimensions but the cross-section of the space that is a gift of grace, which we use not to exploit but to cultivate our relations with others and creation wherever we are. It is to be acutely aware of God's permeating holy presence in all things and through all things.

God's presence is the place where we take time to develop the relations of justice, love, and mercy that God has required of us "from the beginning." To partake of God's eternity is synonymous with being under the reign. The reign of God is the place where God's vision of the restoration of community and the joy of the Trinitarian perichoretic dance takes place.

38. Keller, *Apocalypse*, 118–19.

39. Hahn, "Kairos," 833.

Ada María Isasi-Díaz captures this aspect when she refers to the reign as the "kin-dom" of God.[40] For *evangélicas*, however, it is more than just *un proyecto histórico* (a historical project), and much more than relations. It is that, but it is also God's saving work taking place in and through us. It is place—divine space and divine *kairos* intersecting creation space. It is *eschatos*, a border crossing that leads to transformation. It is more than "kin-dom" precisely because it is grace, an outpouring of the Spirit of God, who has been faithful to the vision "from the beginning."

¡VEN, ESPÍRITU SANTO![41]

A hallmark of *evangélica* theology in general, and of its eschatology in particular, is the prominent role of the Holy Spirit. The Spirit is the *arrabon*, the kairotic evidence of God's perichoretic dance. Through the outpouring of the Spirit, God's fullness is experienced in concrete ways. The congregation sings, and people—especially the women, whether young or old—raise their hands in a joyous dance, speak in tongues, prophesy, weep, and hug. Lives are transformed. People dream dreams and have new visions of what God is doing and will continue to do. These experiences are not escapist, privatistic affairs. Each of these experiences counters their experiences of injustice. For those left voiceless can now speak in tongues. Those with no future now prophesy. Those torn from their countries, communities, and families have forged a new family amid the congregation. Women, who are often barred from pulpits, are anointed and given authority to go forth and speak in the name of God. Healing, in particular, is an important eschatological sign for those whose bodies are often exploited and abused, but who are hindered from access to proper care. Just as important, the dreams and visions empower them to develop new ministries to fight for justice and transformation for their communities: they see what is and know what should be. Villafañe describes these as "spiritual power encounters" that give rise to "signs and wonders" that provide "legitimate expectations in the Spirit's total liberation."[42] Here salvation as personal transformation and salvation as structural transformation intersect. The eschatological indeed has permeated *lo cotidiano*. Yet the Spirit has done more than that.

---

40. Isasi-Díaz, *En la Lucha*; Isasi-Díaz, "Mujerista Narratives," 228–29.

41. Come, Holy Spirit!

42. Villfañe, *Liberating Spirit*, 187.

When Spirit moves in our midst, Spirit exposes the lies and constant myths that bombard our colonized theologies and cultural mores. The Spirit exposes the lie that women are somehow less than men, or that women of color are less human then their white counterparts. Spirit reminds us that the earth is not the plaything of corporate interests who determine who is and is not deserving of its spaces. Spirit reminds us that the earth indeed is the Lord's and not the property of those who erect borders. The earth does not belong to the minutemen who violently repel those who cross. Those who believe they are in control should be careful that they not rob people of the spaces that God, not they, created. Spirit is the one who makes space where there is none, and who pours life where there is death. Through the power of the Spirit, God is present in the peripheric places of suffering, among the least. In these spaces, God reigns. Life, not death, has the last word. This is *evangelio* (good news). The sense of joy and expectation that this imparts is reflected in the coritos evangélicas sing, such as the one based on Jeremiah 31:13:

> Entonces la novia se alegrará en la danza,
> Los jóvenes y ancianos también.
> Cambiaré su lloro en gozo y os consolaré,
> Os consolaré, consolaré, de su dolor.[43]

Sammy Alfaro notes that *evangelic@* eschatology is "organic." While seemingly focused on the future, it has its eye on the present, denouncing "the sinful and unjust structures which militate against" the present establishment of God's reign.[44] Latina *evangélica* eschatology in particular has resisted the tendency to escapism. *Evangélicas* are too situated in place to lose their vision in timelines. Rather than looking to the skies for the coming Christ, *evangélicas* have listened to the Spirit's prompting to go the periphery: not *when* but *where*, *what*, and *who*. Spirit empowers as well as invites, grants charisms and provides the resources necessary to carry out the ministries needed to transform our suffering communities. We let God worry about the *when*—after all, it is God's *kairos*—and instead focus on what God has revealed to be God's vision for the world. Rather than wait for the reign to come, evangélicas have chosen to live life as if it were already here. ¡*Presente*! Through the Spirit, we are filled with hope and grace,

43. "Then shall the young women rejoice in the dance as well as the young and old. I will turn their mourning into joy [and] I will comfort them, I will comfort them, comfort them, of their sorrow."

44. Alfaro, "Se Fue con el Señor," 356.

which enable us to confront what should be by all accounts overwhelmingly hopeless situations. We trust and know that as we face "valleys of death," the eternal and therefore ultimate Word of God is life through the Spirit. The Spirit is the One who invites us to join in a dance—not to escape, but to create sacred spaces of life for all of creation, particularly for the forgotten and the outcast.[45]

The Reverend Leoncia Rosado (Mama Leo) and the Reverend Aimee Cortese de García are women who resisted the social and religious restrictions placed upon them because they had a vision given by God's Spirit.[46] They and other *evangélicas* like them did not wait for a future reign to come, but rather asked God what they were to do in the name of that reign now. They developed prophetic ministries that changed their communities in lasting ways, and created living spaces for people who have been told in myriad ways that there is no place for them.[47] When we stop looking at timelines and seek rather the face of the Spirit in the places where we are, and when we realize that where we stand is sacred ground to be treasured as a gift of God, we will begin to discern the reign of God in our midst and rejoice in the vision that God has shared with us. We will finally see. Then we can partner with God in bringing that vision to full fruition in this place.

CONCLUSION

Eschatology is a reign event. It is a fully Trinitarian event. More than *future* time, it is a realization of God's *kairos* and space as it intersects with creation space. It takes place. The limitation of millennialist schemas is that they tend to interpret eschatology solely as a christological event to be pinpointed in human time rather than as a Trinitarian event that takes place within the divine prerogative. Eschatology is the perichoretic fulfillment that takes place between the Trinitarian God we believe in and the creation that groans for that immanent and intimate moment (Rom 8:22). It is the moment when death is destroyed and when what separates us from the love of God is overcome. In this sense eschatology is incarnational: it is the coming together of body and spirit, the coming together of human and divine. In that process, we become fully human even as we are "divinized" (recall

45. Martell-Otero, "Women Doing Theology," 77–78.

46. Sánchez Korrol, "Unconventional Women," 47–63.

47. Conde-Frazier and Martell-Otero, "US Latina Evangélicas," 477–97. Ríos, "Ladies Are Warriors," 197–217.

theosis): the "broken bones are healed" (*katartismos*), and humankind along with creation joins the dance of the triune God. God's ultimate vision for creation is fulfilled. Eschatology is not about returning to Eden, but about fulfilling God's vision for creation. It is an "at-one-ment" moment, a coming together of all of creation with God and with each other.

As *eschatos*, it is a border-crossing event. Therefore the dichotomies often discussed surrounding eschatology become superfluous. Eschatology is not about only either a future fast approaching us or only a present event unfolding before, within, and among us. Like *mestizaje*, eschatology is a both/and event. It transcends the pre-, a-, or postmillennial debates. Forces of death will always resist the moving of the Spirit, seeking to undo the *perichoresis* of God and humankind. These are the antichrist powers and principalities that revel in death. Eschatology does not pit the secular against the religious. History has too often witnessed the power of the antichrist in the very religious institutions that claim Jesus to be Savior! Eschatology is rather about creating a sacred space, a home for those whose lives have been continuously threatened. It is about making a room for everyone. It is not about the *when* but about the *what*. It is about justice, mercy, love, and grace. Above all, eschatology is about bringing life—full and abundant—to this place.

We do well to remember that eschatology is not solely an event that envelops humankind. It is a creation event. We have mortally wounded our planet, although there is more than sufficient evidence that our very existence is dependent on the world's well being. Eschatology means bringing new life to creation. God's vision for community includes human life in intimate or perichoretic relationship with created life. Thus the writer of Revelation can write a vision about a new heaven and a new earth, not as a result of the destruction of this one, but as a fulfillment of God's saving power in this place.[48] It is about life. Jesus' resurrection affirms this promise, not just for humanity but for all creation.

The resurrection was and is an eschatological moment precisely because it was and is God's resounding No! to the very powers of death that have resisted God "from the beginning." The antichrist was present at the cross, the very epitome of the confluence of political, social, and religious powers that resisted God's vision for community. The resurrection was and is the power of God—that reign event taking place outside the gates of humanity and justice—in which death was indeed overcome, and the life of Christ,

48. Cf. Revelation 21:1–6; 22:1–2.

and therefore life itself, was and is affirmed. In Jesus Christ and through the power of the Holy Spirit, the reign of God has indeed come to us. In and through Jesus' life, ministry, death, and resurrection—empowered by the Spirit—we have been brought into God's space and time. In and through Jesus—anointed by the Spirit—we see ourselves and all creation through the eyes of God. We experience life in the power of God. In this sense, eschatology has begun. It is not coming to us; it is here among us. It has taken place. But it is also "promise." It is the vision of what will be when all powers and principalities are destroyed, when death is completely overcome, and when we are living fully cognizant that everything is "God-space." The pneumatic "power encounters" are experiential moments—albeit fleeting and illegible as they sometimes may be—of the power of the Spirit in human history, eschatological *arrabons* of a perichoretic reality that is taking place in our midst.[49] In those moments, we savor what takes place in the fullness of the Trinitarian reality, and what *life* means for all of creation.

This is why eschatology should not and must not be preached in our churches as "scary bedtime stories" of judgment, fire and brimstone, and death. Those narratives are, in fact, the very antithesis of what Christian eschatology is fundamentally about. Nor is eschatology about an escapist future reality, our traditional "pie-in-the-sky" theology. Rather, it is a reality that empowers us and gives us hope and courage. It is the reality that allows us to face death and say, "you do not have the last word." We can read Paul's "eschatological manifesto" in Romans 8:35, 37–39 (NRSV) with new eyes: "Who can separate us from the love of Christ? Tribulation, or anguish, or persecution, or hunger, or nakedness, or danger, or the sword? . . . Rather, in all these things we are more than conquerors through the One who loves us. Therefore, I am more than confident that neither death, nor life, nor angels, nor principalities, nor powers, nor the present, nor the future, nor heights, nor depths, nor any other created things can separate us from the love of God, which is in Christ Jesus our Lord." This same eschatological hope was expressed first by Jesus in his words to Martha in John 11:25–26 (NRSV): "I am the resurrection and the life. Whosoever believes in me, even though that person dies, will live. And all who live and believe in me, will not die eternally. Do you believe this?"

---

49. Cf., Eco, *The Name of the Rose*, 11: "But we see now through a glass darkly, and the truth, before it is revealed to all, face to face, we see in fragments (alas, how illegible) in the error of the world . . . "

This is the message of eschatology: a message of life and hope in the face of death and destruction. Eschatology is an affirmation that God indeed is sovereign over all things, all creation, all time, and all space. It is a reminder that we do not live according to human standards, but according to God's reality. This is why eschatology can never be divorced from the reign of God, which is, after all, about God's sovereignty and God's reality as it intersects with our own. Eschatology is not about timelines, nor is it a message of fear about death and destruction, unless you are a purveyor of death. Eschatology is a message of life and a response to the socioeconomic, political, religious, and cultural powers and principalities that their reign is over, their time is past, and that God has come home to bring us home.

QUESTIONS FOR DISCUSSION

1. How is eschatology taught and preached in your church?

2. If we change the paradigm of eschatology from a temporal to a spatial one (that is, from concerns about time to focus on sacred spaces), how would such a change affect how eschatology is preached and taught in the church? In our classrooms?

3. Why might some fear that this paradigm shift would rob eschatology of its sense of transcendence?

4. How does our eschatology influence soteriology—that is, our concept of salvation—our evangelism, and the overall mission of the church?

eight

Epilogue

Hablando Se Entiende la Gente

LOIDA I. MARTELL-OTERO

In the introduction, I proposed the concept of *teología en conjunto*—a collaborative and dialogical approach to theological reflection—as one of the characteristics of *evangélica* theology. I believe that this book embodies that spirit well. Elizabeth Conde-Frazier, Zaida Maldonado Pérez, and I chose to write this book collaboratively, rather than to make it a solo project, in spite of our differing geographical locations and work demands. From the beginning it has been a work of passion for us. We write about *evangélica* theology from our experiences and contexts as *evangélicas*. Nevertheless we are clear that this does not give us the right to speak *for* all Protestant Latinas. Rather we write out of the wisdom we have gained from them, not solely in the past but also in our ongoing interactions: more than ourselves, we are an integral part of the *evangélica* community.

Yet the dialogue also goes beyond that *evangélica* community in many ways, for we are also part of a larger Latina community residing in the United States. All of us know what it means to live in poor communities, and each of us continues to minister to the poor and oppressed men, women, and children who reside there. They are not statistics but rather sisters and brothers who leave profound *huellas* (marks) on us—pastoral concerns, tears, and admiration for their courage and faith in our hearts.[1] In a true spirit of *teología en conjunto*, we learn from them as much as we share our knowledge with *nuestro pueblo* (our people). Throughout this book, we have kept our conversations with them very much in the forefront of our thinking. Furthermore, the nature of the book and of our calling as theologians keeps us open to hear the voices of those who do not belong to the Latina community—European and Euro-American, African American, Asian and Asian North American, and Native American theologians—and others who do not necessarily belong to the guild. We acknowledge and desire to learn from still others. We are especially attentive to the voices at the margins, the silenced ones, whom no one else wants to hear. Like the eschatological banquet table, the conversation is only complete when *all* are welcome and *all* are heard. Nevertheless, we do not forget that this book is about *evangélica* theology. We hear the voices, share in the dialogue; yet its content must in the long run inform readers about the thinking and theologies of *evangélicas* residing in the United States.

Like other Latinas, *evangélicas* are not uniform. We are diverse not just culturally, religiously, socioeconomically, and politically as a group, but also individually like any other individual human being. We have points of agreement and disagreement. So too the three of us are aware that even though there are points of commonality among us (all three of us are Puerto Ricans who grew up in the northeast United States, and each of us has pastoral experience), there are also points of divergence that we honor, which we believe helped enrich the dialogue among us: we come from different family dynamics: one of us has a Pentecostal rather than a Baptist background, one of us spent a significant amount of time residing on the West Coast and another of us in Puerto Rico, and we each have different specialties in the general field of theological studies. We expected that our theological understandings would have points of convergence and divergence, and we welcomed all this. I say "welcomed" because the dominant culture at times believes that diversity implies division and precludes harmony; or that harmony and unity demands uniformity. Yet the fact is that in the world of music, harmony requires diversity! You cannot have harmony unless you have different notes. Scripture seems to point to the same conclusion: diversity and disagreement do not signal division, but rather are part of what it means to live in a healthy, living body (1 Cor 12:14–27).

1. *Huellas* literally means "footsteps" or "tracks" that mark the path of persons or animals.

Throughout this project we took time to share in a reflective process and engage in *teología en conjunto*. In this wonderful world of Internet connectivity, cell phones, and other means of telecommunication, the *how* was never as difficult as the *when*. Teleconferencing and frequent e-mails proved a boon for us. We read each other's chapters. We reflected on the book that we had birthed over the past year and a half. We had much upon which to comment. Quite a few questions were stirred up by our reflection, and we agreed that the best way to conclude the book was to respond to the most important ones. We believe our responding is a way that readers can also reflect with us and thus raise other questions that help enrich this dialogue that is the crux of theology or God-talk.

Imagine us, if you will, sitting around a kitchen table sharing a light snack or full meal, chased down by either a cold drink or *una tacita de café* (a cup of coffee). Puerto Rican culture is a very hospitable one, and we always welcome each other with food or drink. Good conversation inevitably drifts toward the kitchen or dining room table for this very reason. In my particular case, my father was a pastry maker, so our home was usually filled with the smells of fresh doughnuts, cakes, and cookies, and freshly brewed *cafecito* (coffee). Conversations of this sort are punctuated with laughter, arguments, people interrupting each other, and always done with respect. *Hablando se entiende la gente.*[2] So we invite you to join us at the table as we briefly reflect on these questions. They do not signal an end, but rather the starting point for future writing projects.

1. What makes our theology distinctively "evangélica"?

- *Conde-Frazier*: The dynamics of every relationship are distinct. The way that *evangélicas* have shaped their understanding of their relationship with God and their expressions of faithfulness to Jesus, guided by his Spirit and the biblical witness, have been the foundation of our theology. The circumstances of our lives, the barriers, challenges, creative problem solving, and biblical arguments are the threads that have fashioned our theology. Each of these is a distinct expression of how we have lived in relationship with God, ourselves, and our communities.

---

2. A Puerto Rican proverb that roughly translates as, "By talking [with each other], people come to an understanding."

- *Maldonado Pérez*: While the following may not be distinctive only of *evangélicas*, it is, however, a key characteristic of the way we do theology. I refer mainly to our Word-centered approach to theology. For instance, although I do not always quote or refer to Scripture directly throughout my chapters, it permeates everything I write, affirming as well as challenging assumptions and biases. This does not mean that I read the Scriptures from a contextual void, however. As an *evangélica*, I do not set aside my experience and context as a Latina woman living in the *va y ven* between Puerto Rico and the US when I read and study the Scriptures. *Evangélicas* are keenly aware that theology is a subjective task, that it is always contextual. We also know that theology is impoverished without our voices and the experiences that make us who we are. This means that while we claim Scripture as central to our life as people of God, we also know that our experiences enable us not only to reflect upon the text but also to enter into a dialogue with it. Experience works with our reason and, through the enabling work of the Holy Spirit who we believe is present in our reading, the Word becomes alive; it becomes Word for us.

- *Martell-Otero*: I concur with my colleagues that the role that Scripture plays is certainly an important mark of *evangélica* theology. Orlando E. Costas once described this as the rule of faith and practice, a common enough Protestant principle. Yet he added the caveat that it was the rule of a contextualized faith that was birthed out of a faithful praxis, and therefore was historically transformative.[3] Conde-Frazier's chapter, I think, delineates this very well: what makes this distinctively *evangélica* is the contextual lens through which it is read, interpreted, and lived out. I think it is readily apparent to the reader that the consistent thread of our "pneumatological nuance"—as Maldonado Pérez describes it in chapter 4—is one of the most distinctive marks of *evangélica* theology. It is not so much that the Spirit is another item to be thought about in our theology as that the Spirit permeates all *evangélica* belief, practice, and theological reflection. A third aspect of *evangélica* theology that is distinctive is the crucial role that "church"— and what that means specifically in *evangélica* faith praxis—plays in its formation. I believe that Conde-Frazier's chapter 6 has captured well that the life of the church becomes an integral part of the life of the community in a real sense. It seemed to me that our friends,

3. Costas, *Liberating News*, 11.

family, and social life are intertwined with church life so that the two become almost indistinct. It impacts a certain way of thinking, believing, and behaving; in short, our worldview. It shapes our theologies in profound ways. We three, in many ways, are the products of our church upbringings even as we now go back and shape the formation of the very faith communities that we love, and which continue to support us with their prayers and faith. Yet again I want to stress that each of these elements—Scripture, pneumatological permeation, and ecclesial and communal bonds—are distinctively *evangélica* insofar as they are incarnated in a particular context and lived out of a specific worldview, which I hope we have conveyed throughout this book.

2. *What were the commonalities shared among us, and where did we diverge as we shared our theological outlooks? What surprised us?*

- *Conde-Frazier*: The influence of the biblical legacy runs throughout the writings as does the description of the work of the Spirit. It is the Spirit that leads Latina *evangélicas* to trespass and to create a space for their faithful witness and defense of this witness. It is in the faithful practice and its defense that our theological reflection takes place. I was pleasantly surprised by the poetry of my colleagues as they described the Spirit: the wild child and *presencia* as understood by the Taínos and woven into our daily expressions of worship.

- *Maldonado Pérez*: It was not surprising to find that the three of us claimed the Scriptures as central, even as we acknowledged the role of experience, reason, and tradition. We claimed the importance of our *abuelitas* or other significant women as sources of inspiration as they exhibited grace and a holy *coraje* in their call to serve God with all their heart, soul, strength, and mind (Luke 10:27). We also alluded to some of the same experiences and their power to shape us. Yet we claimed also the power of God over such experiences transforming them into a witness to the work of God and the affirmation of ourselves as loved of God. We all shared what I would call our "redeemed experiences" in the hope that these will provide a nexus between the reader and the God that makes such great and wild things happen! Epistemologically speaking, I think too that we would agree on an *evangélica* commitment to look a question in the eye and take on the challenge that inevitably ensues when one dares to move the question forward. We are sure that our engagement cannot do without the wisdom and the challenge that comes from critical theological reflection. We are called to raise and entertain questions, welcome insights, and test conclusions, even as we are called to test the spirits. We experienced this thrust for depth and theological clarity in our engaging phone conversations—some of which took hours. I think that one of the places that I would find some nuance between us is related to our understanding of the reign of God. While Justo González and I refer to God's reign as a "new order," Dr. Martell-Otero refers to it as a new "order of place." Her emphasis on place is in distinction to the lack of place for those who, like Jesus, are told there is no "room at the inn," or "place at the table." I believe that is beautifully stated by her and would further nuance it by saying that God's reign implies a new place especially because it is a "new order." In this new order all have a place marked by the fully manifested will of God for us and all God's creation.[4] Because of this, as Martell-Otero indicates, it truly will be "sacred space." Thus, in the end, this too turns out to be more of a commonality of thought between us then a divergence in views.

- *Martell-Otero*: In a sense what surprised me initially was the degree of commonality that we exhibited, particularly with regard to our description of the role that the Spirit played, not just in a particular theological expression, but its centrality in the lives of *evangélicas*. To be sure it was a pleasant surprise, one that affirmed for me that this project was a valid one, and that we were certainly on the right track. Our phone conversations were enriching as we had long conversations about the Trinity or the church or some other topic—whether related to the book or not. The role of *coritos* and testimonies also came up for each of us, albeit in different ways and at different times. In terms of differences, we each have our particular styles of writing and approaching the theological task. That difference in style is important, however. It is, I think, integral to what makes the book an *evangélica* expression and hopefully an enriching experience for readers. What I

4. González and I state in the book that God's reign is "not a different place, but rather a different order. It is not a matter of going to heaven and leaving earth behind, but of a new heaven and a new earth (Rev 21:1)." González and Maldonado Pérez, *Introduction to Christian Theology*, 148. See also 145 for further information on early church tendencies to confuse the message of the Bible about God's reign with Platonic and Gnostic teachings about "another place" that is "up there" in the "beyond."

think was most striking for me in terms of a divergence was how we wrote about Jesus and salvation. I believe that I tended to focus on its more incarnational aspects, and my colleagues still tended to use the more traditional atonement language, which I believe reflects the Western-Anselmanian atonement soteriologies that have influenced evangelical preaching and teaching. I think that surprised me because when we dialogue about these things, those more traditional aspects are not so readily apparent. In fact, I would venture to say that our soteriologies probably reflect more the Irenaean/incarnational paradigm that I discuss in chapter 3, more so than what the language used in their respective chapters reflects. I believe that this more incarnational aspect is indirectly represented in Conde-Frazier's Scripture chapter. Thus I want to emphasize that I am referring to what I believe is a *linguistic* divergence, more than a theological one. Nevertheless, I think this is an area that bears greater conversation. Another area of divergence took place early on when we were planning the book: As a systematician, I wanted to begin with the Trinity, whereas my colleagues believed it was crucial to begin with the Holy Spirit. My argument was that *evangélica* theology is in danger of becoming reductionist by being too christocentric and losing sight of the Trinitarian relations; their argument was that pneumatology is what marks *evangélica* theology as distinctive. In retrospect, I am glad I lost the initial argument. There is wisdom in collaborative work and in communal reflection.

3. *After reviewing our chapters, what topics are missing that you think we should have addressed?*

- *Conde-Frazier:* While we gave narratives describing how women are involved in social and political activism, we did not articulate a theology per se that informs this action. We spoke about how women have expressed their faith in their communities but did not name or define a theology of social justice as such. The description allowed this subject to stand as it is in the lives of the women; a place of passionate obedience to the Spirit as they seek to be faithful. Other writers take the opportunity to insert their voices as Latina *evangélica* scholars to begin the definitions of such a theology. While we have each been involved in social action, we did not take the moment to express ourselves more deeply about it. I have been involved at the level of participatory-action research and for this reason have played the role of a facilitator or cathartic agent rather than the role of a leader. I am hoping not to usurp the voices of those who reflect on their own practice for themselves in their own religious language. It is still a developing theology. The women do not use the language of liberation theology. They use words that expand their understanding of family and caring for the less fortunate in the community. They may use the biblical language of the Matthew 25 passage: "I was hungry and you gave me food. I was thirsty and you gave me to drink . . ." (Matt 25:35 NRSV). Younger women use political language about oppression, while educators use the language of bilingual education or of their particular professions accompanied by the Bible verses that come to mind. It is not a systematic thinking yet. I struggle with inserting myself ahead of those voices. I wish to allow them to speak for themselves. This is why I used narrative to portray the dialogue as it is emerging in their own words.

- *Maldonado Pérez*: There are many things that I would have liked to have addressed in the chapters. I would have liked to engage more of the writings of the early church fathers on the Trinity to show how we have, especially in the West, minimized the importance of the role and person of the Holy Spirit. This myopia, in turn, has led to a concrete parsing of the Trinity that favors Christology over pneumatology—a Son that sits at the right hand of the Father, over the Spirit that calls (and empowers!) us to "go" and "make disciples." I fear that with the taming of the wild Child of the Trinity, churches have booted out also the sense of urgency that would otherwise have us on our knees daily calling on God to help us follow the one we claim as our Lord. While *evangélica* churches have had to depend on the power of Spirit to get them through each day, they are also prone to falling prey to a culture-Christianity that will leave them with spiritual amnesia. Another area that we did not have time to explore further and elaborate was on an *evangélica* epistemology. I think that reading through the book and our responses to these questions sheds some light on what still needs definition. Finally, I also wished we had time to include a chapter on creation (and God's providence). Creation is an area often neglected in church teaching and preaching and one that reveals in very personal ways our inexorable connectedness to and dependence on the rest of the world. This, in my mind, is a topic that holds great promise as a platform for conversation across many lines. As expressed throughout the chapters, we aimed for prophetic expression as much as theological discourse. We hope, in the end, that we captured *alguito* (something) of the essence of *evangélica* understanding in the themes in this book.

- *Martell-Otero*: One of the topics that I think bears thinking about is that of theological anthropology, particularly since so many of us grew up with a colonized and colonizing theology that viewed the "flesh" pejoratively. Such a theology gave room for women to allow themselves to be exploited, and to not value themselves in important ways. Theological anthropology is intimately linked to creation. Thus I can very well envision a chapter that discusses these two topics, and which, in turn, links them with soteriology and eschatology. Recently my own research interests have led me to articulate a theology of spirituality, particularly examining the influence of our African and indigenous legacies. I am not so much interested in "spiritual practices" per se; I think there are so many excellent works about that already. I believe, however, that not as much is written about the theological foundation of the notion of spirituality. What is it, and why is it important? What is behind the practices that we associate with spirituality? What is the role of spirituality in *evangélica* theological formation? This would have been an important contribution to this book. One last topic that at first glance seems to be missing is that of sin, and this leads us to our last question.

4. *It is startling that this book has no chapter on sin. Why did we not include a specific chapter on this? Should we have, or did we need to? If not, why not?*

- *Conde-Frazier*: This is indeed quite an observation, especially given that women often can be portrayed as the door through which sin entered into the history of humanity. Several things come to mind as to why we may have left out this category: the women themselves do not speak to the issue of sin but speak of healing. Sin is a given, and the women do not focus on it but move to the next step in their ministry and work, that of healing and restoring. Their sermons on sin do not harp on the *do*s and *don't*s but on the issue of salvation. It is as if the women live a step closer to the realm of God. This is the focus. Since their understanding of their relationship with God and their expressions of faithfulness to Jesus, guided by his spirit and biblical witness, have been the foundation of our theology, this also gives witness to the focus on the grace of God in that relationship. When sin is spoken of, the conversation turns into one about judgment that eats at women's self-esteem. To speak of sin is to define the nature of the human being. I believe we have spoken to the issue of sin differently by describing the affliction of sin imposed upon us as Latina *evangélicas* in the church and how the Holy Spirit has brought reconciliation in the midst of the brokenness. As I read our chapters over, I also realize that salvation is seen in a much broader sense than just salvation from personal sin. Having said all this, the more I reflect on this omission, the more I recognize the need to speak more directly about sin as a way of addressing the ways that the traditional theological arguments connecting women with sin are the ones used to keep women from feeling like fully equal members of the church. We needed to address this for the sake of the women, and for the purposes of addressing the structural sin of the church.

- *Maldonado Pérez*: Although this first book does not contain a chapter on sin, I believe that we began from the premise that we are sinners in need of grace. "The Bible," which is central to us, "affirms what daily experience confirms: evil is real, that it is powerful, that it corrupts God's good creation. Between creation as it exists stands sin."[5] Following an eschatology of hope that is God's *¡presente!*, we wanted to focus the work of this book on the expectation, power, and call that is ours through the difference—the wonderfully subversive One—given to us through the work of the triune God. Thus our aim here went beyond giving expression to our thoughts about the different components in a systematic theology, however important that is. Much of the passion behind this book arose from our desire to provide, at the very least, a prolegomena, an opening to what we hope will follow. We wanted especially to provide a platform for *evangélica* voices, a bridge to further dialogue as we seek to understand and develop a theology that is truly *de nosotras*. Above all, we wanted to inspire. This explains our very personal approach. Theology is deeply personal. In short, if sin is about brokenness, then we have admitted and claimed our own—even while we speak against the kind of structural sin that

5. González and Maldonado Perez, *Introduction to Christian Theology*, 70.

pervades and impacts all creation. But we have done this from the very start by standing squarely on the answer—our aim, our mark, our hope, our foundation—: the gift and liberatory power of God in Christ through the work of the Holy Spirit. Having said this, since we do not have a chapter on anthropology, it is my sense that we focus more on structural/systemic sin/evil than on personal sin. I think that we do right not to dismiss the omission. But, as we also discussed, we were working from the assumption that we are all sinners in need of God's saving grace and that we received this grace that also empowers us to envision life, and thus also a theology, in new ways. We worked from the place of daughtership. All of this is to say that we are deeply aware of the impact of our understanding of evil/sin upon our theology, upon mission upon ecclesiology, Christology, and so on. Thus, while we wrote of its pernicious effects, we focused on the call and experience of the power of divine redemption.

- *Martell-Otero*: Though it would seem that we ignored the topic of sin, it actually permeates most of the chapters of the book from its inception, much as it does in the real lives of *evangélicas*. Unfortunately, sin is part of the subtext of the *evangélica vida cotidiana* and social context. As Conde-Frazier has pointed out, we did not treat the subject in its more classic evangelical approach. We certainly did not approach it from the more classic Pietistic view as an individualized, privatized reality. Rather, our discussions focused on its more structural manifestation. We see how it deforms the lives of women, particularly poor and oppressed women, as well as how it affects the lives of our communities and society as a whole, including the church! Yet I believe that ultimately we wanted this initial foray, this opening dialogue not to be so much about sin and death. Thus it is not surprising that we begin our theological discussion with the topic of the Holy Spirit, the *ruach*—God's creative breath of life that sustains all of creation in hope and grace. This book is about life. It is, as on that memorable Pentecost day (Acts 2), about dreaming dreams and having visions. It is an expression of the lives of women who dared to hope when there should be no hope, who pass on dreams to their children even in the face of five hundred years of colonized oppression, who continue to teach us that grace, courage, and fortitude are necessary, *pase lo que pase* (no matter what may come to pass). As authors, we envision this book to be an opening salvo, a beginning conversation. We hope to continue the dialogue. We did not want to begin it with death but with life. We wanted to introduce you to our *madres, abuelas, tías,* and *comadres* not in the framework of sin and destruction but in the framework of creativity, of "behold all things are made new" (2 Cor 5:17).[6] We wanted readers to experience the pneumatological ethos of life and hope that has sustained our faith, not only at the margins, but also when we find ourselves isolated at the centers of power. There is sin, of course. We neither deny it nor ignore it. How can we, when we live its consequences daily? Yet we rely on the promise that where sin is present, grace abounds.

Evangélica theology is not a static set of beliefs. It is not a codex written in stone. It is not a story that is clearly marked and accurately chronicled and archived, to be easily documented by a meticulous scholar. It is a living, breathing faith that grows, changes, and gives birth even as it is birthed in the peripheric spaces of the Spanish *barrios*, storefront churches, *evangélica* communities, and believing hearts of men, women, and children. As authors we bear witness to that faith. We sought to make visible a people whom society has ignored, and to give flesh to a theological way of life that heretofore has been disregarded.

This has been a labor of love and a personal story. We bear *testimonio* that we are literally alive—we survived death-dealing neighborhoods and conditions—because of the life-giving spirit of the women who were determined to see us through. We are who we are because they believed in the triune God who is faithfully *presente*. We are who we are because we believe and experience that *presencia*, as Latinas as well as scholars, both in the spaces of *lo cotidiano* as well as in the halls of academia. This book is a *testimonio* about the grace that abounds among *evangélicas*. Yet it is not a conclusion, but rather a beginning. We hope to continue the God-talk. Come and join us at the table. *Tenemos un cafecito listo.*[7]

---

6. Mothers, grandmothers, aunts, and godmothers.

7. We have a cup of coffee ready.

Glossary

Ad alium—(Latin) "to another" or "to the other."

Ahorita—(Spanish) in Puerto Rico, "later"; in other Spanish-speaking countries, "now."

Arrabon—(Greek) pledge or guarantee. Paul describes the Holy Spirit as God's pledge or guarantee that the promises of eternal life and blessings promised in the eschatological reign are true. The Spirit is also an *aparche*—a down payment—of life under the reign.

Authority—trust that a faith or faith community will deposit in a text in order to submit to the instruction and guidance of that text.

Ave María Purísima—(Spanish) Hail, Mary most pure. A common exclamation often said with no religious connotation or intention to call upon the Virgin Mary.

Bachata—a kind of music and a style of dance from the Dominican Republic, which has spread throughout Latin America.

Basileia—(Greek) reign. Often translated "kingdom" but better translated as a verbal noun (the act of reigning), though it also implies the area over which a monarch reigns.

Cappadocians—term referring to the three great fathers of the church who were born in Cappadocia. They were Basil the Great, Gregory of Nyssa (his brother), and Gregory of Nazianzus.

Christology—doctrine of Jesus Christ and his messianic role as savior.

Corito—a short musical refrain, usually based on a biblical text, either of praise or lament.

Cotidiano, lo—literally, the everyday. An epistemological and theological category that refers to the spaces where the poor and voiceless live out their lives, know God, and encounter both grace and sin.

Dabar—(Hebrew) "word as event."

De nosotras—(Spanish) belonging to us. This is also used to mean "characteristic of us." That is, it reflects something of who we are.

Discernimiento—(Spanish) discernment.

Dios Trino—(Spanish) triune God.

Donum—(Latin) gift, implies divine grace.

Encarnada—(Spanish) incarnational, embodied, or enfleshed.

Epistemology—the study of knowledge; a philosophy or field that seeks to discern how we know, particularly, how we discern truths and types of knowledge.

Es y son familia—(Spanish) is and are family. Refers to the Trinity as being One but also a plurality of Persons. Thus, the Trinity "is and are family."

Evangélica/o—a particular popular Protestantism that arose in the Americas originally colonized by Spain and Portugal as a result of the convergence of religious and spiritual influences of Iberian Catholic, African, and indigenous beliefs and their later encounter with various Protestant influences.

Eschatology—doctrine of the "last things."

Fiesta—(Spanish) party, celebration, or feast.

Fiestas Patronales—(Spanish) patron saints' festivals.

Godhead—refers to the triunity of God. The Godhead is three Persons and one substance. This unity of Persons is called the Godhead.

Gratia—(Latin) grace.

Hermeneutics—the theories and methods for interpretation (in this case, of the biblical text).

Hijas e hijos en el Espíritu—(Spanish) daughters and sons in the Spirit.

Hijas de Dios—(Spanish) daughters of God.

Illumination—the process whereby the Holy Spirit enlightens the mind of the receiver of the word so that the meaning for one's life may be clear.

Jíbaro/a—a distinctive Puerto Rican term for a country peasant. Elsewhere in Latin America, the term *campesino* is used. In modern parlance, *jíbaro/a* is also a slang term used to denote an unsophisticated person.

Kairos—(Greek) divinely appointed time in the right place.

Katartismos—(Greek) Originally it meant "mending a torn fishing net" or "healing a broken bone." In Ephesians 4 the word is rendered as "equip" in English and as *perfeccionar* in Spanish. We are given the gifts of the Spirit to heal the brokenness in the created Body as we move towards the fulfillment of God's reign in our midst.

Kyrios—(Greek) lord.

Locus theologicus—(Latin) social location and context from which one reflects upon God and the things pertaining to God.

Madres de la iglesia—(Spanish) mothers of the church.

Manera de ser—(Spanish) way of being; implies a distinctive culture and worldview.

Macedonianism—This is the name given to the view that denied the divinity of the Holy Spirit. The name is taken from Bishop Macedonius of Constantinople (d. c. 362). Another name for this group was the Pneumatomachi.

Mestizaje—(Spanish) a process in which the encounter (often due to social upheaval or violence) of two parent biological or cultural groups leads to the formation of a distinctive third, which nevertheless retains the characteristics of the parents. While *mestizaje* usually refers to the encounter between European and indigenous groups, *mulatez* includes Africans.

Millennialism—a theological view (held by variety of movements) based on the belief that Jesus Christ will establish a reign of one thousand years either prior to a time of tribulation or afterwards. Amillennialists reject any such schema.

Parousia—(Greek) Often defined as "second coming of Christ." The term translates literally as "presence."

Perichoresis—(Greek) literally, to dance around. Refers to the mutual interpenetration or interdependence of the Persons of the Trinity.

Pneumatology—doctrine of the Holy Spirit.

Praxis of accompaniment—the belief that the majority Latin@ theologians do not speak simply on behalf of a faith community but rather speak from and have experienced the very life of an oppressed community. They reflect upon what they themselves experienced and continue to experience as an integral part of the communities they represent.

Presencia—(Spanish) presence, being; implies that one's full attention is being given.

Ruach elohim—(Hebrew) Spirit of God.

Quicumque vult—(Latin) The first words of the Athansian Creed, meaning "whosoever wishes."

Quinceañero (Spanish)—A celebration of a girl's fifteenth birthday highlighting her passage from girlhood to womanhood.

Reactualize—To use the tradition not to invoke the past but to see what it reveals about the present and the future.

Sata/o—(Spanish) A Puerto Rican slang term that usually refers to mutts but that can be name a person who practices immoral behavior.

Sentido—(Spanish) sense, but also implies direction, purpose.

Sobraja—(Spanish) leftovers; a reference to how the dominant culture treats people as "other," as if they had no inherent worth, and can be easily discarded.

Santo/a—(Spanish) holy, sanctified. In the Protestant understanding, it refers to someone "set aside" by God through grace to serve God. In Protestantism, Christians who have accepted Christ are understood to be a "holy priesthood" and therefore to be *santos*.

Soteriology—doctrine of salvation.

Subsistence or subsistences—referring to the three Persons of the Trinity. While it implies substance, it relates more to their mode or state of being.

Theos agraptos—(Greek) "the God about whom we are silent." Cited by Gregory of Nazianzus.

Trabajo personal—(Spanish) personal work. A personal, face-to-face ministry that happens outside the walls of the church. This is further explained in the chapter on the Holy Spirit.

Testimonio—(Spanish) witness or act of witnessing. Narratives, usually shared by women, of how the divine has been experienced *en lo cotidiano*.

Teología en conjunto—(Spanish) a collaborative approach to theological reflection; an understanding that theology should be done in and among community, particularly among diverse voices.

Theosis—(Greek) divinization; the early patristic and Eastern Church notion of salvation that Jesus became human in order to divinize humanity. That is to say, that one is to become Christ-like, to achieve holiness and perfection, and thus be able to become one with the Holy Trinity. This is not to claim that human beings can be God, but rather that they can join in God's eternal life and joy. It is truly "comm-union."

Yada—(Hebrew) A relational knowledge of God

Vínculo—(Spanish) a tie that binds, a relation. The word implies intimacy.

Bibliography

Abalos, David T. *Latinos in the United States: The Sacred and the Political.* 2nd ed. Latino Perspectives. Notre Dame: University of Notre Dame Press, 2007.

Agosto, Efraín. "Reading the Word in America: US Latino/a Religious Communities and Their Scriptures." In *Mis-Reading America: Mimicry, Interruptions, Reorientation and US Communities of Color,* edited by Vincent L. Wimbush. New York: Oxford University Press, forthcoming.

Alegría, Ricardo E. *Apuntes en Torno a la Mitología de los Indios Taínos de las Antillas Mayores y Sus Orígenes Suramericanos.* [Santo Domingo]: Centro de Estudios Avanzado de Puerto Rico y el Caribe, 1978.

Alfaro, Sammy. "'Se Fue con el Señor': The Hispanic Pentecostal Funeral as Anticipatory Celebration." In *Perspectives in Pentecostal Eschatologies: World Without End,* edited by Peter Althouse and Robby Waddell, 340–60. Eugene, OR: Pickwick Publications, 2010.

Althouse, Peter. "'Left Behind'—Fact or Fiction: Ecumenical Dilemmas of the Fundamentalist Millenarian Tensions within Pentecostalism." *Journal of Pentecostal Theology* 13/2 (2005) 187–205.

Aquino, María Pilar. "Theological Method in US Latino/a Theology: Toward an Intercultural Theology for the Third Millennium." In *From the Heart of Our People: Latino/a Explorations in Catholic Systematic Theology,* edited by Orlando O. Espín and Miguel H. Díaz, 6–48. Maryknoll, NY: Orbis, 1999.

Arana-Quiroz, Pedro. "Integral Mission in the Framework of Grace, World, and Church." In *The Local Church, Agent of Transformation: An Ecclesiology for Integral Mission,* edited by Tetsunao Yamamori and C. René Padilla, 179–204. Buenos Aires: Kairos, 2004.

Arrón, José Juan. "La Lengua de los Taínos: Aportes Lingüísticos al Conocimiento de Su Cosmovisión." In *La Cultura Taína,* edited by La Comisión Nacional del Quinto Centenario del Descubrimiento de América, 55–65. Colección Encuentro. Serie Seminario. Las Culturas de América en la Época del Descubrimiento. Madrid: Turner, 1989.

Atkinson, Clarissa W. *The Oldest Vocation: Christian Motherhood in the Middle Ages.* Ithaca, NY: Cornell University Press, 1994.

Augustine, Saint. *Confessions.* Translated by Henry Chadwick. Oxford World's Classics. Oxford: Oxford University Press, 1991.

———. *On the Trinity.* Translated by Arthur West Haddan. In *The Nicene and Post-Nicene Fathers,* 1st ser., 3. Buffalo: Christian Literature, 1887. Online: http://www.newadvent.org/fathers/130108.htm/.

Balasuriya, Tissa. "Liberation of the Holy Spirit." *Ecumenical Review* 43 (1991) 200–205.

Barndt, Joseph. *Understanding and Dismantling Racism: The Twenty-First-Century Challenge to White America.* Minneapolis: Fortress, 2007.

Barth, Karl. *Church Dogmatics*, vol. 3/1: *The Doctrine of Creation.* Edited by G. W. Bromiley and T. F. Torrance. Translated by J. W. Edwards et al. Edinburgh: T. & T. Clark, 1958.

Barth, Markus. *Ephesians 4–6.* Anchor Bible 34A. Garden City, NY: Doubleday, 1974.

Basil the Great, Saint. *On the Holy Spirit.* In *The Nicene and Post-Nicene Fathers*, 2nd ser. Vol. 8. Translated by Blomfield Jackson. New York: Scribner, 1894. Online: http://www.myriobiblos.gr/texts/english/basil_spiritu_9.html/.

Bataillon, Marcel. *Erasmo y España: Estudios sobre la Historia Espiritual del Siglo XVI.* Sección de obras de historia. Translated by Antonio Alatorre. Mexico City: Fondo de Cultura Económica, 1966.

Belleville, L. L. "A Ministry of Reconciliation." Online: http://www.biblegate.com/resources/commentaries/IVP-NT/2Cor/ministry-reconciliation.htm/.

Besançon Spencer, Aida. *Beyond the Curse: Women Called to Ministry.* Nashville: Nelson, 1985.

Bird, Phyllis A. "The Authority of the Bible." In *The New Interpreter's Bible*, 1:33–64. 12 vols. Edited by Leander Keck. Nashville: Abingdon, 1994.

Boff, Leonardo. *Ecclesiogenesis: The Base Communities Reinvent the Church.* Translated by Robert R. Barr. Maryknoll, NY: Orbis, 1986.

———. *Trinity and Society.* Translated by Paul Burns. Maryknoll, NY: Orbis, 1988.

Bonhoeffer, Dietrich. "Costly Grace." In *The Cost of Discipleship*, 45–60. New York: Collier/Macmillan, 1959.

Boys, Mary C. *Educating in Faith: Maps and Visions.* Kansas City, MO: Sheed & Ward, 1989.

Brondos, David A. *The Fortress Introduction to Salvation and the Cross.* Minneapolis: Fortress, 2007.

Burgos, Raúl. "Dios de Mi Sustento." In *Siempre Hay Motivos*, 1990, by XXXIII DC. New Creation Records. Casette NCR002.

Byasee, Jason. "Enraptured: What's Behind 'Left Behind'?" *Christian Century*, April 20, 2004, 18–22.

Cardoza-Orlandi. "Qué Lindo Es Mi Cristo: The Erotic Jesus/Christ in the Caribbean, Latin America and Latino/a Protestant Christian Music." In *Jesus in the Hispanic Community: Images of Christ from Theology to Popular Religion*, edited by Harold J. Recinos and Hugo Magallanes, 157–70. Louisville: Westminster John Knox, 2010.

Chung Hyun-Kyung. "Welcome the Spirit: Hear Her Cries—The Holy Spirit, Creation, and the Culture of Life." *Christianity & Crisis* 51 (July 15, 1991) 220–23.

Clouse, Robert G, editor. *The Meaning of the Millennium: Four Views.* Downers Grove, IL: InterVarsity, 1977.

Comblin, José "The Holy Spirit." In *Systematic Theology: Perspectives from Liberation Theology*, edited by Jon Sobrino and Ignacio Ellacuría, 146–64. Maryknoll, NY: Orbis, 1996.

Conde-Frazier, Elizabeth. "Hispanic Protestant Spirituality." In *Teología en Conjunto: A Collaborative Hispanic Protestant Theology*, edited by José David Rodríguez and Loida I. Martell-Otero, 125–45. Louisville: Westminster John Knox, 1997.

———. "Latina Women and Immigration." *Journal of Latin American Theology* 3/2 (2008) 54–75.

Conde-Frazier, Elizabeth, and Loida I. Martell-Otero. "US Latina Evangélicas." In *Encyclopedia of Women and Religion in North America*, edited by Rosemary Radford Ruether and Rosemary Skinner Keller, 1:477–97. 3 vols. Bloomington: Indiana University Press, 2006.

Conde-Frazier, Elizabeth et al. *A Many Colored Kingdom: Multicultural Dynamics for Spiritual Formation.* Grand Rapids: Baker Academic, 2004.

Congar, Yves. *I Believe in the Holy Spirit.* Translated by David Smith. New York: Crossroad, 2001.

Costas, Orlando E. *Christ Outside the Gate: Mission beyond Christendom.* Maryknoll, NY: Orbis, 1982.

———. "Evangelism from the Periphery: A Galilean Model." *Apuntes* 2/3 (1982) 51–59.

———. "Hispanic Theology in North America." In *Struggles for Solidarity: Liberation Theologies in Tension,* edited by Lorine M. Getz and Ruy O. Costa, 63–74. Minneapolis: Fortress, 1992.

———. *The Integrity of Mission: The Inner Life and Outreach of the Church.* San Francisco: Harper & Row, 1979

———. *Liberating News: A Theology of Contextual Evangelization.* Grand Rapids: Eerdmans, 1989.

———. "A Radical Evangelical Contribution from Latin America." In *Christ's Lordship and Religious Pluralism,* edited by Gerald H. Anderson and Thomas F. Stransky, 133–56. Maryknoll, NY: Orbis, 1981.

Council of Scientific Affairs. "Hispanic Health in the United States." *Journal of American Medical Association* 265/2 (1991) 248–52.

Culpepper, R. Alan. "Luke 13:10–17, The Stooped Woman." In *The New Interpreter's Bible,* edited by Leander Keck, 9:274. Nashville: Abingdon, 1995.

De La Torre, Miguel. *Trails of Hope and Terror: Testimonies on Immigration.* Maryknoll, NY: Orbis, 2009.

Deloria, Vine Jr. *God is Red: A Native View of Religion.* 3rd ed. Golden, CO: Fulcrum, 2003.

Dodd, Charles H. *The Apostolic Preaching and Its Developments: Three Lectures.* New York: Harper, 1944.

Durber, Susan. "Political Readings: Jesus and the Samaritans—Reading in Today's Context." *Political Theology* 4/1 (2002) 67–79.

Eco, Umberto. *The Name of the Rose.* Translated by William Weaver. 3rd ed. San Diego: Harcourt, 1994.

Elizondo, Virgilio. *Galilean Journey: Mexican-American Promise.* Rev. and exp. ed. Maryknoll, NY: Orbis, 2000.

———. *Guadalupe: Mother of the New Creation.* Maryknoll, NY: Orbis, 1997.

Espín, Orlando. "An Exploration into the Theology of Grace and Sin." In *From the Heart of Our People: Latino/a Explorations in Catholic Systematic Theology,* edited by Orlando O. Espín and Miguel H. Díaz, 121–52. Maryknoll, NY: Orbis, 1999.

———. "Pentecostalism and Popular Catholicism: The Poor and the *Traditio.*" *Journal of Hispanic/Latino Theology* 3/2 (1995) 14–43.

Espinosa, Gastón. "Changements Démographiques et Religieux Chez les Hispaniques des Etats-Unis." *Social Compass* 51 (2004) 303–20.

Fiddes, Paul S. *Past Event and Present Salvation: The Christian Idea of Atonement.* Louisville: Westminster John Knox, 1989.

Figueroa, Loida. *Breve Historia de Puerto Rico.* Vol. 1, *Desde Sus Comienzos Hasta 1892.* Río Piedras, PR: Edil, 1979.

Foulkes, Irene. "Desde la Mujer Centroaméricana, Hacia una Teología de Paz." In *Teología desde la Mujer Centroaméricana,* edited by Irene Foulkes, 9–21. San José, Costa Rica: Sebila, 1989.

García, Sixto J., and Orlando O. Espín. "'Lilies of the Field': A Hispanic Theology of Providence and Human Responsibility." *Proceedings of the Catholic Theological Society* 44 (1989) 70–90.

García-Johnson, Oscar. *The Mestizo/a Community of the Spirit: A Postmodern Latino/a Ecclesiology.* Princeton Theological Monograph Series 105. Eugene, OR: Pickwick Publications, 2009.

Gonzales, Felisa. "Hispanic Women in the United States, 2007." Pew Hispanic Center (Revised May 14, 2008) 1–27. Online: http://pewhispanic.org/files/factsheets/42.pdf/.

González, Justo L. *Mañana: Christian Theology from a Hispanic Perspective.* Nashville: Abingdon, 1990.

———. "How the Bible Has Been Interpreted in Christian Tradition." In *The New Interpreter's Bible,* edited by Leander Keck, 1:83–106. Nashville: Abingdon, 1994.

———. *Luces Bajo el Almud.* Miami: Caribe, 1977.

———. *Santa Biblia: The Bible through Hispanic Eyes.* Nashville: Abingdon, 1996.

González, Justo L., and Pablo Jiménez, editors. *Púlpito: An Introduction to Hispanic Preaching.* Nashville: Abingdon, 2005.

González, Justo L., and Zaida Maldonado Pérez. *An Introduction to Christian Theology.* Nashville: Abingdon, 2002.

Greenwald, Robert, producer and director. *Walmart: The High Cost of Low Price.* Produced by Jim Gillam and Devon Smith. DVD. New York: Retail Project L. L. C. Distributed by Brave New Films. 2005.

Gregory of Nazianzus, Saint. *The Third Theological Oration: On the Son.* In *The Nicene and Post-Nicene Fathers,* 2nd ser. Vol. 7 §2. Edited by Phillip Schaff. Online: http://www.ccel.org/ccel/schaff/npnf207.iii.xv.html/.

——— *The Fifth Theological Oration: On the Holy Spirit.* In *The Nicene and Post-Nicene Fathers,* 2nd ser. Vol. 7. Edited by Philip Schaff. New York: Cosimo, 2007.

———. "To Cledonius against Apollinaris (Epistle 101)." In *Christology of the Later Fathers.* edited by Edward R. Hardy, 215–24. The Library of Christian Classics 3. Louisville: Westminster John Knox, 1954.

———. "God in Trinity." In *The Mystical Theology of the Eastern Church* by Vadimir Lossky. Crestwood, NY: Vladimir's Seminary Press, 1976.

———. "The Fifth Theological Oration—On the Spirit." In *Christology of the Later Fathers,* edited by Edward R. Hardy, 194–214. Library of Christian Classics 3. Louisville: Westminster John Knox, 1954.

Grenz, Stanley J. *The Millennial Maze: Sorting Out Evangelical Options.* Downers Grove, IL: InterVarsity, 1992.

Guardiola-Sáenz, Leticia "Reading from Ourselves: Identity and Hermeneutics among Mexican-American Feminists." In *A Reader in Latina Feminist Theology: Religion and Justice,* edited by María Pilar Aquino et al, 80–97. Austin: University of Texas Press, 2002.

Gutiérrez, Gustavo. *A Theology of Liberation: History, Politics, and Salvation.* Translated by Sister Caridad Inda and John Eagleson. Rev. ed. Maryknoll, NY: Orbis, 1988.

Haacker, K. "Samaritan." In *The New International Dictionary of New Testament Theology*, edited by Colin Brown, 3:449–66. Grand Rapids: Zondervan, 1986.

Hahn, H. C. "Kairos." In *The New International Dictionary of New Testament Theology*, edited by Colin Brown, 3:833–39. Grand Rapids: Zondervan, 1986.

Hasenhuttl, Gotthold. *Charisma, Ordnungsprinzip der Kirche*. Ökumenische Forschungen 1. Ekklesiologische Abteilung 5. Freiburg: Herder, 1969.

Hellwig, Monika. "Eschatology." In *Systematic Theology: Roman Catholic Perspectives*, edited by Francis Schüssler Fiorenza and John P. Galvin, 2:349–72. 2 vols. Minneapolis: Fortress, 1991.

Heron, Alasdair I. C. *The Holy Spirit*. Philadelphia: Westminster, 1983.

Heschel, Abraham J. *The Prophets: An Introduction*. New York: Harper & Row, 1961.

Isasi Díaz, Ada María. *En La Lucha / In the Struggle: A Hispanic Women's Liberation Theology*. Minneapolis: Fortress, 1993.

———. *La Lucha Continues: Mujerista Theology*. Maryknoll, NY: Orbis, 2004.

———. "Mujerista Narratives: Creating a New Heaven and a New Earth." In *Liberating Eschatology: Essays in Honor of Letty M. Russell*, edited by Margaret A. Farley and Serene Jones, 227–43. Louisville: Westminster John Knox, 1999.

———. *Mujerista Theology: A Theology for the Twenty-First Century*. Maryknoll, NY: Orbis, 1996.

Jenni, Ernst. "Eschatology of the OT." In *The Interpreter's Dictionary of the Bible*, edited by George Arthur Buttrick, 2:126–33. Nashville: Abingdon, 1962.

Kärkkäinen, Veli-Matti. *An Introduction to Ecclesiology: Ecumenical, Historical and Global Perspectives*. Downers Grove, IL: InterVarsity, 2002.

Keller, Catherine. *Apocalypse Now and Then: A Feminist Guide to the End of the World*. Boston: Beacon, 1996.

Kendall, Diana. "Families and Intimate Relationships." In *Sociology in Our Times: The Essentials*, edited by Diana Kendall, 476–509. 8th ed. Belmont, CA: Wadsworth, 2010.

Kim, Yong-Bock. *Education for the 21st Century in Asia*. Hong Kong: Christian Conference of Asia, 2001. Online: http://admiralty.pacific.net.hk/~egy/resource/aref-kyb.htm.

Kirsteen, Kim. "Spirit and 'Spirits' at the Canberra Assembly of the World Council of Churches, 1991." *Missiology* 32 (2004) 349–65.

Kinukawa, Hisako. "The Miracle Story of the Bent-over Woman (Luke 13:13–17): In Interaction-Centred Interpretation." In *Transformative Encounters: Jesus and Women Reviewed*, edited by Ingrid Rosa Kitzberger, 292–314. Biblical Interpretation Series 43. Leiden: Brill, 2000.

Kümmel, Werner Georg. "Futuristic and Realized Eschatology in the Earliest Stages of Christianity." *Journal of Religion* 43 (1963) 303–14.

Kwok Pui-lan. "Mending of Creation: Women, Nature, and Eschatological Hope." In *Liberating Eschatology: Essays in Honor of Letty M. Russell*, edited by Margaret A. Farley and Serene Jones, 144–155. Louisville: Westminster John Knox, 1999.

———. *Postcolonial Imagination and Feminist Theology*. Louisville: Westminster John Knox, 2005.

Lacueva, Francisco. *Curso de Formación Teológica Evangélica: Un Dios en Tres Personas*. Vol. 2. Barcelona: CLIE, 1989.

Lakey Hess, Carol. *Caretakers of Our Common House: Women's Development in Communities of Faith*. Nashville: Abingdon, 1997.

Lavastide, José I. *Health Care and the Common Good: A Catholic Theory of Justice.* Lanham, MD: University Press of America, 2000.

Levine, Daniel H. *Popular Voices in Latin American Catholicism.* Studies in Church and State. Princeton: Princeton University Press, 1992.

Libánio, Juan B., and María Clara L. Bingemer. *Escatología Cristiana: El Nuevo Cielo y la Nueva Tierra.* Series 3, La Liberación en la Historia. Translated by Alfonso Ortiz García. Argentina: Paulinas, 1985.

Lillie-Blanton, Marsha D., and Charisse Lillie. "Re-examining Federal and State Roles in Assuring Equitable Access to Health Care." In *Achieving Equitable Access: Studies of Health Care Issues Affecting Hispanics and African Americans,* edited by Marsha D. Lillie-Blanton et al., 163–200. Washington, DC: Joint Center for Political and Economic Studies, 1996.

Machado, Daisy L. "Abre Mis Ojos a la Realidad de la Mujer Hispana." *Apuntes* 19/2 (1999) 35–41.

———. "The Unnamed Woman: Justice, Feminists, and the Undocumented Woman." In *A Reader in Latina Feminist Theology: Religion and Justice,* edited by María Pilar Aquino et al., 161–76. Austin: University of Texas Press, 2002.

———. "Voices from *Nepantla*: Latinas in US Religious History." In *Feminist Intercultural Theology: Latina Explorations for a Just World,* edited by María Pilar Aquino and María José Rosado-Nunes, 89–108. Studies in Latino/a Catholicism. Maryknoll, NY: Orbis, 2007.

Maduro, Otto. "Notes toward a Sociology of Latina/o Religious Empowerment." In *Hispanic/Latino Theology: Challenge and Promise,* edited by Ada Maria Isasi-Díaz and Fernando F. Segovia, 151–66 Minneapolis: Fortress, 1996.

Maldonado, David Jr., editor. *Protestantes/Protestants: Hispanic Christianity within Mainline Traditions.* Nashville: Abingdon, 1999.

Maldonado Pérez, Zaida. *The Subversive Role of Visions in Early Christian Martyrs.* Asbury Theological Seminary Series in World Christian Reviatlization Movements in Early Church Studies 1. Lexington: Emeth, 2011.

———. "The Trinity." In *Handbook of Latina/o Theologies,* edited by Miguel de La Torre and Edwin Aponte, 32–39. St. Louis: Chalice, 2006.

———. "US Hispanic/Latino Identity and Protestant Experience: A Brief Introduction for the Seminarian." *Perspectivas* 7 (Fall 2003) 93–110.

Marcus, Joel. *Mark 1–8.* Anchor Bible 27. Garden City, NY: Doubleday, 2000.

Marsden, George, editor. *Evangelicalism and Modern America.* Grand Rapids: Eerdmans, 1984.

Marshall, Molly T. *Joining the Dance: A Theology of the Spirit.* Valley Forge, PA: Judson, 2003.

Martell-Otero, Loida I. "Creating a Sacred Space: An Iglesia Evangélica Response to Global Homelessness." *Dialog* 49/1 (2010) 9–18.

———. "Encuentro con el Jesús Sato: An Evangélica Soter-ology." In *Jesus in the Hispanic Community: Images of Christ from Theology to Popular Religion,* edited by Harold J. Recinos and Hugo Magallanes, 74–91. Louisville: Westminster John Knox, 2009.

———. "Liberating News: An Emerging US Hispanic/Latina Soteriology of the Crossroads." PhD diss., Fordham University, 2005.

———. "My GPS Does Not Work in Puerto Rico: An Evangélica Spirituality." Online: https://files.me.com/doc2rev/cvsrjh.

———. "Of Satos and Saints: Salvation from the Periphery." *Perspectivas* 4 (Summer 2001) 7–38.

————. "Woman Doing Theology: Una Perspectiva Evangélica." *Apuntes* 14/3 (1994) 67–85.

Martin, David. *Tongues of Fire: The Explosion of Pentecostalism in Latin America*, with a foreword by Peter Berger. Oxford: Blackwell, 1990.

Martin, Joan M. "A Sacred Hope and Social Goal: Womanist Eschatology." In *Liberating Eschatology: Essays in Honor of Letty M. Russell*, edited by Margaret A. Farley and Serene Jones, 209–26. Louisville: Westminster John Knox, 1999.

McDermott, Gerald R. "Martin Luther: The Monk Who Rose Up against Heaven and Earth." In *The Great Theologians: A Brief Guide*, 79–95. Downers Grove, IL: IVP Academic, 2010.

McDonnell, Killian. "The Determinative Doctrine of the Holy Spirit." *Theology Today* 39 (1982) 142–61.

McGrath, Alister E. *Christian Theology: An Introduction*. 2nd ed. Cambridge: Blackwell, 1997.

Migliore, Daniel L. *Faith Seeking Understanding: An Introduction to Christian Theology*. Grand Rapids: Eerdmans, 1991.

Moltmann, Jürgen. *The Coming of God: Christian Eschatology*. Translated by Margaret Kohl. Minneapolis: Fortress, 1996.

————. "The Crucified God." Lecture presented at the School of Theology and Ministry Public Lecture Series at Seattle Pacific University in 2008. Online: http://dcimos. apple.com/WebObjects/Core.woa/Browse/seattleu.edu.1974012462.01974012468.2 319708322?i=2076601705/.

————. "Liberating and Anticipating the Future." In *Liberating Eschatology: Essays in Honor of Letty M. Russell*, edited by Margaret A. Farley and Serene Jones, 189–208. Louisville: Westminster John Knox, 1999.

————. *The Source: The Holy Spirit and the Theology of Life*. Minneapolis: Fortress, 1997.

Moore, Donald T. *Puerto Rico para Cristo: A History of the Progress of the Evangelical Missions on the Island of Puerto Rico*. Cuernavaca, Mexico: Centro Intercultural de Documentación, 1969.

Morales, Beatriz. "Latino Religion, Ritual and Culture." In *Handbook of Hispanic Cultures in the United States*, edited by Thomas Weaver, 4:191–207. Houston: Arte Público, 1994.

Nhat Hanh, Thich. *Living Buddha, Living Christ*. 2nd ed. New York: Riverhead, 2007.

Oberman, Heiko A. *Luther: Man between God and the Devil*. Translated by Eileen Walliser-Schwarzbart. New Haven: Yale University Press, 1989.

O'Day, Gail R. "The Gospel of John." In *The New Interpreter's Bible*. Vol. 9, *Luke–John*, edited by Leander E. Keck. Nashville: Abingdon, 1995.

Omi, Michael, and Howard Winant. *Racial Formation in the United States: From the 1960s to the 1990s*. 2nd ed. New York: Routledge, 1994.

Otaño, Blanqui. "Nueva Identidad de la Mujer Encorvada: Exégesis de Lucas 10: 13–17." In *Teología desde la Mujer Centroamericana*, edited by Irene Foulkes, 125–32. San José, Costa Rica: Sebila, 1989.

Otto, Rudolf. *The Idea of the Holy*. Oxford Paperbacks. London: Oxford University Press, 1958.

Padilla, C. René "Introduction: An Ecclesiology for Integral Mission." In *The Local Church, Agent of Transformation: An Ecclesiology for Integral Mission*, edited by Tetsunao Yamamori and C. René Padilla, 19–49. Buenos Aires: Kairos, 2004.

Pannenberg, Woflhart. "The Task of Christian Eschatology." In *The Last Things: Biblical and Theological Perspectives on Eschatology*, edited by Carl C. Braaten and Robert W. Jenson, 1–13. Grand Rapids: Eerdmans, 2002.

Passel, Jeffrey S. et al, "Census 2010: 50 Million Latinos—Hispanics Account for More Than Half of Nation's Growth in Past Decade." Pew Hispanic Center (March 24, 2010) 1–7. Online: http://pewhispanic.org/files/reports/140.pdf/.

Pedraja, Luis G. "Guideposts along the Journey: Mapping North American Hispanic Theology." In *Protestantes/Protestants: Hispanic Christianity within Mainline Traditions*, edited by David Maldonado Jr., 123–39. Nashville: Abingdon, 1999.

———. *Teología: An Introduction to Hispanic Theology*. Nashville: Abingdon, 2003.

Peek, Monica E. et al. "Racism in Health Care: Its Relationship to Shared Decision-making and Health Disparities: A Response to Bradby." *Social Science and Medicine* 71/1 (2010) 13–17.

Pérez y González, María. "The Heresy of Social Justice: Latinas in the Barrio." Paper presented at Latin American Studies Association, Washington, DC, 1995.

———. *Latinas in Ministry: A Study on Pioneering Women Ministers, Educators and Students of Theology*. New York: New York City Mission Society, 1993.

Peters, Ted. "Where Are We Going? Eschatology." In *Essentials of Christian Theology*, edited by William C. Placher, 347–64. Louisville: Westminster John Knox, 2003.

Pew Hispanic Center, "Statistical Portrait of Hispanics in the United States, 2009." Table 8. Online: http://pewhispanic.org/files/factsheets/hispanics2009/Table%208.pdf.

Ramírez, Daniel. "Migrating Faiths: A Social and Cultural History of Pentecostalism in the U.S.–Mexico Borderlands." PhD diss., Duke University, 2005.

Ramírez de Arellano, Annette B., and Conrad Seipp. *Colonialism, Catholicism, and Contraception: A History of Birth Control in Puerto Rico*. Chapel Hill: University of North Carolina Press, 1983.

Recinos, Harold J. *Hear the Cry!: A Latino Pastor Challenges the Church*. Louisville: Westminster John Knox, 1989.

Reverby, Susan M. "'Normal Exposure' and Inoculation Syphilis: A PHS 'Tuskegee' Doctor in Guatemala, 1946–1948." *Journal of Policy History* 23/1 (2011) 1–28. Online: http://www.wellesley.edu/WomenSt/Reverby,%20Normal,%20JPH.pdf/.

Revuelta Sañudo, Manuel, and Ciriaco Morón Arroyo, editors. *El Eramismo en España*. Santander, Spain: Sociedad Menéndez Pelayo. 1986.

Ríos, Elizabeth D. "'The Ladies Are Warriors': Latina Pentecostalism and Faith-Based Activism in New York City." In *Latino Religions and Civic Activism in the United States*, edited by Gastón Espinosa et. al., 197–217. Oxford: Oxford University Press, 2005.

Rodríguez-Trías, Helen et al. *Eliminating Health Disparities: Conversations with Latinos*. Eliminating Health Disparities. Santa Cruz, CA: ETR Associates, 2003.

———. *Women and the Health Care System: Sterilization Abuse*. New York: Women's Center of Barnard College, 1978.

Rogers, Frank. "Dancing with Grace: Toward a Spirit-Centered Education." *Religious Education* 89 (1994) 377–95.

Rosenblatt, Marie-Eloise. "Gender, Ethnicity, and Legal Considerations in the Hemorrhaging Woman's Story Mark 5:25–34." In *Transformative Encounters: Jesus and Women Re-viewed*, edited by Ingrid Rosa Kitzberger, 137–61. Biblical Interpretation Series 43. Leiden: Brill, 2000.

Russell, Letty M. *Church in the Round: Feminist Interpretation of the Church.* Louisville: Westminster John Knox, 1993.

———. *Household of Freedom: Authority in Feminist Theology.* The 1986 Annie Kinkead Warfield Lectures. Philadelphia: Westminster, 1987.

Sales, Rubén. "Somebody Touched Me." *The Other Side* 39/6 (2003) 10–13.

Sánchez Korrol, Virginia. "In Search of Unconventional Women: Histories of Puerto Rican Women in Religious Vocations Before Mid-Century." *Oral History Review* 16/2 (1988) 47–63.

Schaff, Philip. "The Holy Trinity." In *The History of the Church: From the Birth of Christ to the Reign of Constantine, A.D. 1–311.* New York: Scribner, 1859. Online: http://www.ccel.org/ccel/schaff/hcc2.v.xiv.xiii.html/.

Schüssler Fiorenza, Elisabeth. *Discipleship of Equals: A Critical Feminist Ekklesia-logy of Liberation.* New York: Crossroad, 1993.

———. *The Power of Naming: A Concilium Reader in Feminist Liberation Theology.* Concilium Series. Maryknoll, NY: Orbis, 1996.

Schwarz, Hans. *Eschatology.* Grand Rapids: Eerdmans, 2000.

Schotroff, Luise. "The Samaritan Woman and the Notion of Sexuality in the Fourth Gospel." Translated by Linda M. Maloney. In *What Is John?*, vol. 1, *Literary and Social Readings for the Fourth Gospel*, edited by Fernando F. Segovia, 157–81. Society of Biblical Literature Symposium Series 7. Atlanta: Scholars, 1998.

Segovia, Fernando F. "Hispanic American Theology and the Bible: Effective Weapon and Faithful Ally." In *We Are a People! : Initiatives in Hispanic American Theology*, edited by Roberto S. Goizueta, 21–50. Minneapolis: Fortress, 1992.

———. "Toward a Hermeneutic of the Diaspora: A Hermenuetics of Otherness and Engagement." In *Social Location and Biblical Interpretation in the United States*, edited by Fernando F. Segovia and Mary Ann Tolbert, 57–73. Reading from This Place 1. Minneapolis: Fortress, 1995.

Silva, Moisés. "Contemporary Theories of Biblical Interpretation." In *The New Interpreter's Bible*, edited by Leander Keck, 1:107–34. Nashville: Abingdon, 1994.

Soliván, Samuel. "The Holy Spirit—Personalization and the Affirmation of Diversity: A Pentecostal Hispanic Perspective." In *Teología en Conjunto: A Collaborative Hispanic Protestant Theology*, edited by José David Rodríguez and Loida I. Martell-Otero, 50–85. Louisville: Westminster John Knox, 1997.

Suicide Prevention Resource Center. "Suicide among Racial/Ethnic Populations in the U.S.: American Indians/Alaska Natives." Newton, MA: Education Development Center Inc., 2011. Online: http://www.sprc.org/sites/sprc.org/files/library/Hispanics FactSheet_2012.pdf /.

———. "Suicide among Racial/Ethnic Populations in the U.S.: Hispanics." Newton, MA: Education Development Center, Inc. Online: http://www.alamonurses.org/ attachments/File/HispanicsFactSheet.pdf/.

Suro, Roberto et al. "Changing Faiths: Latinos and the Transformation of American Religion." Pew Research Center (2007) 1–151. Online: http://www.pewhispanic.org/ files/reports/75.pdf/.

Támez, Elsa "Women's Rereading of the Bible." In *Feminist Theology from the Third World: A Reader*, edited by Ursula King, 190–200. Maryknoll, NY: Orbis, 1994.

Tertullian. "Against Praxeas." In *Early Christian Writings*, edited by Peter Kirby. Translated by Peter Holmes. Website. Online: http://www.earlychristianwritings.com/ text/tertullian17.html.

Tinker, George E. *American Indian Liberation: A Theology of Sovereignty.* Maryknoll, NY: Orbis, 2008.

Torgerson, Heidi. "The Healing of the Bent Woman: A Narrative Interpretation of Luke 13:10–17." *Currents in Theology and Mission* 32 (2005) 176–86.

Uhlein, Gabriele, editor. *Meditations with Hildegaard of Bingen.* Santa Fe: Bear & Co. 1984.

US Department of Education, National Center for Education Statistics (2012). *The Condition of Education, 2012* (NCES 2012-045). Table A-33-1. Washington, DC: National Center for Education Statistics

————. "Status Dropout Rates." *The Condition of Education 2011 in Brief* (NCES 2011-034). Washington DC: Government Printing Office, 2011.

Washington DC: National Center for Education Statistics, 2011. Online: http://nces.ed.gov/pubs2011/2011034.pdf/.

Velazquez, Jaci. "Little Voice Inside." Written by Chris Harris, Joey Elwood, and Toby Mckeehan. In *Jaci Velasquez.* CD. Sony, 1998. B000007NB3

Villafañe, Eldin. *The Liberating Spirit: Toward an Hispanic American Pentecostal Social Ethic.* Grand Rapids: Eerdmans, 1993.

Wesley, John. "Preface to the Old Testament." In *John Wesley's Commentary on the Bible: A One Volume Condensation of His Explanatory Notes,* edited by G. Roger Schoenhals, 15–20. Grand Rapids: Zondervan, 1990.

————. *Sermons on Several Occasions.* Hudson, NY: Norman, 1810.

————. "Wesley's Notes on the Bible." Online: http://wes.biblecommenter.com/acts/2.htm/; http://www.ccel.org/ccel/wesley/notes.i.vi.iii.html/.

Wink, Walter. *Naming the Powers: The Language of Power in the New Testament.* The Powers 1. Philadelphia: Fortress, 1984.

Witt, Marcos. From the CD, "Poderoso: En Vivo," produced by CanZion Group/ Word Record and Music Group, Nashville, TN, 1993, CD#7019466605.

Wood, A Skevington. *The Expositors Bible Commentary.* Vol. 2, *Ephesians.* Grand Rapids: Zondervan, 1978.

"Word and Spirit, Church and Word: The Final Report of the International Dialogue between Representatives of the World Alliance of Reformed Churches and Some Classical Pentecostal Churches and Leaders, 1996–2000." *Pneuma: The Journal of the Society of Pentecostal Studies* 23/1 (2001) 9–43.

Zizioulas, John D. *Being as Communion: Studies in Personhood and the Church.* Crestwood, NY: St. Vladimir's Seminary Press, 1985.

————. *Communion and Otherness: Further Studies in Personhood and the Church.* Edited by Paul McPartlan. London: T. & T. Clark, 2006.

————. *Lectures in Christian Dogmatics.* Translated by Douglas Knight. London: T. & T. Clark, 2008.

Subject and Name Index

A

abuelas, 2, 4, 138
  See familia
adoption, 8
  adoptionist, 55
  See familia
agency, 40, 86, 95
  and authority, 85
  moral, 79
  and self-identity, 82
ahorita, 119, 120, 139
aliens, 78
St. Anselm of Canterbury, 35
  Anselmanian, 133
anthropology, theological, 135
antichrist, 110, 124
aparche, 27, 139
  See Holy Spirit
apocalyptic, 110, 115
Aquino, María Pilar, 2, 5, 79, 148, 150
arrabon, 27, 51, 121, 125, 139
  See Holy Spirit
astheneia, 48
atonement, 35, 59 n.31, 133
ausencia, 117
Ave María Purísima, 7, 139

B

bachata, 14, 18, 28, 139
Baptist, 128
  American, 6
as Anabaptists, 8
baptistery, 117
barrios, 93, 138
Basil the Great, 15, 139, 146
basileia, 26, 94, 100, 112
  and relation with *dabar*, 105
  tou theou, 112
  See reign of God
Besançon-Spencer, Aida, 80
Bible, 74, 75, 76, 77, 78, 79, 94, 98,
    110, 112, 134, 136
  authority of, 74, 84,
  and illumination, 75
  and inspiration, 75
  Institute, 83, 84, 87
  Scofield Study Bible, 110
  See also Scripture
biblical, 11, 12, 18, 31, 40, 41, 45, 53,
    75, 79, 80, 81, 82, 85, 86, 87,
    88, 89, 91, 92, 97, 98, 103, 105,
    112, 129, 131, 134, 136
  and discernment, 26
  and hermeneutics or
    interpretation, 78–81, 83
  scholars, 73, 111
bibliography, 145–54
Boff, Leonardo, 58 n.23, 61, 98
Bonhoeffer, Dietrich, 49, 146

C

café, 129
  cafecito, 129, 138

calling, 9, 21, 22, 24, 32, 40, 70, 96,
  97, 128
  as *trabajo personal*, 23
  See llamadas
Cappadocians, 57 n.20, 61, 139
census count, 4
  of Puerto Rico, 4
Christology, 10, 34, 37, 82, 85, 95,
  134, 137, 139
  See Jesus Christ
church(es), 4, 5, 7, 9, 11, 12, 15, 17,
  19, 20, 22, 24–26, 29, 30, 31,
  33, 34, 35, 40, 50, 51, 52, 54,
  60, 66, 69, 70, 74, 76, 79, 80,
  90–101, 103, 104–7, 108, 110,
  114, 117, 125, 126, 130–32,
  134, 136, 137–39, 141, 142
  community of faith, 27, 32, 75, 100
  as *dabar*, 105
  as familia, 11
  Free, 8
  as holistic ministry, 91
  Pentecostal, 86, 93
  storefront, 138
  tasks of, 103
  and *testimonios*, 98
  World Council of, 19
  See ecclesiology, iglesia
chronos, 108, 111, 119, 120
ciego, 113
  in saying: que no quiera ver, 113
cielo, 62, 63, 64
  See heaven
colonized, 2, 6, 12, 37, 42, 74, 122, 135,
  137, 140
  See also postcolonial
comadres, 2, 138
  See familia, madres
communal, 2, 6, 10, 13, 19, 22, 24, 26,
  27, 34, 35, 59, 60, 65, 95, 105,
  106, 131, 133
  narrative, 40, 86
  See also community
community, 4–7, 11, 12, 22, 24–25,
  27, 34, 39, 41, 46–47, 51, 60,
    67 n.53, 72, 73, 74, 75, 76, 77,
    87, 88, 89, 90, 96, 98–103, 105,
    106, 109, 110, 113, 115, 120,
    124, 130, 134, 139, 141, 142
  as community-based organizations,
    91
  church as, 95
  as familia sana, 20
  as Triune, 51, 59, 61, 62, 113
compassion, 11, 25, 57, 69, 83, 94, 99,
    100–105, 106, 115
  passion and, 101, 104
Conde-Frazier, Elizabeth, 1, 9, 11–12,
    24, 45, 127, 130, 133, 137, 146
consubstantial, 17
  Co-divine or co-equal, 17
coraje, 131
coritos, 10, 21, 33, 40–41, 46, 61,
    62–64, 122, 132, 139
Cortese de García, Amy, 123
Costas, Orlando E., 7 n.22, 37, 58–59,
    78, 117, 130, 147
cotidiano, 10, 12, 35, 79, 121, 138,
    139, 142
  explanation of, 6, 41
  Scripture and, 12
  as source of theology, 79
creation, 13, 28, 29, 31, 34, 52, 55,
    58, 60, 65, 80–81, 93, 94, 95,
    100, 103, 109, 112, 113, 115,
    118, 120, 123–26, 132, 134,
    135, 136, 137
  as new, 100–102
  relation to Spirit, 20
  as space, 12, 109, 120, 121, 123
culture, 6, 27, 31, 69, 77, 87, 90, 98, 99,
    104, 117, 118, 129, 134, 141, 142
  definition of, 81
  as dominant, 26, 116, 119, 128
  as oral, 105
  See Taíno

D

dabar, 11, 105, 140

death, 16, 20, 21, 27, 28, 38, 49, 65–66, 82, 102, 105, 109, 110, 112, 122–26, 137, 138
   death-bearing institutions, 16, 38
   death-dealing powers, 10, 50, 116
   injustice as, 116–17
   of Jesus, 38, 50, 53, 70, 92, 106
   as vicarious, 35
denominations, 7, 90, 93
diakonia, 22, 100, 101
didache, 22
discernment, 11, 12, 24–27, 32, 95, 99, 110, 140
Dios, 16, 21, 39–40, 45, 49, 51, 57, 62–64, 74, 113, 120, 140
   See also God
diversity, 13, 55, 90, 113, 128
divine filiation, 56
divinization, 20, 34, 51, 113, 142
   See theosis
donum, 21, 140
doctrine(s), 10, 20, 34, 51, 74, 79, 86, 115
   of patripassianism, 55 n.11

E

ecclesiology, 8, 11, 90–91, 93–95, 97, 100, 105–6, 137
   See church
ecstatic, 19
Elizondo, Virgilio P., 37, 41, 147
epistemology, 134
eschatology, 12, 13, 23, 72, 90, 108–15, 117, 120, 122, 123–26, 135, 140
   consistent vs. realized, 111
eschatos, 108, 118, 121, 124
Espín, Orlando O., 4, 6, 147, 148
Espíritu Santo, 15, 29, 30, 61, 62, 64, 121
   See Holy Spirit
espíritu, 60
euangelion, 39, 42
Eucharist, 50
   as Communion, 99

Eurocentric, 79
evangélica, *passim*
   definition of, 8
   historical development, 7–8
   theological emphases, 10–11
evangélic@, 2, 8, 9, 34, 110, 122
evangelicals, 8
evangelio, 2, 8, 38, 122
exegesis, 76

F

Falcon-García, Ana María, 97
familia, 11, 19, 46, 51, 53, 54, 60–62, 66–71, 90, 140
   de Dios, 40
   as reconstituted, 11, 66, 68–71
   sana (holistic), 20
   Trinity as, 53, 66
fiesta(s), 30, 114, 140
   patronales, 69, 140
   primera communion, 69
   quinceañeros, 69
Fitzpatrick, Joseph, 66
flor y canto, 41

G

García-Johnson, Oscar, 106, 148
García, Sixto J., 4, 148
gender(ed), 17, 18, 22, 32, 40, 71, 80, 93, 98
glossary, 139–43
God, *passim*
   as Abba, 68
   ad extra, 61. *See* Trinity
   as aliento, 62, 64
   as bearing, 59–60
   as Creator, 28, 45, 54, 57, 85, 115
   crucified, 65
   and gender, 17–18, 54–55
   of history, 64
   image of, 60, 80, 86, 103, 113; *see also imago Dei*
   as Jesus Christ, 34, 47, 57

God (*continued*)
  knowledge of, 94, 100, 103, 143
  as mission, 58–59
  as provisión, 62–64
  as pure act, 59
  Redeemer, 54–55
  Reign of, 12, 17, 32, 34, 38, 50, 51,
      94, 105, 107, 109, 111, 113–16,
      121–23, 125, 132, 140
  Sanctifier, 54–55
  sovereignty of, 65, 112, 126
  space of, 109, 118, 121, 122, 125
  as Spirit, 10, 16, 17, 20–22, 39–40,
      51, 59, 96, 121–23
  Word of, 75, 76, 123. *See* Scripture
  as Triune, 10, 11, 51, 55–58, 70,
      123, 136. *See* Trinity
god(s), 65, 74, 118
Godhead, 15, 17, 28, 29, 52, 53,
    54–55, 56, 57, 61, 62, 140
God-talk, 129, 138
Goizueta, Roberto, 5
Gonzalez, Justo L., 2, 4, 76, 117, 119,
    132, 148
Google maps, 118
grace, 16, 31–32, 39, 41, 70, 74, 85,
    98, 100, 112, 120–21, 122, 124,
    131, 136, 137, 138
  cheap, 49
  costly, 50
  grace-full, 21, 113, 115
gratia, 21, 140
Great Awakening, 75
Gregory of Nazianzus, 18, 20, 52, 54,
    71, 139, 142, 148
Guardiola-Saenz, Leticia, 81

H

hablando, 127, 129
  in saying: se entiende la gente, 129
healing, 13, 23, 25–27, 34, 39, 40, 45,
    50, 51, 87–88, 93, 102, 106,
    107, 117, 119, 121, 135
  See sanidad

health, 3, 36, 93, 104, 128
  care, 45, 46
heaven, 10, 28, 35, 38, 49, 50, 52, 62,
    63, 64, 77, 112, 113–16, 124
hermandad, 67, 69, 71
  See familia
hermeneutic(s), 78, 80, 85, 140
  hermeneutical, 6, 7, 12, 74, 80,
      81, 89
  See biblical, interpretation
Heschel, Abraham, 102, 149
hesed, 39, 100
Hispanic, 2, 4, 19, 31 n.39, 39, 78, 79,
    83, 119
  See Latinas
Hispanic Theological Initiative, 1
holistic, 12, 20, 34, 35, 39, 40, 51, 91,
    95, 104, 109
holy, 17, 23, 28, 30, 32, 56, 58, 68, 87,
    102, 118–20, 131, 142
  Holiness movements, 35
  versus unholy, 27
  Voice of, 98
  See Pietism
Holy Spirit (or Spirit), 2, 9–11, 13,
    14–21, 28–32, 34, 35, 38, 41,
    42, 43, 45, 47, 51, 53, 55–57,
    59–64, 68, 70–73, 76, 89, 90,
    94–98, 100–102, 107, 121–25,
    129–34, 136, 137
  as Advocate, 16
  as breath, 20
  and call, 96–97
  charisms or gifts of, 21–25, 28, 51,
      91, 95, 97, 98
  as *donum*, 21
  discernment of, 26–28
  gone native, 28–29, 32
  and illumination, 76–77
  and Jesus Christ, 38
  personhood and, 19–20, 39
  presencia de, 17–19, 21, 26, 39
  and salvation, 33, 39, 47, 48, 51, 59
  as Wild Child, 9, 14, 21, 28, 31

See arrabon, *gratia*,
Macedonianism,
pneumatology, *ruach*
huellas, 127, 128 n.1

I

iglesia, 47, 60, 69, 97, 141, 150
illumination, 15, 75–77, 89, 140
imago Dei, 103, 104
See God, image of
immigrants, 67, 69, 76, 84, 103
Incarnation(al), 7, 10, 11, 21, 28, 34,
35, 37, 50, 57, 105, 111, 119,
123, 133
encarnada, 140
incarnated word, 89, 105
See Jesus Christ
interpretation, 24, 42, 73, 74–75, 77,
79–81, 83–85, 110
interpreter, 41, 73, 77, 81, 82, 85, 87
See hermeneutics, Scripture
Isasi-Díaz, Ada María, 2, 6, 12, 121,
149

J

Jenni, Ernst, 111, 149
Jesus Christ
as enfleshed Word, 77
Jesús jíbaro, 37, 38
Jesús sato, 37–43, 45–48, 50
See Christology, jíbaro, sato
jíbaro, 10, 37, 38, 140
justice, 11, 13, 24, 34, 35, 39, 41, 46, 47,
50, 51, 78, 80, 82, 88, 91, 93, 94,
99, 101, 109, 112, 114, 115, 116,
117, 120, 121, 124, 133
injustice, 6, 7, 10, 11, 26, 50, 83,
84, 101, 116, 117, 121

K

kairos, 12, 48, 109, 118, 119, 120, 122,
123, 140
definition of, 120

relation with place, 120–21
katallage, 92
See reconciliation
katartizō, 45
katartismos, 10, 50, 124, 140
kerygma, 22
koinonia, 22, 100, 120
kyrios, 94
Kwok Pui-Lan, 79, 114, 149

L

Latinas, 1–4, 6, 11, 12, 19, 35–37,
39–41, 43–45, 47, 48, 54, 73,
88, 90–93, 95, 106, 113, 116,
117, 119, 120, 127, 128, 138
Latin@s, 1–8, 36
Latinas/os, 66, 67, 119
Latinos, 4, 19, 39, 54, 78, 116
See Hispanic
Left behind, 44, 108, 110
LaHaye, Tim, 111
leitourgia, 22
Líbanio, Juan B., 109, 150
liberación, 34, 39, 40, 41, 46, 50
liberation, 28, 39, 47–49, 74, 81,
85, 89, 98, 102, 121, 134
llamada, 9, 42–43
See also, calling(s)
love, 2, 10, 11, 14, 15, 18, 19, 21, 25,
29, 32, 38, 39, 41, 42, 47, 51,
55, 58–62, 64, 65, 70, 71, 81,
83, 92, 93, 96, 98, 100, 104–7,
112, 114, 120, 123, 124, 125,
131, 138
locus theologicus, 35
Luther, Martin, 65, 75, 77, 151
lyein, 48

M

Macedonianism, 56, 141
Machado, Daisy L., 1, 43, 47, 82, 150
madres, 2, 69, 70, 138
de la iglesia, 60, 141
See familia

Maldonado Pérez, Zaida, 1, 4, 10, 12, 117, 127, 130, 150
Mama Leo. *See* Rosado, Leoncia
mañana, 2, 21, 119–20
manera de ser, 6, 8, 141
Mapquest, 118
marginalized, 6, 36, 37, 39, 40, 41, 47, 94
    marginality, 4, 78
    See periphery
Marquez, Brixeida, 102
Martell-Otero, Loida I., 10, 12, 23, 90, 132, 150
menospreciadas, 47
Messiah, 37
mestizaje, 5, 37, 78, 124, 141
    mestiza, 7
    mestizo, 6, 8, 37
    and pluriform, 5
Migliore, Daniel L., 34, 151
millennial, -ism, 110, 124, 141
    amillennial, 124, 141
    Dispensational premillennial, -ism, 12, 110, 124
    postmillennial, 124
ministry, 11, 17, 22, 24, 29, 35, 38, 39, 44, 47, 80, 91–106, 114, 125, 135, 142
    definition of holistic, 91
    of reconciliation, 11, 92, 94–96, 98, 100, 104, 106
miracle(s), 14, 19, 29, 60, 61, 84
modalist, 55
Moltmann, Jürgen, 22, 59, 111, 151
monarchianism, 55
mujerista, 9, 40, 78
    See Isasi-Díaz, Ada María
mulatez, 5, 78, 141
    See pluriform
mystery, 25, 52, 53, 65, 71, 81, 94

N

Naht Hanh, Thich, 46
Nazareth, 83

nepantla, 5, 8
    See mestizaje, pluriform, sata
Nicene (-Constantinople) Creed, 10, 15, 56, 68
normatizing myths, 40

O

Oberman, Heiko, 65, 151
O'Day, Gail, 105
oppression, 27, 34, 46, 65, 83, 86, 115, 116, 134, 137
    oppress(es), 27, 47, 48
    oppressed, 3, 6, 11, 23, 30, 35, 37, 38, 43, 48, 49, 99, 112, 115, 127, 137, 141
    oppressive, 20, 81, 102
    oppressor, 81, 83
Otto, Rudolf, 52
outside the gate, 49, 125

P

Paraclete, 65
    See Holy Spirit
parousia, 110–11, 114, 141
pastoras, 90, 95, 100, 103
patriarchal, 9, 10, 42, 66, 77, 78, 79, 115, 117
    patriarchy, 16, 18, 98
Pentecostal, 5, 19, 29, 86, 93, 97, 99, 105, 128
    Pentecost, 105, 137
    Pentecostalism, 7
Pérez, Altagracia, 26
Pérez y González, María, 91, 93, 152
perichoresis, 12, 13, 113, 124, 141
periphery, 36–38, 43, 49, 50, 78, 122
    peripheral(ly), 8, 36, 37, 40, 78
    peripheralized, 35, 47
    peripheric, 116–17, 122, 138
perro, 38
person(s), 9, 19, 20, 22, 25, 29, 36, 37, 46, 50, 54, 62, 67, 76, 84, 86, 91, 93, 103, 104, 106, 118, 125

depersonalization, 19, 83

nonperson, 19

Person of

Holy Spirit, 9, 10, 15, 18, 19, 20, 26, 29, 39, 134

Trinity, 10, 17, 18, 21, 54–58, 61, 63, 68, 71, 140

personal, 9, 10, 17, 18, 20–22, 47, 49, 51, 59, 61, 62, 66, 80, 93

personhood, 17, 19, 23, 26, 39, 42, 43, 47, 61

personalization, 19, 39

Pietism, 7, 18, 35, 75, 137

place(s), 9, 11, 19, 24, 35, 37, 48, 49, 52, 67, 70, 71, 78, 87, 90, 91, 94, 96, 97, 100, 109, 113, 114, 117–23, 124, 132, 133, 137, 140

displaced, 13, 115, 116, 117

as sacred, 118–19

takes place, 5, 7, 13, 19, 46, 50, 81, 82, 87, 89, 102, 103, 105, 106, 108, 111, 120, 121, 123, 124–25, 131, 133

See periphery, space (sacred)

Placher, William C., 34

pluriform, 5, 6, 8, 34

See mestizaje, sat@

pneumatology, 10, 19, 20–21, 39, 133, 134, 141

pneumatological, 9, 10, 20, 65, 131, 138

nuance, 64, 130

See Holy Spirit

postcolonial, 2, 9, 12, 79, 81

poverty, 4, 78, 93, 104

the poor, 38, 43, 48, 49, 50, 60, 78, 83, 84, 94, 95, 99 112, 116, 127, 139

powers, 10, 15, 19, 50, 63, 74, 102, 116, 124, 125, 126

definition of, 103

principalities, and, 27, 30, 50, 51, 124, 125, 126

praxis, 6, 7, 13, 103, 106, 130

of accompaniment, 5, 141

presencia, 8, 11, 17–19, 21, 26, 27, 32, 47, 48, 131, 138, 141

presence, 8, 9, 11–13, 17, 19–21, 23, 27, 29, 36, 39, 40, 41, 48, 53, 62, 65, 66, 86, 106, 111–16, 119, 120, 141

presente, 9, 17, 21, 30, 53, 62, 64–66, 120, 122, 136, 138

proceeds, 55, 56, 57

prophecy, 23–24, 32, 39

prophet(s), 24, 32, 51, 102, 113, 114

propheteia, 22

prophetic, 2, 3, 12, 24, 39, 94, 99, 102, 104, 105, 114, 123, 135

Protestant, 1, 2, 5–9, 12, 23, 35, 73–76, 78, 79, 93,96, 119, 127, 130, 140, 142, 142

provisión, 62, 63, 64, 67

provision, 61–64

See Trinity

pueblo, 128

R

Ramírez, Julia, 97

rapture, the, 110

Recinos, Harold, 116, 152

reconciliation, 11, 92–96, 98, 100–101, 104, 106, 115, 136

Reformation, 75

Reign of God, 12, 34, 38, 107, 109, 111–12, 115, 120, 123, 125, 126, 132

relations, 19, 57, 59 n.29, 61, 68, 79, 80, 82, 109, 118, 120–21, 133

relational, 17, 57, 61, 62, 77, 94, 100–101, 143

relationality, 113, 118

Revelation, book of, 110

Rosado, Leoncia, 101, 123

ruach, 18, 20, 27, 137

ruach elohim, 15, 142

See Holy Spirit

Russell, Letty M., 99, 115, 153

S

salvation, 6, 7, 10, 20, 33–35, 37,
    39–42, 44, 46, 48–51, 59, 91,
    109, 112, 113, 115, 120–21,
    126, 133, 135, 136, 142
relation with other doctrines, 34
    See soteriology
Samaritana(s), 43–44
sanidad, 34, 39–41, 44, 46, 50
santa(s), 10, 33, 42–43, 51, 78
santidad, 34, 39, 40, 41, 50
sanctificada, 9
    sanctification, 15
    sanctified, 9, 17, 30, 142
    Sanctifier, 54–55
sata, 6, 10, 33, 36, 42, 43, 51
    sata/o, 5, 142
    sat@, 8, 3, 37, 38, 42
    sato, 10, 36–39
    Jesús sato, 37–43, 45–48, 50
    See pluriform
Scripture(s), 7, 10, 11, 12, 17, 18, 20,
    27, 29, 31–33, 40, 41, 40, 61, 62,
    64, 67, 68, 71, 73–77, 79, 85–89,
    94, 96, 128, 130, 131, 133
    sola scriptura, 75
    See Bible
secularism, 111
sentir, 21, 26, 62
    sentido, 21, 142
Segovia, Fernando F., 79, 153
sermon(s), 33, 42, 76, 78, 83, 84, 86,
    135
shalom, 34, 39, 46, 49, 106, 113
Schotroff, Luise, 42, 153
Silva, Moisés, 77, 153
sin, 7, 21, 27, 28, 30, 31, 32, 35, 41, 43,
    47, 49, 50, 60, 61, 64, 65, 70,
    113, 114, 135, 136, 137–38
    sinful, 38, 42, 61, 65, 122
    sinner, 59, 65, 136, 137
    structural sin, 41, 136
sobraja, 3, 10, 33, 38, 39, 2, 43, 46,
    48, 51
    definition of, 36, 114, 142

Soliván, Samuel, 19, 39, 153
soteriology, 10, 33–35, 41, 49–51,
    126, 135, 142
    sōter, 34
    See salvation
sōzein, 46
space, 6, 11–13, 18, 21, 22, 28, 33–35,
    39–41, 43, 47–50, 68, 80, 86, 89,
    90, 91, 100, 102, 108–9, 113–15,
    117–26, 131, 132, 138, 139
    God-space, 125
    sacred, 118, 119
    spatiality, 118
    See spirituality
Spics, 36
Spirit (*See* Holy Spirit)
spirit(s), 8, 15, 17, 19, 26, 27, 28, 32,
    46, 48, 60, 64, 65, 80, 88, 93,
    97, 102, 103, 104, 117, 123,
    128, 132, 136, 138
spiritual, spirituality, 8, 22–27, 30,
    48, 60, 63, 69, 76, 91, 94, 95,
    99, 101, 101–5, 110, 119, 121,
    134, 135
subsistence(s), 55, 142
subversion, 71
sufficiency, 103, 104
sufrimientos, 38
synechō, 92

T

Taíno, 118–19, 131
    indigenous culture, 118
Tamez, Elsa, 88, 153
testimonio, 10, 12, 40–41, 50, 96–98,
    138
    definition of, 33, 93–94, 142
teología en conjunto, 1, 6, 9, 13, 42,
    127–29, 142
    collaborative theology, 6
theos agraptos, 18, 142
theosis, 20, 34, 113, 124, 142
    See divinization
tías, 2, 138
    See familia

tongues, 23, 28, 29, 31, 39, 43, 121
   See Holy Spirit
trabajo personal, 9, 17, 22, 23, 142
tradition, 2, 3, 7, 9, 12, 18, 20, 24, 34,
   37, 51, 53, 64, 72, 73, 75, 78, 80,
   81, 83–86, 97, 98, 119, 131, 142
transcendence, 12, 21, 64, 101, 111,
   126
Trinity, 10, 11, 14, 15, 17, 20, 29, 31,
   32, 34, 52–62, 64–68, 70–71,
   132, 133, 134, 140, 141, 142
   ad alium, 58, 60
   as Being-for-the-other, 53, 57–58
   distinctions, 54, 55, 56, 73
   economic Trinity, 54, 61
   as Emmanuel, 53
   as interrelations, 17 n.11, 57, 68
   unity, 55, 56–57, 59, 61
   as wholly other, 53
   See God, relations, unity

U

unity, 22, 53, 55–57, 59, 61, 98, 101,
   128, 140
   See Trinity

V

va y ven, 58–60, 130
   as missional, 58, 60
   as Trinitarian, 58–59

vicarious, 35
   See death
Villafañe, Eldin, 30, 66, 69, 116, 121,
   154
vínculo, 20, 143
violence, 36, 40, 46, 50, 65, 82, 117
   as erotic, 114
   associated with mestizaje, 141
vocation, 11, 22, 34, 38, 42–44, 106
   bivocation, 99

W

Wesley, John, 22, 29, 154
   Wesleyan, 7
wetbacks, 36
Wild Child, 14, 18–19, 21, 27, 28, 31,
   32, 131, 134
   See Holy Spirit
Wink, Walter, 102, 154
wisdom, 15, 23, 24, 25, 102, 104, 127,
   132, 133
   Spirit as, 28

Y

yada, 94, 100, 143
Yunque, el, 118–19

Z

Zizioulas, John, 58, 154

www.ingramcontent.com/pod-product-compliance
Lightning Source LLC
Chambersburg PA
CBHW030307100426
42812CB00002B/606